The Illustrated Art Of Learning & Teaching Rink Hockey Fundamentals

By Bob Swope
1st Edition 2005

Jacobob Press LTD.

Cover photo Courtesy of Mike Beck and Jeff Heubner from "St. Louis Skatium" In-Line Roller Hockey teams. The old St. Louis University jersey was loaned courtesy of Lindsay Middlebrook when he played goalkeeper there from 1974 - 1976. Lindsay now works at Johnny Mac's Sporting Goods Store in St. Louis.

Published and distributed by:
Jacobob Press LTD.
St. Louis, Mo.
(314) 843-4829
E-Mail: jacobobsw@msn.com

Jacobob Press LTD.

ISBN: 0-9705827-8-1
Copyright 2005
All Rights Reserved
Including the right of reproduction in whole or in part in any form.

Printed and Bound by:
Hardbound, Inc.
Earth City, Mo. 63045

First Edition 2005

AUTHORS ACKNOWLEDGMENTS

My thanks to the 2004/2005 edition "Afton Pee Wee House #1" boys Ice Hockey team, and their coach's Joe Evola, and Brian Naeger from St. Louis, Mo. Also the 2005 edition of the "St. Louis Skatium" boys In-Line "Bullets" Roller Hockey team and their coach Dale Schuhwerk from St. Louis, Mo, Jeff Heubner, and rink manager Rob Grimm for all their help in putting together the pictures for this book. The pictures will really help illustrate what I am trying to get across to everyone using this book, and that is to help children improve on their ice and roller hockey skills.

ICE HOCKEY TEAM

ROLLER HOCKEY GROUP

TABLE OF CONTENTS

1. Introduction..8

2. Attitude & Behavior Development..10
   Influence...10
   Their Improving 10
   Respect 11
   Hustle 12
   Health Habits 12
   Fitness..13

3. The Fundamentals..14
   What are They..14
   Low Forwards and Centers...15
   High Forwards and Wings...15
   Defensemen...16
   Goalkeepers...16

4. Games Training..17

5. Organize your Teaching..17

6. Where they Play on the Rink...18

7. Drills and Exercises 19
   How do they help..19
   Warm up and Stretching 19
   Coordination and Agility 25
   Controlled Falling & Rink Presence...28
   Power & Strength 30
   Running, Leg Strength, and Balance 36
   Cool downs 39
   Games Approach to Learning Hockey..40
   Skating and Movement 40
   Communicating 53
   Puck/ Ball Handling...56
   Passing and Receiving..60

Shooting..67
Checking...71
Carrying the Puck/ Ball...77
Faking..78
Rebounding...80
Protecting the Puck/ Ball.....................................82
Pressuring...84
Blocking, Catching, Stopping..............................84
Reading and Reacting..85
Facing Off...87
Goaltending..90

8. Tactics and Strategies..114
    Team Tactics..115
    Offensive Strategies..116
    Defensive Strategies...120
    Transition Strategies...122
    Power Play Strategy..124
    Penalty Killing Strategy......................................134

9. Hockey Terminology..138
    Key (Legend) for Diagrams................................146

10. New Parent Orientation..147

11. The Playing Rink..150

12. General Game Rules..151

13. Hockey Age Groups...160

14. Officials..160

15. Penalties...164

16. Equipment...166

17. Other Available Books..174

*******WARNING*******

If your child or the participant has any physically limiting condition, bleeding disorder, high blood pressure, pregnancy or any other condition that may limit them physically you should check with your doctor before participating in these drills and exercises.

Be sure participants, making hard contact, are of the same weight and size to avoid injury.

All drills and exercises should be supervised by an adult. **AUTHOR ASSUMES NO LIABILITY FOR ANY ACCIDENTAL INJURY OR EVEN DEATH THAT MAY RESULT.**

EXTRA CARE AND CAUTION SHOULD BE TAKEN WITH ANY OF THE BLOCKING DRILLS, CHECKING DRILLS, AND EXERCISES AROUND THE NET, AS THEY ARE PROBABLY THE MORE DANGEROUS ONES.

ABOUT THE AUTHOR

Bob Swope, is a long time youth sports coach and teacher. He has 18 years experience coaching, managing, and teaching kids, both boys and girls. His teams are known for their knowledge and use of the fundamentals. His philosophy is kids will have more fun out there when they know the basic fundamentals, and how to apply them. He has taken a team of left over kids, after a draft had been performed, and taken them to a championship and playoffs in just three years. This was basically accomplished just by teaching them the fundamentals, and getting good knowledgeable coaches to work on them every day with the kids. He has coached and managed in four different sports. Taking a lot of training and teaching techniques from one sport and using them in another. He has been a member of the "Youth Football Coaches Association of America", and is currently working with the "National Youth Sports Coaches Association" to get certification in several sports.

Introduction

My real interest in ice hockey started when I came to St. Louis, Missouri. I became a fan of the St. Louis Blues hockey team when Mike Shanahan was the president of the team. Hockey was exiting then when the team played at the old arena across from forest park. Up until then I only knew about "Roller Derby" where they skated around a track using quad skates. I came to St. Louis from the Los Angeles, California area. Most of the time I lived there we did not have ice or roller hockey. So I learned a lot about ice hockey from watching the Blues play. I try to be a knowledgeable person in sports, so I tried to learn a little about how hockey is played, so I could discuss it with my friends at work. At least I would know a little bit about hockey. Well I still don't know everything about hockey, but I am learning because I do a lot of research. And I'm very lucky because just about a mile away from my house there is an ice hockey rink where select teams and the little kids play. You can learn a lot by watching what the coaches are doing as they train the real little kids.

I have been following ice hockey since about 1980 in the Olympics. The USA win over the Russians in the "miracle on ice" was very exiting. Even people who did not know much about hockey got exited. Most of my experience has been working with local teams and their coaches to learn more about the rules and how kids play the game these days. Since this book is mostly for young boys, and girls, in the 5 to 12 year old range, their next step from youth sports will probably be to a select team or a high school team. Some of the things I will be illustrating is what the coaches on those teams would like the kids to already basically know when they get there. Recently the experts have studied many of the old standard conditioning exercises in youth sports, and they came up with better ways to accomplish the same thing. So what you are reading in this book is some of the latest information on how to teach kids simple stretching, strengthening, and endurance exercises, with less chance of them getting an injury.

The idea of a hockey fundamentals reference book for young boys and girls has that certain appeal for me because when I was at that young age there were no books out there for my dad to refer to, so he could help me learn about a sport such as hockey. And he was not into athletics much anyway, since he came from an era when men started to work at a young age. And so I guess he actually never even thought much about sports or helping me learn. So this book is dedicated to all those mothers and fathers who would like their children to be the best they can be at playing hockey, and also have some fun while learning the sport.

Usually mom and dad would like to see their kids get involved in sports in some way either for the exercise, or maybe to just keep them busy and out of trouble. But they probably don't know what sport to get them into. Well maybe ice or roller hockey is the sport. It's different. Most kids naturally think it's cool to skate around on the ice. The boy or girl that more than likely doesn't want to play youth baseball, basketball, or soccer, might be just be afraid they don't have the skills to play those sports. Or you may just have a boy, or girl, that just does not like those sports. And some of you single moms, maybe you have a son or daughter that you would like to get out there and do something with. But maybe you just don't know how to go about it. All of you that are in this situation can use this book to help learn more about how to get them ready to play hockey. The average mom and dad don't know what they can do to have some fun with their son or daughter, and also teach them something about hockey while doing it. Well for all of you out there, here is a book you can use as a guide or reference manual with lots of pictures. Take it with you out to the driveway or parking lot, and use it as you go about teaching and having some fun. It's very hard for most parents to find an open ice rink to use for practicing. You are probably saying to yourself though "What is he talking about, there is no ice in those places". What you do is use "in line" roller skates to practice with. It's very similar to skating on ice.

As a member of the "Youth Football Coaches Association of America", I was sent to coaching clinics to learn coaching techniques, and how to treat injuries. I have been interested for a long time in conditioning for sports. Due to careful team training, other than minor bumps and bruises, I can only remember two injuries on football teams I have been directly connected with. And this was over a six year period. One boy had bruised ribs, and my oldest son had a broken wrist. This would be only two injuries out of a possible 1380 boys playing, over a six year span. It's not perfect, but I am proud of being associated with this kind of record.

No book can not turn a boy or girl into a STAR player in a sport, unless they have at least some talent. I can't think of any book that could do that. However this book will help them to improve their basic hockey skills, and grow up to be a better person, and a team player in life. And also it will be a lot of fun for you to get out and work with your son or daughter. I can recall that these were some of the best times of my life. My kids and I still talk about them sometimes when we get together. Playing hockey will also teach them how to work with other kids as a team. And it follows that the game will be more fun for them as they learn more about the basic fundamentals. They will feel good because their knowledge of hockey will impress all of their friends. All the hours of practice might also keep them out of trouble as long as you don't over do it because they won't have a lot of free time to get into trouble. Another thing that will help them is, some youth hockey leagues they join might have a policy that they keep their grades up in school while playing. And this is very important as they go into the higher grades in school. When you stop and think about it, with you and your son or daughter *working together*, this could become a turning point in both of your lives in many ways.

Attitude & Behavior Development

Influence

Boys and girls from the age of *five through eight* are very impressionable, and mom and dads influence can be important in their development at this stage of learning. They learn by watching you mom and dad. It is also important to teach young boys, and girls that youth hockey is only a game, and what is most important for them to realize is to develop good sportsmanship, have fun, play the game, and learn. Explain to them that they should always try their best, and if they don't do well every time there is always another day. One of the things I have learned though is, that if something is worth doing then why not try to be the best you can be at it. Don't goof off out there just because you are there. I realize this is very hard for some young kids to learn. Most of them just want to have fun. And that's ok as long as it does not get out of hand in a bad way. Sometimes that fun is not fun for the coaches trying to get their attention to make a teaching point.

Their Improving

What I always told the kids, on my teams, was have someone watch you (hopefully you mom or dad) to see what it is you might be doing wrong. Then that person should work with them, over and over, to correct these things (repetition). I explained to them that if they worked hard, they would begin to see that they were getting better and better. If your son or daughter has a good attitude then this will usually be reflected to the rest of the kids on the team. In other words it can be contagious, to everyone else on the team.

Also part of the learning process is improving their attitude towards other players on the team, their coaches, their managers, and officials. This will depend a lot on how YOU mom or dad normally act. Your son or daughter will most often reflect your attitude towards these people. So, be very aware of what you say when they are present, or nearby. Many times I have seen parents screaming from the sidelines at officials, or another kid on the team, when they think that person has made a mistake. Then, following your example, during practice, your son or daughter will belittle or bad mouth one of their team mates or the coach. This is really just learned behavior from YOU. And as parents we have to be honest with ourselves, we are not perfect, so why should we expect everyone else to be. Think about it, if a team has to rely on a referee's call, or a team being perfect to win the game, then maybe they didn't deserve to win. A parents bad attitude just makes things worse not better. My advice to you is when you have a gripe just bite your tongue so to speak, until you cool off a bit, and you find that you will have a lot more fun out there.

So please instruct him or her to get along with their team mates. Because if they are a better player than their team mates, they can help them more by encouraging them than by belittling them. It will also help in showing their team mates how they can become a better player, like your son or daughter is. This way the whole team gets better. And when that happens, everyone has more fun out there. No one wants to lose every game they play. It's very discouraging, and there is just no way it will be fun for them.

On my Gardnerville football team I had one boy that became so good at this, and he had so much respect from the other boys, I could let him run the drills while I went over to talk to a parent or one of my coaches. He was like an extra coach on the team. Do you know what he is doing now? He coaches, and works with the local youth football teams in his area.

Respect

Explain to your son or daughter the roles of the officials, and the head coach. Only the head coach should question the referee when he or she believes that a there has been a mistake, or a rules interpretation problem.

Sometimes the official was just out of position to see what happened. When you teach your son or daughter respect for the rules, then you teach them respect for law and order later in their life. Remember mom and dad the example YOU set by your actions may influence the way THEIR life turns out. Many times, at the youth hockey level as a coach if you are reasonable with a official, and ask only for a clarification, he or she may even reverse their call. They may just have had a different view of the play. What usually happens though is when the players, coaches, and parents start screaming, and complaining about the call, they will start to favor the other team on any call that is questionable or close. It's just human nature. In the long run it is better to just let the referee make their call. After the game is over, or the next day, then go to your head coach and tell them why you think the officiating was poor. Your head coach should then go to the head of officials, and explain the complaint. It might just be that the official is inexperienced, new, or just doesn't understand the rules. But they will never improve if the head of officials does not know that the official had problems, then helps him or her to correct them. Believe me, they never will change by your hollering, and screaming, at them. And it will just aggravate you and everyone else watching the game.

Hustle

Hustle will improve their attitude, and make the game better to watch. A little game you can play, with your young son or daughter, is whenever you are working with them say, "Lets see how fast you can do this, maybe you can beat me". Then do it yourself as fast as you can, and afterwards ask them to try. Then no matter how fast they do it say, "Gee your almost as fast as me". When you see that they are getting faster, offer them some kind of reward like taking them to a movie on the weekend. In hockey your son or daughter needs to be taught how to move around fast. When substitutions or line switches are made they need to move, on and off the rink, fast to avoid being scored upon or delaying the game. When there is a lot of hustle the game goes faster, and mom that will sometimes get you home a lot earlier to start supper. And it's always fun for the spectators to see a lot of hustle out there on the rink. I have personally proven to myself that hustling in life, at whatever your job is, impresses the boss also. So it's a good lesson to learn.

Health Habits

It is a very good idea to start them out in life with good health habits. What we are talking about here is plenty of sleep, a good nutritious balanced diet, with timely exercise, and conditioning. What we mean by timely is, don't over exercise them a few hours before game time. Not being tired, or sick, will also improve their mental outlook, and attitude during the game.

Just a few words here about dietary supplements. **DO NOT** let them take anything containing *"Ephedra"*. In some cases it may be ok, but it has very serious side effects. Death being one. So why take a chance. Also stay away from *"Anabolic Steroids"*. They also can have bad side effects such as increased irritability, and possible liver or kidney trauma. They are young, so let them develop naturally for the long term. Also see the section on "Equipment" for some additional health concerns.

Fitness

I have had kids come to a summer afternoon, or early evening, game really dragging their feet, so to speak. And after talking to them I found out mom let them go over to a friends house all morning at their swimming pool for a swim party. Swimming is a good workout, but not the day of a game. They need at least one days rest, from any heavy exercise before a game. As training for a sport these days becomes more complex the trainers, and strength coaches, have found that some exercises can be dangerous. So what I have tried to do is find out the latest techniques, and tailor the exercises to fit young kids practicing, and playing hockey.

In the game of hockey it takes lots of stamina, and endurance, to play at the same level all the way until the end of the game. This means they need to have "*cardiorespiratory fitness*" and "*muscular fitness*". In simple terms, cardiorespiratory fitness has to do with their aerobic and anaerobic capacity. Muscular fitness has to do with their strength, power, speed, muscle endurance, and flexibility. In the later stages of the game, they need a physical and mental advantage going for them. To be able to do this, young kids need to work on their aerobic, anaerobic, and muscle conditioning constantly. When kids have good muscular fitness they tend to have less injuries. And when they are hurt they tend to heal more quickly. Do not over do it though, but keep at it every day, for at least a few repetitions. If your son or daughter is on the overweight side, be extra careful not to over work them, or push them to hard. Especially when they begin to exercise. You only increase repetitions when you see that they are getting into shape, and can handle it. If there is any question, talk to your Doctor about it. If they are a little overweight, it's probably a good idea to have a doctor check them out before starting. They will give you a better idea of what they can or can't do.

We tried all kinds of techniques, to help the kids keep their strength level at or near it's peak. Most teams go through a warm up exercise routine, just before the game starts, to get them loosened up. So don't worry about exercising them before they leave for practice or a game. We had some kids that appeared to lose stamina, during the game, eat a banana the day before a game. This was to let the vitamins and minerals get into their systems by game time. The idea being, make sure these vitamins and minerals did not get all sweated out of their system, during practice or a game. Now days they have *"GatorAid"* for that. A suggestion here would be to give your son or daughter some *"GatorAid"*, by taking a bottle with you, when you are out working with them on a hot or warm day. We had one coach that had one of the parents cut up oranges, and hand them out to suck on during break. Both the bananas, and oranges, helped some, but then when they came out with *"GatorAid"*, that worked out much better when they are thirsty during practice, or during a game. Also make sure you give them plenty of water breaks when it's hot out.

The Fundamentals

What are they

Fundamentals are the basic skills needed, to be able to play the game of ice hockey or in line roller hockey. The skills are skating, communicating, puck/ ball handling, passing, receiving, shooting, carrying, faking, checking, blocking, rebounding, facing off, and goaltending. Since hockey has a player rotational system called line changing, each player has to know which line they are on when there is a shift change. This is very important for the younger players. This is because when they have a line change, they have to get on and off the ice or the floor quickly. I am going to break the skills down for you into how they relate to the different positions. All players except goaltenders need to learn facing off. All players need to learn communicating. Also kids need to be taught which are offensive skills and which are defensive skills. The reason being that kids must know which skill they need to be using as they transition from offense to defense. As an example, if you just teach your son or daughter only offensive skills, then they may give up a goal when they transition to defense because they have not learned how to properly defend against an opponent.

Their size is not going to matter too much when they are 5 to 8 years old. If they are already tall for their age, have long arms and legs they might have an advantage as a goaltender. But many times smaller kids are quicker and can move the puck around, and get to it more efficiently.

When they get to their first team, it is very important that they know the basic fundamentals, for all the positions. This is especially true for 5 to 8 year olds. And how those fundamentals relate to offense and defense. This way the coach can spend more time on teaching the plays, tactics, and strategies they will need to know during the game.

Low Forwards, and Centers

Probably the first fundamental skill they need to learn is skating. All the different skating techniques need to become a habit with them. In this position they have to move around in all directions. If they do not learn these skills first, then they will probably be very frustrated when they get to their first team and can't move quick enough to where the coach wants them. Learning all the different skating techniques to move in different directions lets your son or daughter get in the proper position to execute their other required skills. The other skills you need to concentrate on are puck handling first, then passing, then blocking, then shooting, then faking, then rebounding, then checking, then communicating, and last facing off. Followed by quickness, agility, speed, and last power. In the section on "Drills and Exercises", you will find out how to teach your son or daughter these basic fundamental skills.

Learning the different skating techniques will also help your son or daughter with their puck handling abilities. A special skill for you mom or dad to look for here is, a boy or girl that is naturally very coordinated, fast, seems to be always moving, never sets still, and appears to already have an aggressive quality in their character. All of these natural traits will make it easier for them to learn how to become a good low forward or center.

High Forwards, and Wings

Probably the first fundamental skill they need to learn is skating. All the different skating techniques need to become a habit with them. In this position they have to move around in all directions, but mostly they have to skate up and down the side lines of the rink. If they do not learn these skills first, then they will probably be very frustrated when they get to their first team and can't move quick enough to where the coach wants them. Learning all the different skating techniques to move in different directions lets your son or daughter get in the proper position to execute their other required skills. The other skills you need to concentrate on are puck handling first, then shooting, then passing, then faking, then rebounding, then checking, then blocking, then communicating, and last facing off. Followed by speed, quickness, agility, and last power. In the section on "Drills and Exercises", you will find out how to teach your son or daughter these basic fundamental skills.

Learning the different skating techniques will also help your son or daughter with their puck handling abilities. A special skill for you mom or dad to look for here is, a boy or girl that is naturally very coordinated, fast, seems to be always moving, never sets still, likes to throw or kick things around, and appears to already have an aggressive quality in their character. All of these natural traits will make it easier for them to learn how to become a good high forward or wing.

Defensemen

Probably the first fundamental skill they need to learn is skating. All the different skating techniques need to become a habit with them. In this position they have to move around in all directions. If they do not learn these skills first, then they will probably be very frustrated when they get to their first team and can't move quick enough to where the coach wants them. Learning all the different skating techniques to move in different directions lets your son or daughter get in the proper position to execute their other required skills. The other skills you need to concentrate on are puck handling first, then checking, then blocking, then shooting, then faking, then rebounding, then communicating, and last facing off. Followed by quickness, agility, power, and last speed. In the section on "Drills and Exercises", you will find out how to teach your son or daughter these basic fundamental skills.

Learning the different skating techniques will also help your son or daughter with their puck handling abilities. A special skill for you mom or dad to look for here is, a boy or girl that is naturally very coordinated, fast, seems to be always moving, never sets still, has a protective nature in them, and appears to already have an aggressive quality in their character. All of these natural traits will make it easier for them to learn how to become a good defensemen.

Goalkeepers

They need to learn all the special fundamental skills required for goaltending. Their job is very different from the other positions. Because of this you will have to decide whether your son or daughter really wants to, or can become a goalkeeper. Otherwise you may be wasting your time teaching them all these special skills they won't need if they end up playing in any of the other positions. Not to mention buying all the special equipment they have to wear. A special skill for you mom or dad to look for here is, a boy or girl that is naturally very coordinated, agile, maybe extra tall or big for their age, has a protective nature in them, and appears to already have an aggressive quality in their character. All of these natural traits will make it easier for them to learn how to become a good goalkeeper. However, make sure they have the desire to really want to be a goalkeeper. The other skills you can work on with them is puck handling, and blocking. Followed by agility, quickness, and last power. In the section on "Drills and Exercises", you will find out how to teach your son or daughter these basic fundamental skills.

Games Training

According to the "American Sport Education Program" (ASEP), the games approach to training may be better than endless hours of drilling kids on fundamental skills. And knowing todays kids, they may be on to something. However I think the answer is a little of both may be the best way. There are a lot of clever ways to play games with your kids, and they learn some skills without even knowing it. Our suggested approach is play the game(s) with them, then maybe on alternate days, or sessions, go over the fundamentals they were using and how they relate, and how they could improve on them. Todays young kids do have a short attention span. They get bored easy. This is why when you look at the "practice" times we have for a particular fundamental, you will see the times are fairly short. The trick is mixing up the training so that it repeats every week or every other week. Also it keeps them busy with different types of things to do. This is why I suggest organizing a teaching plan. Scattered throughout the book, we have added games to play with them for this purpose.

Organize your Teaching

To organize your teaching, have a plan. My suggestion is sit down, read the section in the book where I talk about what fundamentals your son or daughter needs to learn. Then go through the rest of the book, and read the sections where I show the exercises, drills, and skills, needed. As you go through the book, start a _list_ of what they need to practice. Next to that particular drill or exercise, figure out approximately how much time will be needed to accomplish the teaching and practicing, then write it down. This way you can plan your teaching sessions. I am sure that when you get done, you will see that it takes a lot of hours to go through the fundamentals they need to learn, even for one time through. And with the few hours each week their coach has to go over fundamentals, time runs out, and they have to start working more on strategies, tactics, and formations. So teaching them at home from 5 years old, even a little each year, will really help them improve on their skills, and make it more fun.

Where They Play on the Rink

In youth ice hockey and roller hockey there are usually 5 players and 1 goaltender positioned on the rink for each team (side). In some places they will play 4 vs 4 in roller hockey. In this book we will only cover mostly 5 vs 5 hockey because it is the most popular. Hockey is not like some of the other sports that play on a court or a field. They play on a rink in both ice hockey and roller hockey. The difference is, in roller hockey they play on a floor and not on ice. They start out with the left wing and the left defenseman on the left side, the right wing and right defenseman on the right side, and the center in the middle for the face off *(SEE DIAGRAM 1)*. For 4 vs 4 roller hockey they are in similar positions, except there is only one defenseman instead of two. Goalkeepers usually are positioned right in front of the goal. They can move away from the goal, all the way up to the red line, but they usually do not go too far from the front of the goal. Basically the left wing plays up and down the left side line, and the right wing plays up and down the right side line. The center plays up and

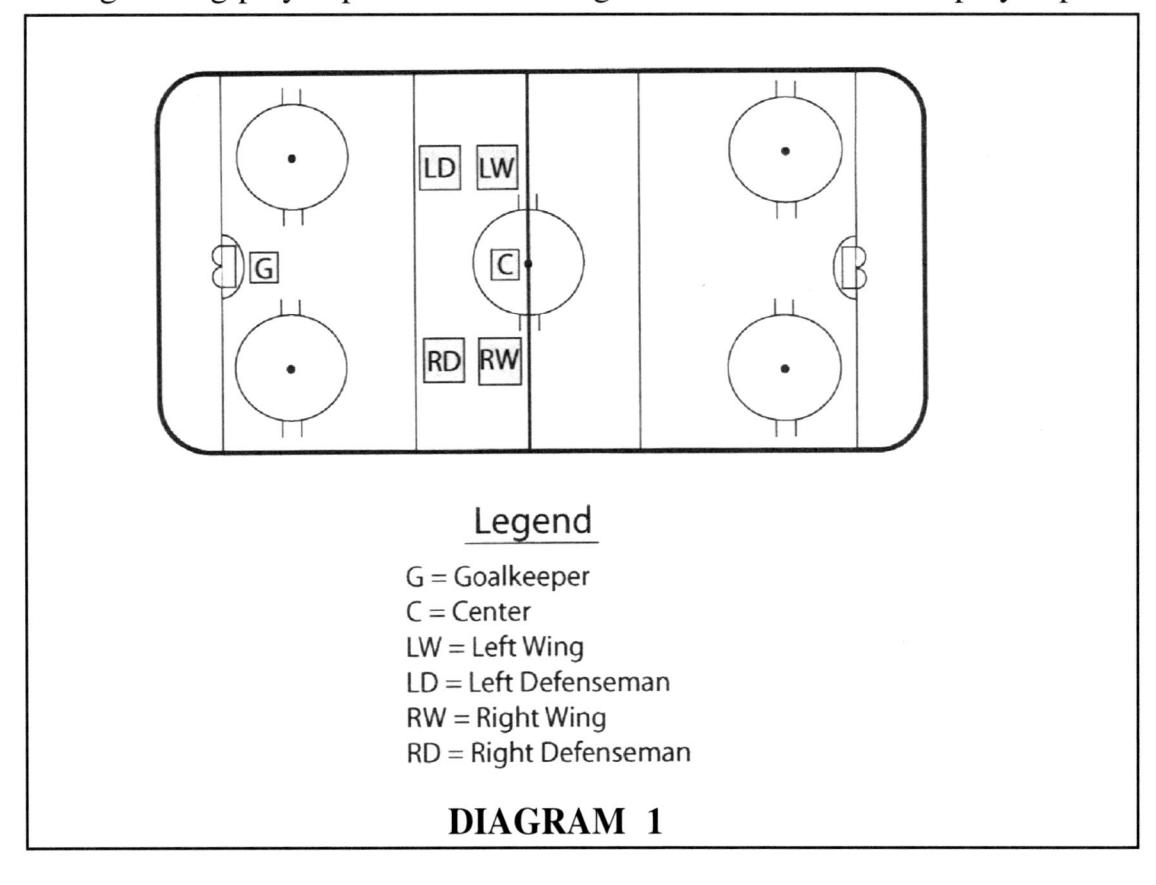

Legend

G = Goalkeeper
C = Center
LW = Left Wing
LD = Left Defenseman
RW = Right Wing
RD = Right Defenseman

DIAGRAM 1

down the middle. Depending on what offense or defense the coach wants to use, they will move to slightly different locations during those phases of the game.

Drills and Exercises

How do they help

Modern hockey training, and conditioning, is advancing all the time. In this book we will follow the latest recommended exercises, and tailor them for the younger kids. Over the past several years, researchers and physicians have identified commonly used exercises that can, in some cases, be potentially harmful to the body of young kids. These exercises can be modified though, to eliminate the undesirable characteristics. In this book we will now use the safer alternatives.

I will break the drills and exercises down into the fundamental categories, and how they relate to what you want to teach. We will use picture figures, and diagrams as much as possible, to eliminate some of the confusion for all mothers, and some fathers, who may never have played the game of hockey. So, bear with us, those of you that have played a lot of hockey. This book was written as a reference book for mom and dad to use in teaching, and training, their son or daughter the fundamental skills of playing hockey. You can take this book right out to the street, parking lot, or rink, with you to look at for reference. I might suggest that if your son or daughter does not seem to be very interested in exercising, then try to make a game out of it. For instance say something to them like, "I bet you can't do this better than me", or "I bet you can't beat me down to the fence". Then do the exercise slow, and let them run a little bit ahead of you. Well you know what I mean. This will keep them interested. Whatever you do, get them into exercising at home. They will need to be well conditioned to play hockey. And, not only that, it will condition them to do exercises even as they grow older in life.

Warm up and Stretching

You need to warm up before doing any flexibility, stretching, or other exercises. Before starting, *slowly* jog around the court, or yard, for about 1 to 3 minutes to get the muscles warmed up. This is required before you start any of these flexibility, strength, or stretching exercises. The shorter time is for the little 5-7 year olds. The longer time is for 12 year olds. Adjust the time accordingly with all the ages in between. Start with the upper part of the body stretches, and end up with the lower body part stretches last. Also after vigorously stretching, and exercising unless you are going to the strengthening exercises next, be sure to do a "*COOL DOWN*" routine, instead of just stopping cold.

Exercise No. 1- Overhead Stretch

This stretching exercise is for the torso, upper back, and rib cage. From the standing position, have them put their feet apart about shoulder width. Put the right hand on the right hip. Put the left arm straight up towards the sky and make a fist. Then keeping the arm as straight as possible, move it over until it touches the left ear. Next twist the wrist so it is pointing to the right. Then bend the whole upper body to the right, and hold the first time, for about 4 seconds. Totally relax for 3 or 4 seconds, in between each stretch. For all following stretches, hold for 7 to 12 seconds each. Next switch arms and do it to the left. Repeat at least 3 times with each arm *(SEE FIGURE 1)*.

FIGURE 1

Exercise No. 2- Seated Pelvic Stretch

This stretching exercise is for the lower back, obliques, and gluteus maximus. From the sitting position, have them put the left leg straight out in front with the toe up. Then put the right leg over the left, just back of the knee, with toes pointed outward. Next put the left arm on the right knee, with the left hand on the right hip. Then put the right arm out to the side, and slightly back. Turn the head to the right, and hold for 4 seconds the first time. Totally relax for 3 or 4 seconds, in between each stretch. For all following stretches, hold for 7 to 12 seconds each. Repeat this at least 3 times to each side *(SEE FIGURE 2)*.

FIGURE 2

Exercise No. 3- Hip Extensor Stretch

This stretching exercise is for the hip extensor muscles. From the lying position head up, have them put the left leg straight out to the front, toe down.

Then lift the right leg up, keeping it as straight as possible with the foot flat. Next grasp the right leg with both hands, and pull back towards the head. Hold that position for about 4 seconds the first time. Totally relax for 3 or 4 seconds, in between each stretch. For all following stretches, hold for 7 to 12 seconds each. Repeat this at least 3 times with each leg *(SEE FIGURE 3)*.

FIGURE 3

Exercise No. 4- Hip Flexor Stretch

This stretching exercise is for the hip flexor muscles. From the kneeling position, have them put their left leg out in front of them. Next put their left hand on the left thigh, and the right hand on their right waist. Put a towel or pad under the down knee for protection. Keeping their back straight have them shift their weight to the front leg. Then they lean forward until they feel a stretch in front of the hip and thigh of the leg they are kneeling on. Have them hold that position for about 4 seconds the first time, then totally relax for 3 or 4 seconds. Then switch legs and stretch the other hip. For all following stretches, hold for 7 to 12 seconds each. Repeat this at least 3 times with each leg *(SEE FIGURE 4)*.

FIGURE 4

Exercise No. 5- Seated Straddle Groin Stretch

This stretching exercise is for the inner thigh groin muscles. From the sitting position, have them put both legs way out to the side, toes up, keeping the knees down and straight. Next have them grasp both hands

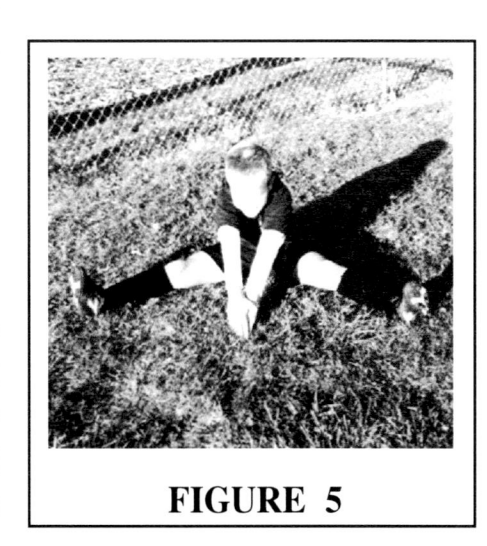

FIGURE 5

together at the thumbs, then keeping the arms straight, lean forward, and reach way out in front. While doing this, try to keep the back straight. Hold that position for about 4 seconds the first time. Totally relax for 3 or 4 seconds, in between each stretch. For all following stretches, hold for 7 to 12 seconds each. Repeat this at least 3 times *(SEE FIGURE 5)*.

Exercise No. 6- Abductors Stretch

This stretching exercise is for abductors in the legs. From the standing position, have them put their right arm down at their side, and extend the left leg out to the top edge of a chair, or some other stationary item. Whatever the item is, the leg has to be as straight out to the side as possible. Then push lightly down, with the left hand just above the left knee. Hold that position for about 4 seconds the first time. Then put the leg down and totally relax for 3 or 4 seconds, in between each stretch. For all following stretches, hold for 7 to 12 seconds each. Repeat this at least 3 times for each leg *(SEE FIGURE 6)*.

FIGURE 6

Exercise No. 7- Triceps Stretch

This stretching exercise is for the tricep and rotator cuff muscles. From the standing position, have them put their right hand behind their head, and touch the top of the opposite shoulder blade. Next hold the elbow of the right hand using the left hand. Then gently push down on the elbow, pushing your right hand down your back. Hold that position for about 4 seconds the first time. Then totally relax for 3 or 4 seconds, in between each stretch. Then switch arms and put the left arm behind them and touch the top of the right shoulder. For all following stretches, hold for 7 to 12 seconds each. Repeat this at least 3 times for each arm *(SEE FIGURE 7)*.

FIGURE 7

FIGURE 8

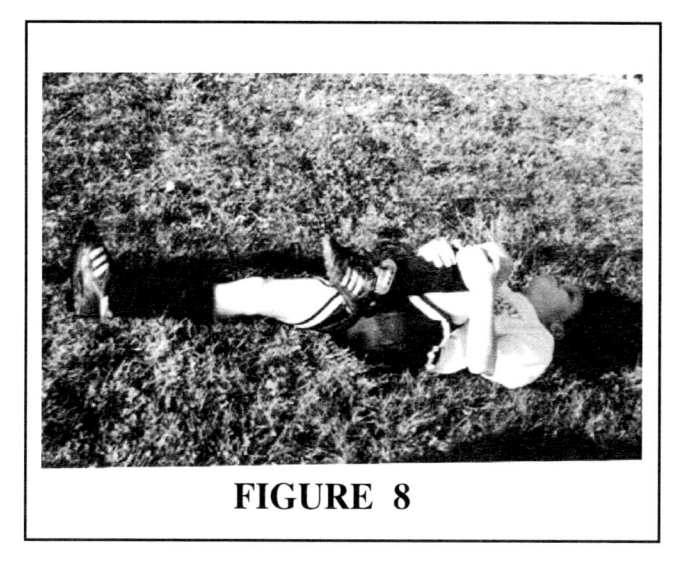

Exercise No. 8- Knee to Chest Stretch

This stretching exercise is for the knee, and lower back muscles. From the lying position face up, have them put the right leg straight out front, with toes up. Then have them pull their left leg up tight to their chest, with both hands grasped together just below the knee. Hold that position for about 4 seconds the first time. Then have them put the left leg down and totally relax for 3 or 4 seconds, in between each stretch. For all following stretches, hold for 7 to 12 seconds. Repeat this at least 3 times for each leg *(SEE FIGURE 8)*.

Exercise No. 9- Calf Stretch

This stretching exercise is for the calf muscles. From the kneeling position, have them lean forward and put both hands out in front, palms down. Next have them extend the right leg straight out to the rear, and up off the ground. Then have them lift up the left knee and move it slightly forward of the hip, with toes bent down. This is like a modified runners start position. They should push to the rear until they feel pull in the right calf muscle. Hold that position for about 4 seconds the first time. Then go back to the kneeling position and totally relax for 3 or 4 seconds, in between each stretch. For all following stretches, hold for 7 to 12 seconds. Repeat this at least 3 times for each leg *(SEE FIGURE 9)*.

FIGURE 9

FIGURE 10

Exercise No. 10- Ankle Stretch

This stretching exercise is for ankle area muscles, and tendons. From the sitting position, have them put both feet, relaxed toes up, out in front of them with feet together. Arms out at their sides, for balance. Next keeping the legs flat to the floor or ground, have them roll both ankles forward, pushing the toes down. Hold that position for several seconds, then relax the feet back to the starting position. Next, keeping the heels flat to the floor, have them roll both ankles back towards their head, with the toes pointing up. This should be a hard pull, with the toes hard towards their head. Hold that position for about 4 seconds the first time. Totally relax for 3 or 4 seconds in between each stretch. For all following stretches, hold for 7 to 12 seconds. Repeat this at least 3 times for each leg *(SEE FIGURE 10)*.

Exercise No. 11- Seated Leg Stretch

This stretching exercise is for the hamstrings, and quadriceps muscles. All players need to do this exercise every day if possible, so they won't pull their hamstring muscle during explosive running or stair climbing drills for building up their jumping strength. From the sitting position have them put both legs together out in front of them. The toes should be pointing straight up. Then keeping the knees down to the floor or ground, have them reach forward and touch their toes with both hands. Hold that position for 2 seconds, then totally relax for 3 or 4 seconds in between each stretch. For all following stretches, hold for 7 to 12 seconds. Repeat the stretch at least 5 times. They can do more than 5 as they get stronger if they like *(SEE FIGURE 11)*.

FIGURE 11

Drills for Coordination and Agility

These drills are designed to teach them how to move around on their feet better, and change directions quickly, without falling down or getting tangled up with their feet. These drills will help their balance, and agility, to improve. Hockey can be a rough game, especially trying to move around to get to another spot, or trying to get to the puck or ball carrier. They should know how to roll over when going down on the ice or floor if necessary *(SEE DRILL No.5)*. In most cases when they do go down on the ice or floor they have to be able to come up to their feet quickly, and keep moving. Coordination also includes good timing. As an example when checking, blocking, or trying to avoid a check or block. They have to have a very good sense of timing in order to get out of the way of a fast closing opponent. Also shooting the puck or ball accurately requires good coordination skills. If they will do these drills every day, even just for a short while, you will notice their coordination and rink sense improving after just a few weeks.

Drill No. 1 Crossover Foot

This is called the crossover foot, and side to side exercise. Take your son or daughter out in the backyard, or down to the park where there is grass and lots of room. Stand in front of them, and face each other, at about three yards apart.

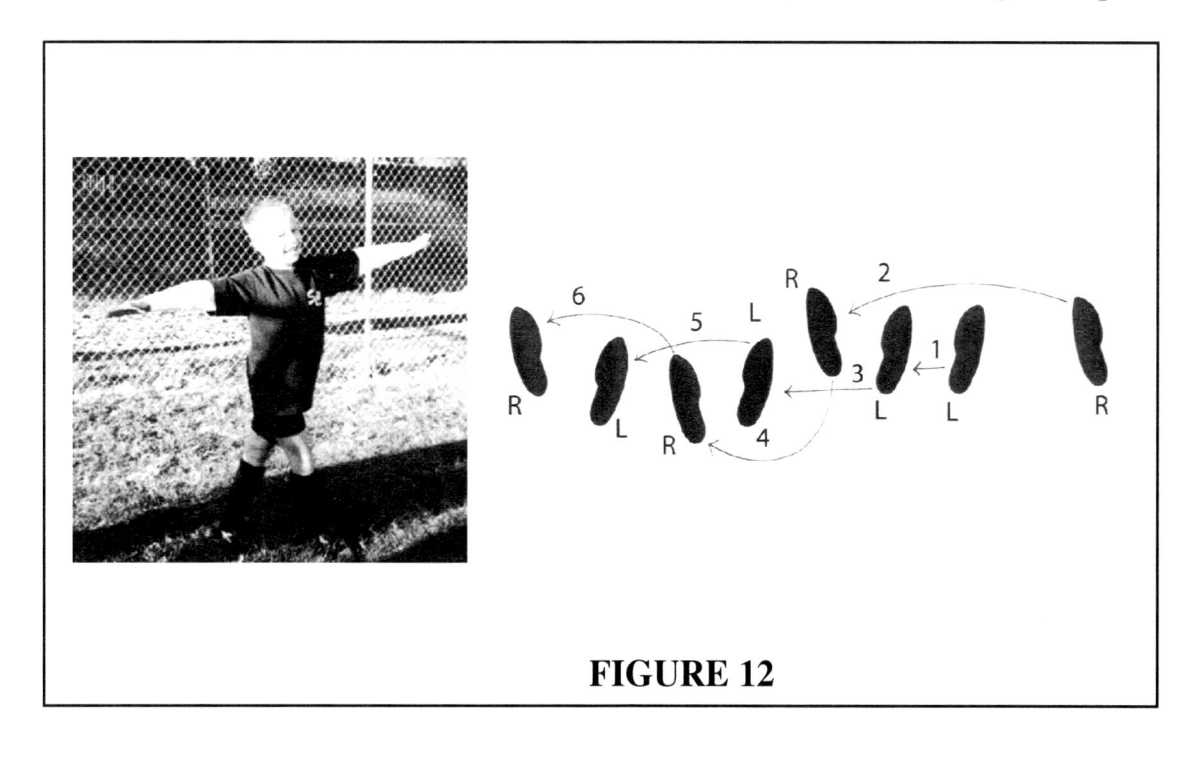

FIGURE 12

You do the same steps they do, except start out to your right (a mirror image). Start by both of you walking through this slowly until you learn how to move your feet, then speed up little by little until you both get better at it. Start with the feet apart, then have them step to the left, with the left foot. Next step to the left, with their right foot crossing over the top of their left foot. Then step again to the left, with their left foot crossing behind their right foot. Next step again to the left, with their right foot crossing behind their left foot. Then step again to the left, with their left foot over the top of their right foot. Then keep repeating this combination of steps to the left, over and over, for about 30 yards. Then stop and reverse these steps, going first to their right, with their right foot, then with their left foot over their right, and so on, for about 30 yards to the right. Keeping their hands straight out to their sides will help them keep their balance. The better they get at doing this, you can speed the process up little by little. After a few weeks, your son or daughter should be able to do this drill on the run, and without falling down. If not, keep working with them, and don't give up because they can learn it *(SEE FIGURE 12)*. They should do this drill for at least 10 minutes at a session.

Drill No. 2 Running Backwards

This is called the running backwards coordination exercise. Here you will need to find a very large back yard, or a big area in a park, with thick grass. The reason I am suggesting thick grass is, it will cushion their fall a little if they fall backwards. This exercise will help them when skating backwards, or changing directions while moving to the puck or ball.

First both you, and your son or daughter, line up side by side about 3 or 4 yards apart, with about 50 yards of clear space behind you. Then both of you start running backwards while pumping your arms up and down. Do this for about 50 yards then stop, turn around, and repeat the drill for about 50 yards, back to where you started. Usually one, or both, of you will fall down the first few times you try this drill. If either of you fall down, laugh and make a joke out of it. If you criticize them too much, they may not want to do it any more. If they are falling down a lot, and you are not, then you may want to fall down a few times yourself so that they will see it is hard for you also, and not be discouraged. This usually works in keeping them interested. Also

FIGURE 13

shout encouragement to them as you are running side by side. The secret for keeping their balance is, raising their knees high while pumping their hands up and down as fast as they can. Once he, or she, can run fast for the 50 yards, and not fall down, you will notice their interest level go up. When they do become good at this, then you can change the drill a little to make it harder. Some suggestions, on how to do this, might be to have them run backwards about 10 or 15 yards, then blow a whistle and have them turn around without stopping, and run forward. Keep doing this, and change directions every 10 or 15 yards. This is one of the best drills for kids, that I have seen, that will really improve their running coordination and agility *(SEE FIGURE 13)*. They should do this drill for at least 15 minutes at a session.

Drill No. 3 Dodge Ball Game

This is a little game they can play out in the back yard, to help them keep away from players trying to make a flying check on them. You will need to have them get 3 or 4 of their friends to come over and help them play this game, so it will be more fun. Start out by marking a 30 or 40 foot diameter ring or square out in the back yard. You can use twine anchored to the ground and spray painted orange, or use colored cones to mark the boundaries. You have boundaries otherwise the game will go all over the neighborhood. Have two of their friends get on opposite sides of the ring or square. Give one of them a light weight beach ball or a volleyball. Your son or daughter and the rest of the players get anywhere inside of the ring or square. The object of the game is for the players on the outside of the ring or square to throw the ball, back and forth, at any of the players inside, and attempt to hit them with the ball. If they miss, the player on the opposite side catches the ball, then throws it back trying to hit any of the players inside of the ring or square. If they hit a player inside, then that player goes outside and becomes a thrower. The player that hit them with the ball gets to go inside, and try to keep from being hit by the ball. The object

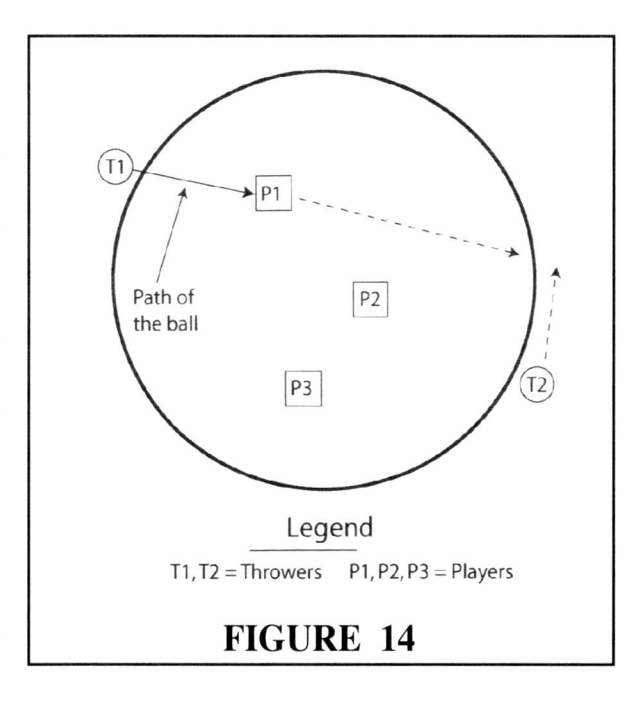

FIGURE 14

for the players inside is to keep from being hit by the ball, and see how long they can stay inside the ring or square. If it's too easy for the players outside to hit the players inside, then you may have to make the ring or square larger in size *(SEE FIGURE 14)*. A <u>TIP</u> is, turn sideways because you present a more narrow, hard to hit, target for the thrower. An alternate version of this game is, have one player start on the outside of the ring or square then run inside of the ring and attempt to tag one of the players. Sort of like the game of "Tag your it". In this method, your son or daughter will have to learn how to shift and contort their body around, to miss being tagged. Playing the game for 20 or 30 minutes at a session should be enough, but they can play longer if they like. Just as long as it does not take up the whole practice time period. All players except the goalkeeper need to play this game once in awhile.

Drills for Controlled Falling & Rink Presence

These drills are designed to help kids control their body, and react to going down on the ice or floor, putting their hands down, or rolling and coming up on their feet so they won't get hurt. No matter what position they are in, they must learn how to control their body while going down to the ice or the floor. The more they do these drills, the more natural it will be for them to go down, put their hands down to stop their fall, or roll and come up on their feet quickly. Repetition of these drills will make these reactions (muscle memory) a habit.

Drill No. 4 Monkey Walk

FIGURE 15

This is called the monkey walk drill. Take your son or daughter out to where there is a large area of grass, and have them get down on all fours, not on their knees though. The fingers of both hands should be spread out, and they should be up on the balls of their feet. Then have them walk on all fours to the front, then backwards, and from side to side. As they get a little more comfortable with this position, then stand in front of them, and point with your hand to all the different directions you want them to go in. Then have them speed it up, little by little until they become very good at reacting to your direction changes. After a few weeks, they should begin to get better at this, and will think it is fun as long as you don't criticize them, or push them to hard. This drill is very good at helping them get up to their feet faster after going down to the ice or floor *(SEE FIGURE 15).* They should do this drill for at least 10 minutes at a session.

Drill No. 5- Roll Over Come Up to Your Feet

This is a drill to teach them to roll over and come up to their feet quickly. What this does is, teach them to be in control when they go down on the ice or floor. You will also need to find a thick soft grass area, in the yard or park, or pads on the gym floor to work on. The grass, or pads, is so they won't get hurt when they go down on their stomach. Wearing their knee pads, and elbow pads, will protect their knees when they go down on the grass or pad on this drill.

Have them get in a ready stance, then say "GO" and have your son or daughter kick their feet back, and drop down to the grass or pad flat on their stomach. As they do this they break the fall with their hands. Next they immediately roll over once to either side, ending up on their stomach with their hands right next to their shoulders. Following that they push up with the hands and bring up their feet so they are in the "Monkey Walk" position in Drill No.3. From this position they come all the way up to their feet into the starting ready position. All the way through this drill, have them look straight ahead, and not to the sides. Doing this also helps them develop their peripheral vision *(SEE FIGURE 16)*. They should do this drill for at least 5 minutes at a session

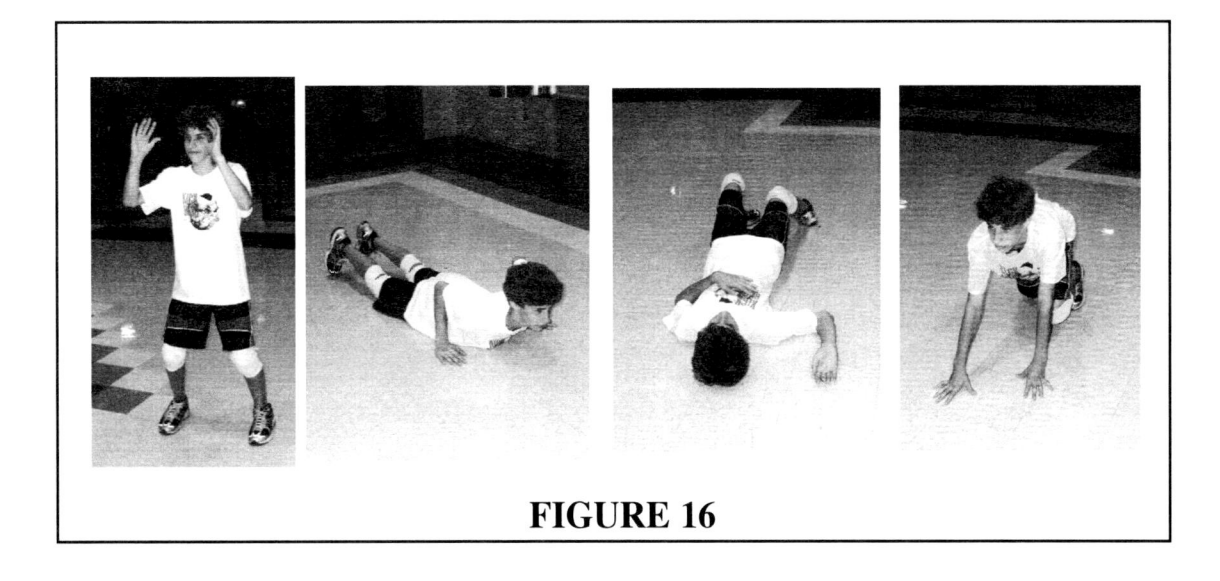

FIGURE 16

29

Drills for Power & Strength

These drills are designed to build up, and strengthen, your son or daughters key body muscles, mainly in their arms and legs. Many young kids these days just sit around home a lot, and <u>don't</u> have a lot of chores to do as they did years ago, possibly on a farm. And because they have very little to do with their arms or legs, like pitch hay, or carry buckets of milk and things like that, they tend to be a little on the weak side. It is important that they do some of these drills every day. If they get tired and quit for a week or two, the drills will not help them as much. Follow all breathing instructions, for they are also important in each drill.

Drill No. 6- Sit up Crunches

This exercise is to strengthen the abdominal, or stomach muscles. Have your son or daughter lay down on the floor face up, on their back, with both knees bent up about 10 to 12 inches high, and feet on the floor. They should then fold both arms, in an "X", across their chest. Next have them raise up just enough to get their neck, and shoulder top, off the floor a little bit. Then hold the raised up position for 5 seconds. Each time, just before they sit up, have them take a deep breath and then exhale it very slowly while they sit up and hold *(SEE FIGURE 17)*. These can be done with someone holding down their feet for balance, ***but only*** if they can't raise up, without the help. An alternative method is to use a "Swiss ball" to do the exercise on *(SEE FIGURE 18)*. They are not too expensive, and the NHL is recommending them. Start out by having them do about 5 or 10 if they can do that many. If they are a large boy or girl, still carrying a lot of baby fat, they may not be able to do that many. In that case start them out with the most they can easily do,

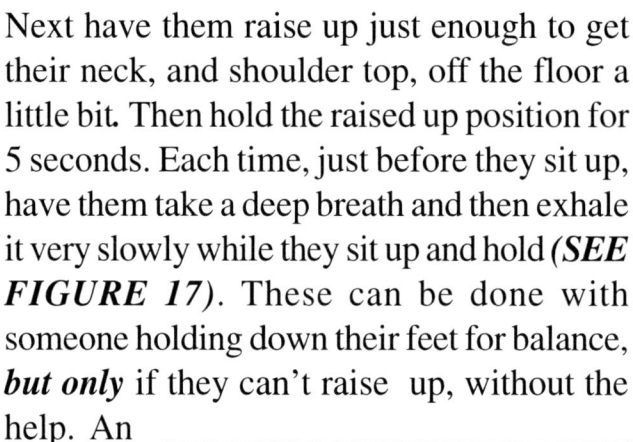

FIGURE 17

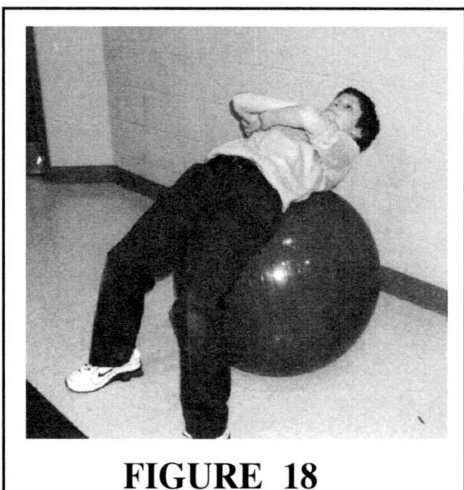

FIGURE 18

30

without struggling too much, then increase the numbers as they get stronger .

Drill No. 7- Half Squats

This exercise is to strengthen the quadriceps (front thigh), hamstrings, gluteal (buttocks), and back muscles. Have your son or daughter stand, with both hands on their hips, and feet slightly apart. Next have them squat halfway down, keeping their balance, with their back as straight as possible. They should take a deep breath before they squat, then hold that position for at least 5 seconds. Also let me point out that they should bend back far enough to feel the tightening in their front, and back thigh muscles. Then as they straighten back up to the starting position, they slowly expel the air. Have them start out by doing about 3 or 5 of these. If they are a large boy or girl, still carrying a lot of baby fat, they may not be able to do that many. In that case, start them out with the most they can easily do, without struggling too much. Then increase the numbers as they get stronger *(SEE FIGURE 19)*.

FIGURE 19

Drill No. 8- Knee Bend Pulls

This exercise is to strengthen the knees. The exercise is going to be a little harder to accomplish because you, mom or dad, will need a resistance type stretch band, and maybe another person to help out. Ideally, you also need an exercise bench in order that they can hold onto the front bar(s), and not slip backwards. The bench also gives you place for the non exercising foot to pull against. The right kind of stretch band is not easy to find. The cheapest, and maybe the best place, is on the "InterNet". Knees are probably near the top of the list for injuries. This means that if you can get set up to do this

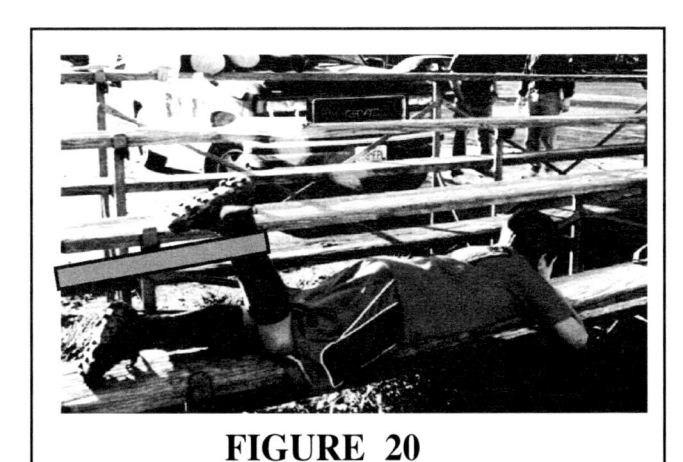

FIGURE 20

exercise with them, it will be a big help, and maybe keep them injury free.

To do the exercise, have your son or daughter lay down on their stomach, on top of the bench. Then have them hold on to the bars, at the front of the bench, with both hands. Attach the stretch band to something permanent. Next have them slip the free end of the band around their right ankle. They should take a deep breath before they pull the leg up, then hold the up position for at least 5 seconds. Then as they lower the leg to the starting position, they slowly expel the air. If you can't afford a bench, but you can get a band, you can still get set up to do this exercise.

In that case, what you might do is, cut off two broom stick handles about 9 inches in length. Find a place out in the back yard with plenty of grass, and space around it. Drive the stakes about 4 inches into the ground, and about 12-14 inches apart. Have them lay down on their stomach, and hold on to the handles with each hand. Next have them extend both feet out behind them, with toes pointed down. Then have a helper get down on their knees, moving their left knee up against the sole of your son or daughters left foot, for support. Next the helper puts your son or daughters right ankle through one end of the stretch band, and holds the other end stationary. Then your son or daughter can go ahead and pull up with the right leg. Have them start out by doing about 3 or 5 of these with each leg *(SEE FIGURE 20)*.

Drill No. 9- Ankle Strengthening

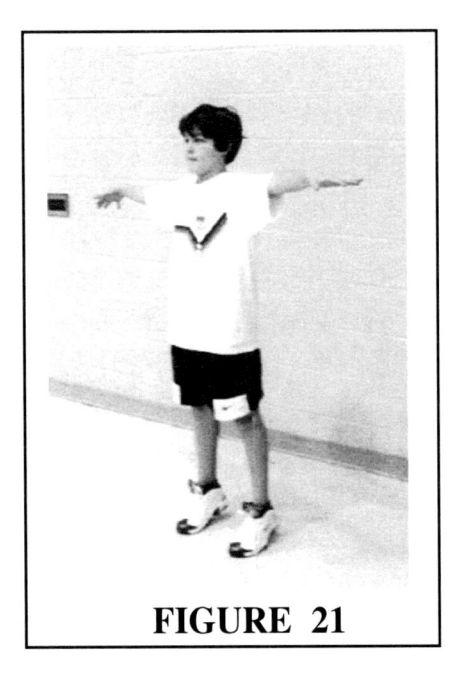

FIGURE 21

This exercise is to strengthen the toes and ankles. This drill is for all players because they need strong ankles and toes to stay up on the skates, and to push off or stop. Ankles are probably near the top of the list for hockey injuries, so this drill is very important for them to do every day if possible. Have them stand up straight, with their feet about shoulder width apart, and put their arms out at their sides for balance. Then they raise up on their toes as high as they can go. Have them hold that position for 5 seconds. Then they come slowly back down to the starting position. Have them take a deep breath, just before they start to push up, then let

32

it out slowly as they come back down to the standing position. Then they totally relax for about 4 or 5 seconds then repeat. 5 year olds should start out by doing 5 of these, with 12 year olds doing about 8. They can increase the number by a few as they get stronger *(SEE FIGURE 21)*.

Drill No. 10- Dumbbell Pullover

This exercise is for the rectus abdominal muscles, and the back of the arms. Again, you will ideally need an exercise bench. However if you don't have a bench, you could do this exercise over the edge of a sturdy bed. You will also need a dumbbell for this exercise. Have your son or daughter lay down on their back, on the bench (or bed), then stretch their legs out, with feet together. Next have them move back, so their arms will be able to extend over the end of the bench (bed). Next take the dumbbell, and grasp with both hands together, just under the end bulb. Then take a deep breath, and lower the dumbbell behind them, over the end of the bench (bed) *SEE FIGURE 22-A*. Then they pull the dumbbell up, to a position just over their throat *(SEE FIGURE 22-B)*.

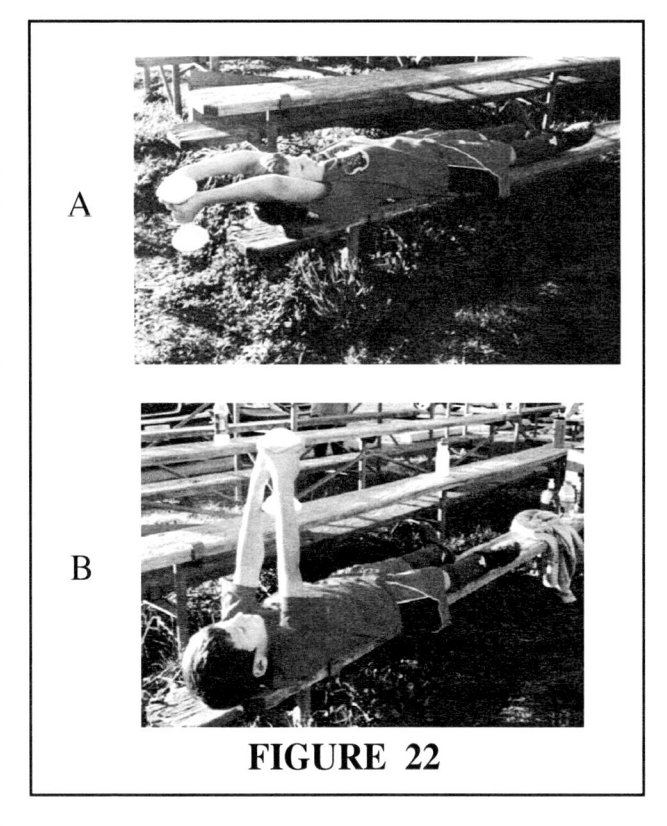

FIGURE 22

Drill No. 11- Wrist Curl

This exercise is useful for building wrist strength for making passes and shots on goal. This is rolling (lifting) up a dumbbell, from the down position, to the up position using the wrist. Lifting weight should not hurt your son or daughter if you don't over do it with too much weight. This drill should improve their wrist strength. Start with 5

FIGURE 23

year olds using two 3.3 or 4 pound dumbbells, and then work up to 6.6 or 7 pound dumbbells as they get stronger and older. Its not so much the amount of the weight, but that your son or daughter is working their muscles and tendons. This drill can be done inside or outside of the house. Start by having them sit on the edge of a utility bench, chair, or couch. Next have them spread their legs apart, then take the dumbbell in their right hand. Then have them put their right elbow on the top of the right knee. Next they will take their left hand, and use it to hold down their right hand at the wrist. To start they should have their right palm facing up, then curl it down towards the floor, then back up again, and hold in the up position for 5 seconds. 5 year olds should do this about 5 times with the right arm, then switch to the left arm reversing the positions, for about 5 times. 12 year olds should start out doing about 10 of these with each arm. As they get stronger, you can increase the number of repetitions with each arm. Caution here, do not over do it with too many repetitions, and hurt their arm or wrist. If they are not strong enough at first, then reduce the number of repetitions and the weight until they get stronger. To judge how strong they are at first, make this observation, they should be just barely able to do the last curl lift on each set, for each arm. And last have them take a deep breath and hold it just before they start on the upward curl motion, and then letting it out slowly as they go to the down position *(SEE FIGURE 23)*.

Drill No. 12- Upper Body Strengthening

This exercise is going to work the entire upper body. Using a "medicine ball" in combination with a "swiss ball" is being recommended by the NHL. Have them lay down on a mat on the floor, and put their legs up on the swiss ball. Next they grab a medicine ball with both hands, and bring it to their chest. Then you, mom or dad, get a few yards out in front of them in position to catch the ball. When you are in position, have them push throw the ball to you, lifting up their head slightly while throwing *(SEE FIGURE 24)*. All players can use good upper body strength, so they should do this drill for at least 6 throws at a training session.

FIGURE 24

Drill No. 13- Finger Strengthening

Here are two drills to strengthen the fingers. They are useful for building finger strength especially for holding onto and gripping the hockey stick. The first one is just taking a sheet of paper in one hand, then crumbling it up into a small wad, or a ball of paper. This is has to be accomplished all with one hand, and with *no* help from the other hand. The second one is just taking a tennis ball in one hand, and then squeezing it as hard as you can, using all the fingers.

One way to practice this is, get a newspaper sheet, tear it in half, then wad it up using just one hand and fingers. Wad up one sheet with the right hand, then take another sheet and wad it up with the left hand. Use at least 3 sheets of paper with each hand at a session. Or take a tennis ball in the right hand and squeeze it hard and hold for a few seconds, relax the hand for a few seconds, then squeeze it again. Do this for several minutes with the right hand, then switch and repeat the same squeezes with the left hand. The time, or number of repetitions, can be increased as they get stronger.

Drill No. 14- Biceps Curl

This is lifting up a dumbbell, from the down position, to the up position. It is useful for building up arm strength for shots on goal, and for muscling up when an opponent tries to knock your stick away from the puck. Have them stand straight up, with their feet about shoulder width apart, and with a dumbbell in each hand. Then have them let their arms hang down at their thighs, with their palms facing out. Next they pull in their abdominal muscles, and stand up straight, with their knees slightly relaxed. Start by having them curl up their right arm to their shoulder, with the palm facing in towards their shoulder at the top of the movement. Next they slowly lower the arm back down to the starting position. Then they repeat the same process with their left arm. 5 year olds should do about 4 of these with each arm if they can, with 12 year olds doing about 8 with each arm. If 10 to 12 year olds have a light weight barbell set, they can substitute it to do their curls. A word of caution here, don't put to much weight on the barbell to where they can't do at least 8 curls easily. They

FIGURE 25

can do a few more when they get a little older or stronger. Have them take a deep breath, just before they start to curl up the dumbbell, or barbell, and let it out slowly as they start on the downward motion to lower the arm *(SEE FIGURE 25)*.

Drills for Running, Leg Strength, and Balance

Drill No. 15- Stair Climbing

This is an exercise is to strengthen the thigh and leg muscles. It is for all players because at some time or another they will all use these muscles. Have your son or daughter find some steps somewhere convenient, maybe a nearby high school stadium after school, or a 3 or 4 story building someplace nearby. What they can do is try several ways. One is, hit each stair with one foot or the other. This developes quick feet while building leg strength and endurance. Another way is, both feet step on one step. This will help your coordination and develop quick feet also. The last way is, run up the steps two at a time. This will lengthen your stride abilities. You can run down the stairs in the same ways. It will help in developing a different area of the quadricep muscle. Running up, and down, the stairs is effective in developing all 4 quadricep muscles. Here is a note of *caution*. Either you mom or dad, or a coach, or adult, should be there at all times while they run the stairs in case they accidentally fall. They could be seriously hurt and no one would be around to help them. Make sure they are properly warmed up and stretched out before doing this exercise.

Drill No. 16- Wind Sprint Ladders Running

This is running out to a set distance, touching down, and going back to the starting point. Then touching down at the starting point, and running out to a longer distance, touching down, and running back to the starting point. The distance they run out keeps increasing as they touch the starting point. It is for all competitors because at some time or another they will all need to use quickness and endurance. If you don't have a football field close by, with white yard line markers, this will take a little work to set up. ***Beware***, before they even start this drill, have them jog around for 3 to 5 minutes to get their muscles properly warmed up. Next, since this is an explosive type drill, have them do at least 8 to 10 hamstring stretches to keep them from getting hurt. To make the yard line markers, try using old white plastic milk bottles filled with sand, kitty litter, or water, to weight it down. You can take a wide tip black felt permanent marker, and mark 0, 10, 20, 30, 40, on them in great big letters. They make great yard markers, and you are recycling for the environment. Next estimate, or measure out a 40 yard distance. Put one bottle, marked "0", down at the starting point. Then go down about 40 yards, and put another one down marked "40". Now in your mind divide the distance between the two bottles into 4 equal spaces, of 10 yards long. Then go out from the start 10 yards, put down the bottle marked "10", then out another 10 yards and put down the bottle marked "20", then 10 more yards and the bottle marked 30. Now you have a 40 yard course set out.

Here is how the ladders work. Have your son or daughter go to the starting point. On the command "GO", have them charge out straight ahead at full speed for 10 yards, then they are to stop quickly and touch either hand down on the ground, turn and run back to the starting line. They will know when they have gone 10 yards, by looking over at the milk bottle. And always looking over at the milk bottles will tell them when to touch down. Now, at the starting point, they stop again, quickly touch either hand down, then they turn and run out to the 20 yard marker. Again they touch down, then turn and run back to the starting point. Then they touch down again, turn, and run out to the 30 yard marker. Then they touch down again, turn, and run back to the starting point. In other words they will be increasing the distance they run, by 10 yards, each time they touch down at the starting point. The last time they will be running the whole 40 yards, then touching down, and running back the 40 yards to the starting point. Have them try to do at least one set of these, every time you practice this drill. Later on if they can do more than one set, and they are not too tired, its ok *(SEE FIGURE 26)*.

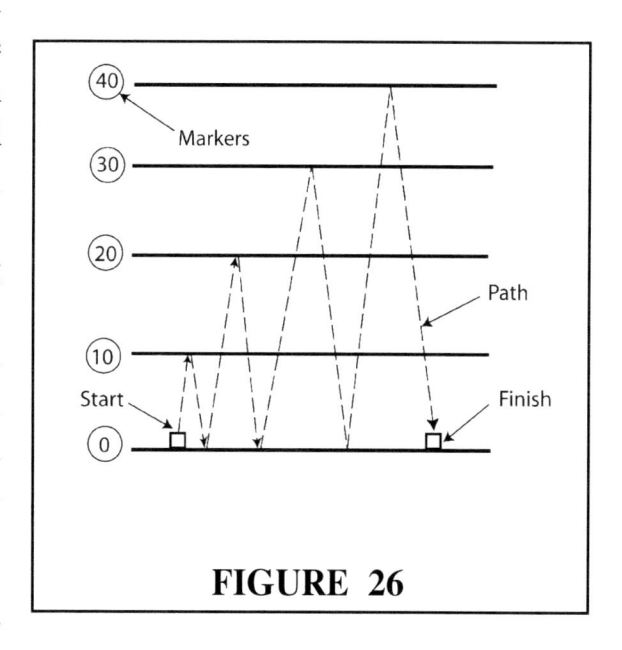

FIGURE 26

Drill No. 17- Speed Burst Running

This is explode out running to a set distance, stopping and walking back to the marker. Resting for a few seconds, then explode out running back to the starting point. Next resting at the starting point for a few seconds, then explode running out to the next longer distance. Then resting again, and explode running back to the starting point. The distance they run out keeps increasing as they explode run out from the starting point. The distance they run for this drill can be tailored to specific training needs. Also if you can find a gradually sloping hill with a reasonable incline, this drill can be run up hill to develop even better lung capacity, and endurance. And after they have been doing this drill for awhile, you can speed up the drill and further improve on their quickness. The beauty of this is when they run in their first game or practice, and you see how fast they are when compared to the other kids their own age, both of you will feel good about having worked with them on this excercise. It is for all competitors because at some time or another they will all need to use quickness and endurance. But it is especially good for helping them get to the puck or ball quickly.

This is a special quickness, and endurance, running drill. It is called speed bursts. It is a drill that is somewhat like ladders *(SEE FIGURE 26)*. There are several variations, but I like this one best for young boys or girls. I have always ended up coaching the littlest kids, so that's why I am recommending this drill, and because I know it works. **Beware** before they ever start this drill have them jog around the yard or park a few times, to get their muscles warmed up properly. Next have them do at least 8 or 10 hamstring stretches. This is to keep them from possibly getting hurt. Start off by marking a 20 yard coarse similar to the one in Drill No. 16 *(SEE FIGURE 26)*, except put the yard markers at 5 yard intervals instead of 10 yards apart. When you have the course marked, have your son or daughter go to the starting point of yard "0". On the command "GO", have them explode out from the starting line. Then they run as fast as they can for 5 yards while pumping their knees, and hands, up and down as high as they can. Then at the 5 yard marker, have them stop and catch their breath, turn, and walk back to the 5 yard marker. Next give them a half minute to rest, then say "GO", and have them run as fast as they can back to the "0" yard marker. Then they turn, and walk back to the "0" yard marker while catching their breath. Then let them stand there at the "0" yard marker, and rest half a minute. Then say "Go", and have them run out to the 10 yard marker the same way and stop, then turn, and come back to the 10 yard marker. Then they rest a half minute, then say "GO", and they run back to the "0" yard marker. They keep doing this until they get all the way out to the 20 yard marker, going 5 yards more each time. Make sure they pump their hands up and down, and get their knees up as high as they can.

If they get too tired, stop the drill until they can build up their stamina, to get all the way through one complete set. This drill will be very tough, on boys or girls that are big for their age, or overweight, so be patient and keep encouraging them. If they are having trouble, then try going just a little bit farther each day or week as you see that their endurance is building up. One time through the whole 20 yards once a day, should be more than enough for a 5 year old. That would be a big accomplishment, for even the best of 5 year olds.

Drill No. 18- Balance Conditioning

This is an exercise to condition players to have good balance. You will have to get a "balance board" for this drill. They are not too expensive if you watch for a "sale" on them. What these boards do is build muscle memory, and develop the inner ear balance mechanism. Have them stand on the board with both feet, knees bent, then move it up and down. After a few "teeter totters" they try to keep the board level to the floor *(SEE FIGURE 27).* They should work on this drill at least 10 minutes at a training session.

FIGURE 27

Cool Downs after Exercising

After their body gets all heated up, it tries to cool itself down after a workout. So make sure they do *"cool downs"* after doing any strenuous exercises, or drills. Cool downs can be as simple as slowly just walking around the yard, or pedaling very slowly and relaxed on an exercise bicycle, for at least 3-5 minutes. Or it could be just a slowed down, and relaxed, version of the strenuous exercise they just finished. The idea is, to get as many parts of the body moving, but in a slower motion for about 3-5 minutes, right after you have completed your exercise routine. Remember though the more intense their exercise pace was, the more gradual their cool down pace should be. Step it down gradually. Another thing to point out is, don't let them get "chilled" right after a strenuous intense exercise routine, by being someplace where the temperature is cool. Such as outside when it's 50 or 60 degrees. The ideal temperature to cool down in is 68-72 degrees.

The Games Approach to Learning Hockey

The better way to teach kids a sport is in this order, play the game, learn the tactics, learn the skills. And that is all well and good, except for one small thing to remember. Not all kids learn the same. Remember in school when some kids memorized the spelling words, and others had to learn by the "Phonics" method. No matter what the experts say, usually when kids just go out there and start playing, they make a lot of mistakes. And not always, but usually that translates into losing the game. And yeah they are busy and not bored, but believe me they are not having fun when they mess up because they don't know what to do. I think the way to blend this all in is to get them out there in the street or driveway, with a few friends, put on some in line skates and play a half rink game using one goal. Explain to them the tactics of what the game is about, and just let them play a little while. Then mix it in with teaching them fundamentals every other day or training session. This way they get the best of both worlds so to speak, by putting into practice what they just learned the day before.

Drills for Skating & Movement

The first fundamental your son or daughter needs to learn is the basic skills for skating. Skating is going to be a little different depending on whether your son or daughter is training for ice hockey or roller hockey. These drills are basically to teach them to move automatically in the direction they wish to go. One of your hardest tasks is going to be teaching your son or daughter how to skate. When they are beginners they will have to work on these drills every day until it becomes a habit with them (muscle memory). They should eventually use all these skills without even thinking about what they are doing. It's going to take lots of practice and repetition though, on your part mom or dad. Don't give up on them, they can learn how to skate. First they have to learn to skate forward, then stopping, then how to make turns, then backwards, and last sideways.

Drill No. 19- Forward Skating
The Basics are:
Start off by getting a hockey stick. Not only do you have to get used to skating around with a hockey stick, but it does give you some support as you are standing up learning to skate. There are 3 phases to the forward skating movement. They are the "drive", "the glide", and the" recovery". Power is developed with

fast short strides. As your speed increases you go to longer strides, and fewer of them. Begin training by getting into a ready position. The feet are about shoulder width apart. The skates are parallel to each other. The knees are slightly bent and just ahead of the toes of the skates (stay low). The body is leaning slightly forward with the head up. Keep the back straight, and the thighs angled back. Both hands are holding the stick with the blade down on the ice and off to one side *(SEE FIGURE 28)*. To start the stride (drive), the push foot is turned about 35 to 40 degrees towards the outside of the body *(SEE FIGURE 29-A)*. Then shift your weight to the push foot. Next the push foot is pushed down and out to the side, with the skate blade or wheels pushed hard against the ice or the floor surface. As the push foot pushes out to the side, the knee of the other leg is pushed forward which extends the push leg way out to the rear *(SEE FIGURE 29-B)*. This action moves you

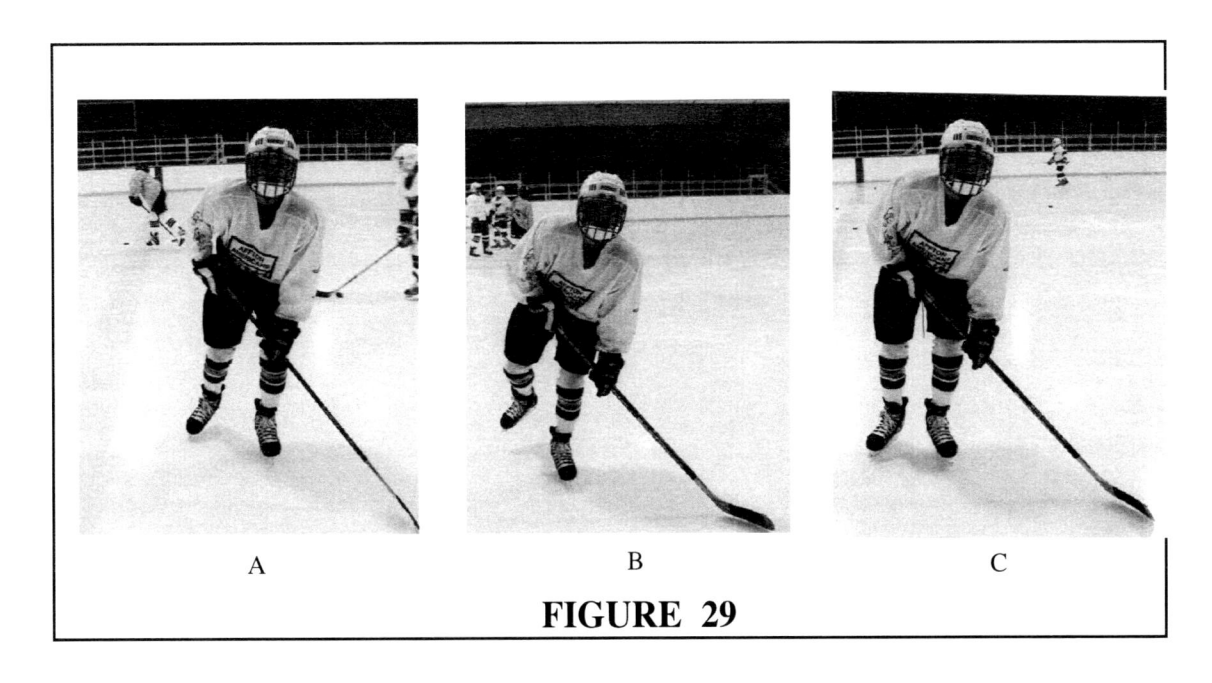

FIGURE 28

A   B   C

FIGURE 29

forward. As you go forward, you "glide" along on the non pushing foot with the toes pointing straight ahead. Your weight is then shifted to the glide leg. At the end of the stride push, the push leg is lifted slightly up off the ice or floor. Then the knee bends as the leg is brought forward up next to the glide leg at the starting position *(SEE FIGURE 29-C)*. This completes the stride movement (recovery) cycle. The next move is a stride using the opposite foot. And the process starts all over again.

Practice:

This can be practiced out in the street, or on a flat driveway. What you want to do is get a cone and place it out ahead of your son or daughter about 20 yards. Have them practice skating forward all the way down to the cone, then stop and skate forward back to the starting point. All skaters should work on this every day until they can skate well enough to move forward with out even thinking about what they are doing. Since hockey is played while the players are on skates, make sure they know how to skate forward before you move on to any of the other training exercises. All players should work on this drill every day for at least 15 minutes.

Drill no. 20- Stopping
The Basics are:

Start off by getting a hockey stick. Not only do you have to get used to skating around with a hockey stick, but it does give you some support as you are standing up learning to make a skate stop. There are 3 basic stopping techniques for skaters. They are, "the one foot drag", "the quick turn", and "the 2 foot stop". The one foot drag is used more for roller hockey. It won't let you stop quickly, but it can be used effectively to slow you down for maneuvering. You start by going into the ready position, then a glide mode

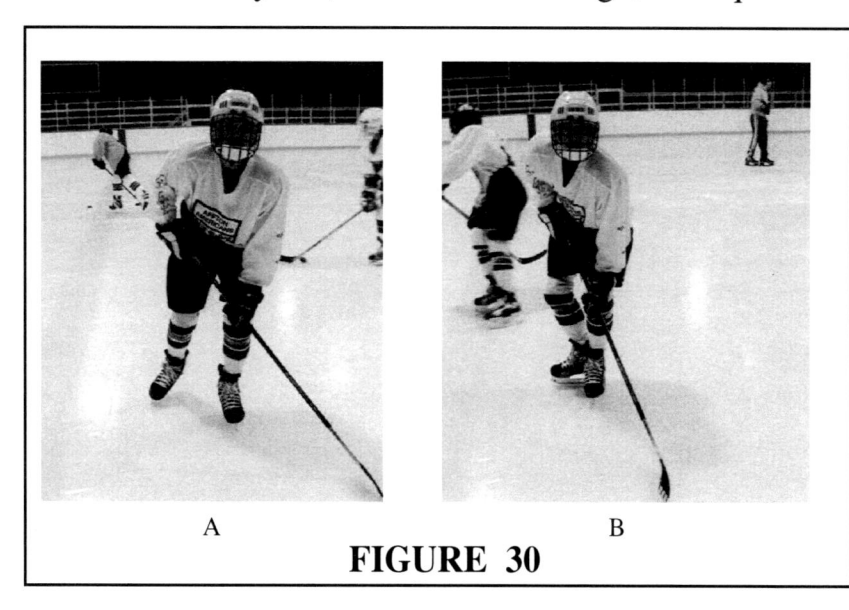

FIGURE 30
A   B

as an approach move *(SEE FIGURE 30-A)*. Then you have to figure out which foot will be the glide foot, and which foot will be the drag foot. Next you put the drag foot behind the glide foot. Then you turn the drag foot 90 degrees to the direction you are going, and drag it behind you on the inside edge of the blade or wheels. Putting pressure on the blade or wheels by pushing downward is what slows you down *(SEE FIGURE 30-B)*.

    To execute the quick turn stop, you stop skating and go into a glide mode for your approach. Next go into the ready position *(SEE FIGURE 31-A)*. From there you put the foot, on the side you wish to turn to, in front of the other skate in a heel toe arrangement. You then start the turn by turning the head and shoulders in the direction you wish to turn toward. Next you bring the arms and the stick towards that same side. Then as you turn, you distribute your weight as evenly as possible to both skates. Make sure they lean forward and don't sit back on their skates though *(SEE FIGURE 31-B)*. Next you exert pressure on the outside edge of the leading foot skate, and on the inside edge of the back skate. The skates should be kept at shoulder width apart around on fourth of a semi circle turn radius. Once the turn starts you have to apply a hard force of pressure down on both skates. This is what causes the skates to make a quick turn *(SEE FIGURE 31-C)*. As you start to stop you will feel a force trying to pull you out of stopping. So you have to be ready with the proper lean in, to counter that force.

    The two foot, or sometimes called the hockey stop technique, is more of an advanced move to use on the ice. You start out in the ready position, then go into a glide towards the stopping point *(SEE FIGURE 32-A)*. You next turn your body 90 degrees sideways to the direction you are moving. Then you begin

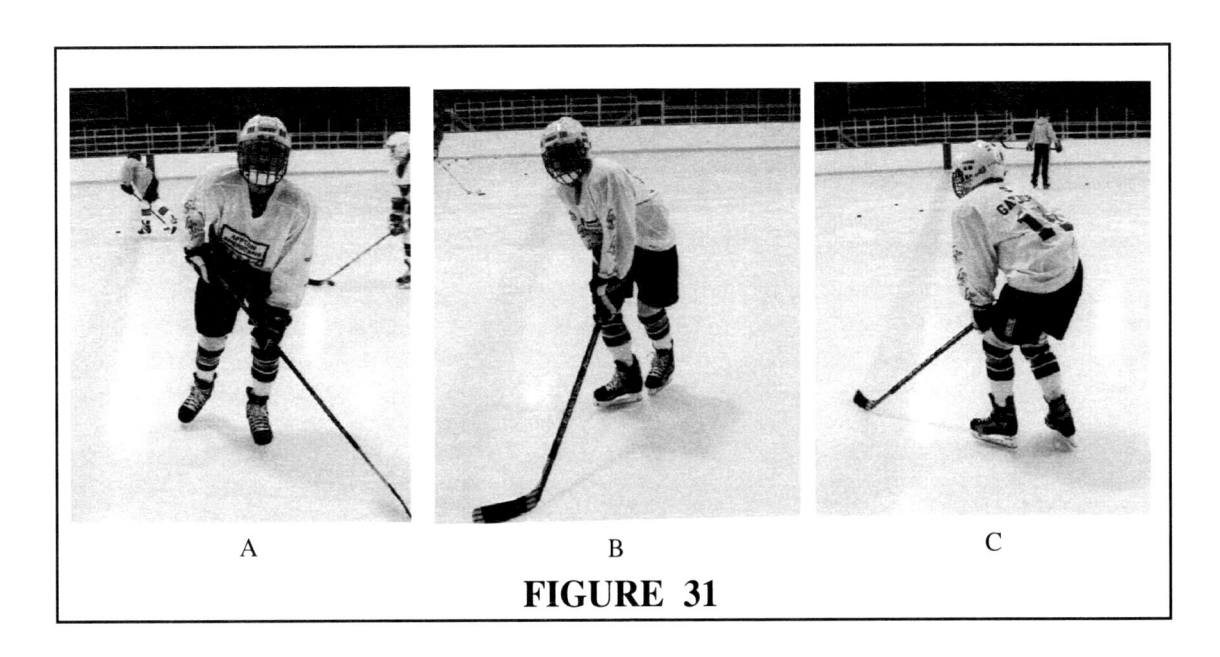

FIGURE 31

your stop by turning the shoulders, then the hips, as you swing either leg into the front breaking position *(SEE FIGURE 32-B)*. The inside leg acts as a pivot, and travels slightly ahead of the outside leg in a heel toe position. Your weight wants to be evenly distributed on both feet. Next both legs are extended forward with hard pressure being put on the front part of the skates, using the inside edge of the outside skate, and the outside edge of the other skate *(SEE FIGURE 32-C)*. It is most important to put the pressure on the front part of the leading skate inside edge. This is the action that really makes you stop on the ice. Make sure they keep both hands on the stick, but don't lean on it.

Practice:

This can be practiced out in the street, or on a flat driveway if you are using the in line roller skates. You will have to find an available ice rink though to practice the "two foot" ice hockey stop. What you want to do is put a cone down where they start, then get another cone and place it out ahead of your son or daughter about 20 yards. Have them skate forward down towards the cone, then first work on their "one foot drag" stops right at the cone, using it for a stopping point. Then turn around and skate back towards the starting point, and making another stop there. Follow this by working on the "quick turn" stop, then the "two foot" stop. All skaters should work on these 3 techniques every day until they can skate well enough to make their stops without even thinking about what they are doing. Since hockey is played while the players are on skates, make sure they know how to make all the stops on their skates before you move

A B C

FIGURE 32

on to any of the next training exercises. All players should work on these drills every day for at least 30 minutes.

Drill No. 21- Turning on Skates
The Basics are:

Start off by getting a hockey stick. Not only do you have to get used to skating around with a hockey stick, but it does give you some support as you are standing up on your skates learning to make turns. All players are going to have to learn how to make turns. There are 3 different basic techniques for making forward direction turns on skates. They are, "the glide turn", "the stride turn", and the "crossover turn".

FIGURE 33

The glide turn is similar to the glide turn used for stopping. Everything is the same, except after making their turn, they use a crossover start move by bringing the back leg around and over the front leg to power out of the turn and continue skating forward ***(SEE FIGURE 33)***.

For the stride turn, the skater stops skating, goes into the ready position, and glides to their approach ***(SEE FIGURE 34-A)***. Next they lean into the direction they wish to turn to, then shift their weight over to the support (inside) leg. Then they stride with the inside leg and start pumping with the outside leg skate just like it was an oar rowing a boat ***(SEE FIGURE 34-B)***. The outside

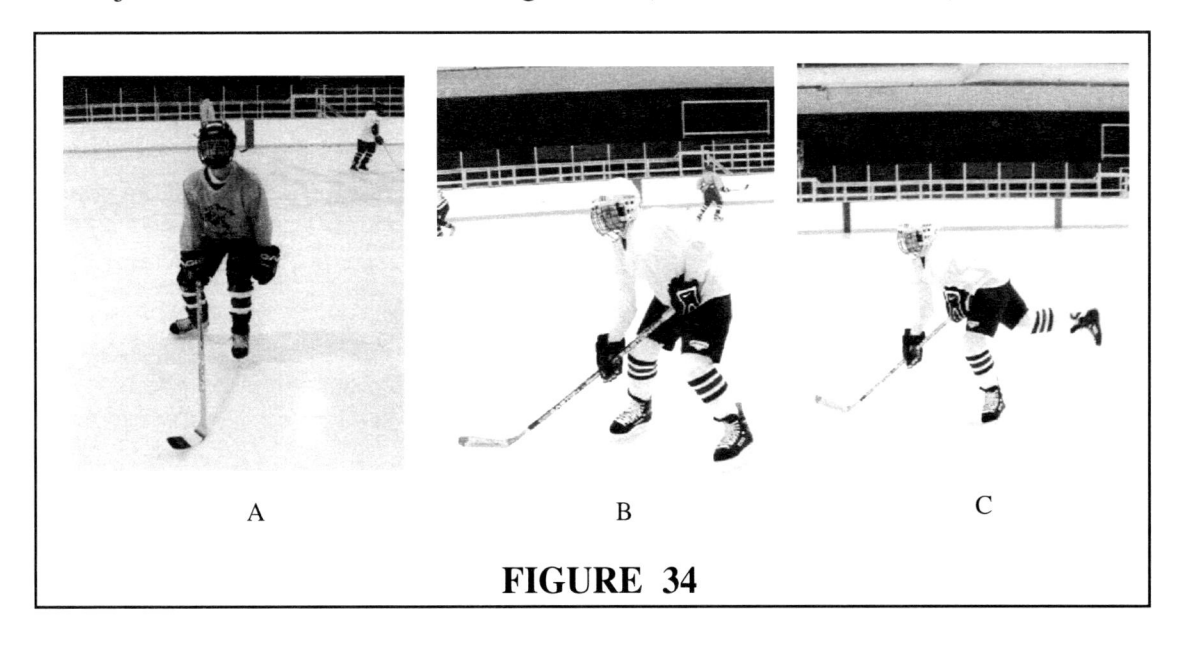

A   B   C

FIGURE 34

edge of the inside (gliding) leg, and the inside edge of the pumping leg is what pushes the skater through the turn. They finish the turn with a low recovery move with the pumping leg by bringing it up, and then a strong hard toe kick action as they come out of the turn *(SEE FIGURE 34-C)*.

For the crossover turn, the skater stops skating, goes into the ready position, and glides to their approach *(SEE FIGURE 35-A)*. This is a turn a player would use when they want to increase or maintain their speed through the turn. The first move is to push the outside leg of the turn all the way out to the side until it is fully extended *(SEE FIGURE 35-B)*. All through the push move, the skate should stay in contact with the ice surface. At the end of the push, the skater pushes down hard on the ball of the foot, to get that extra push from the stride. After the leg has been extended, the skater swings the outside leg over the inside leg skate. The outside leg skate should now be parallel to the inside skate, but slightly ahead of it *(SEE FIGURE 35-C)*. Next the skater pushes the inside skate (other leg) to its full extension outward and under the body, using the outside edge of the skate *(SEE FIGURE 35-D)*. Once it has been extended, the leg is recovered by being brought back in next to the outside skate. Then the process starts all over again, with the outside leg pushing you farther through the turn. The skater then keeps repeating this technique sequence over and over as they go through the turn, using an equal force with each stride.

Practice:
This is basically an ice hockey turn, so you will have to find an available rink someplace. You can try to practice these 3 turning techniques using in-line

FIGURE 35

skates out in the street or driveway, but it's going to be harder for the little kids. You probably want to put the cones out just like the previous drills, so you will have a reference for making the turns. Have them practice making all 3 turns if possible. Also have them practice turning to the right and to the left. You are probably going to find that with the little kids, turning one way is going to be easier than turning the opposite way. And which way that is will probably depend on whether they are right or left handed. You can't always turn only one way though so keep working with them on learning to turn in either direction. Don't give up on them, they can learn how to do this. If they are having trouble learning this technique, and they are discouraged, just drop it and come back another day to try. If you push the little kids, they are probably not going to want to try it again. Depending on whether they are catching on to this technique or not, they should work on this drill for at least 30 minutes to an hour at each training session.

Drill no. 22- Skating Backwards
The Basics are:

Start off by getting a hockey stick. Not only do you have to get used to skating around with a hockey stick, but it does give you some support as you are standing up on your skates learning to skate backwards. The players that really have to know how to skate backwards are "defensemen". However all players should know how to skate backwards. This is going to take some time and a lot of patience on your part, mom or dad, to teach the little kids how to skate backwards. Whatever you do don't give up on them, they can learn how to do this. There are 5 different technique moves to get the skater moving backwards. They are, "backward striding", "Push and glide backward", "pivoting backward to forward", "backward crossover stride", and the "backward one foot stop and T-Push".

For the "backward striding" technique, have them start by getting into the ready position *(SEE FIGURE 28)*. Next have them shift their weight to the starting foot. Then using the front part of the blade, or the front two wheels of the skate, they push the starting foot straight out to the side until it is fully extended *(SEE FIGURE 36-A)*. To make the correct push, they should apply a direct downward force, using a ball of the foot to heel thrusting action. This would form a C-cut shape if you are on an ice surface. After that foot is fully extended, the skater lifts it up and steps to the other foot. Next they bend the knee of the leg just lifted (free leg), and while keeping it close to the ice or floor surface, brings it in towards the other leg (opposite stride leg) *SEE FIGURE 36-B*. As it nears the other foot (opposite stride leg), they stride straight out to the side with the

FIGURE 36

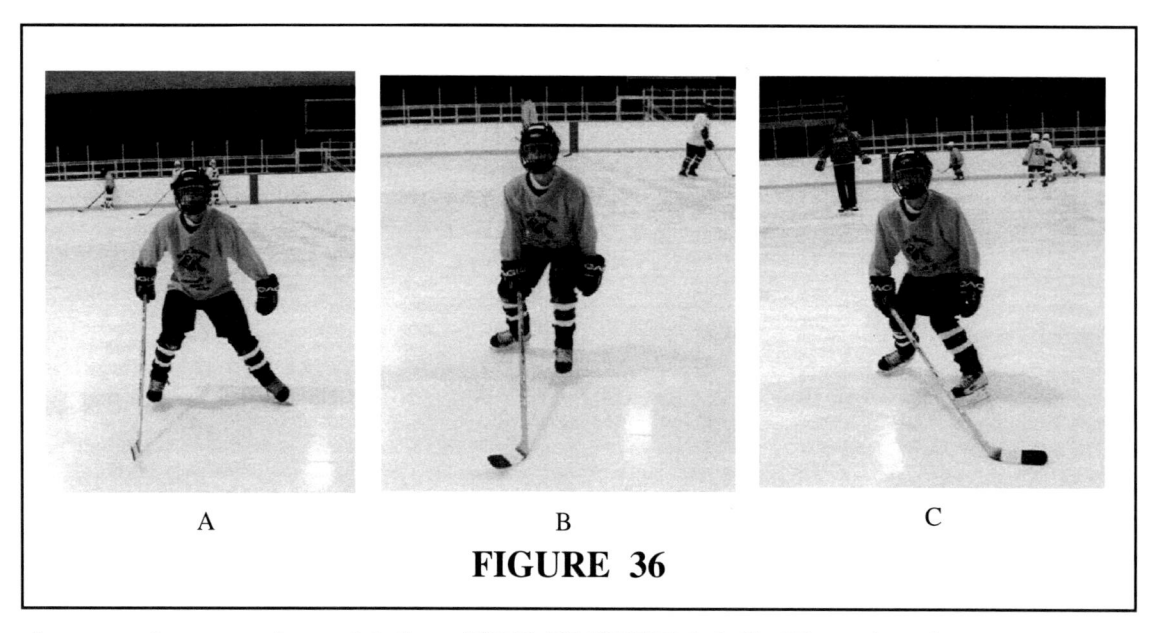

skate on the opposite stride leg *(SEE FIGURE 36-C)*. Then they keep repeating this alternating back and forth action, with both skates, always keeping the weight on the striding leg. This will get them moving backward. If they are having trouble it's probably because they are leaning forward too much. They have to bend a little at the knees, but stay more upright, and maintain a sitting type position.

The "push and glide" technique is sort of an extension of the striding backward technique. When they are moving backwards, what they do is after they make the stride out to the side *(SEE FIGURE 37-A)*, they glide backwards while the push leg recovers and moves back in next to the other leg *(SEE FIGURE 37-B)*. As in the previous technique, the stride makes a C-cut shape in the ice if performed properly *(SEE FIGURE 37-C)*. Then they keep repeating this

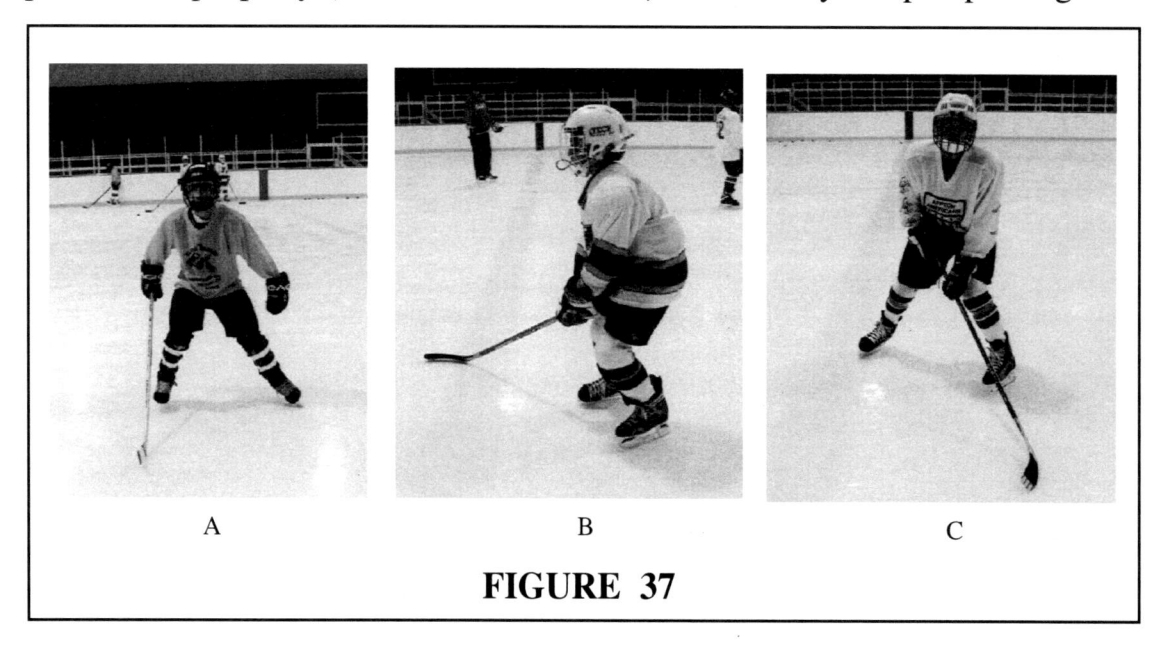

FIGURE 37

A   B   C

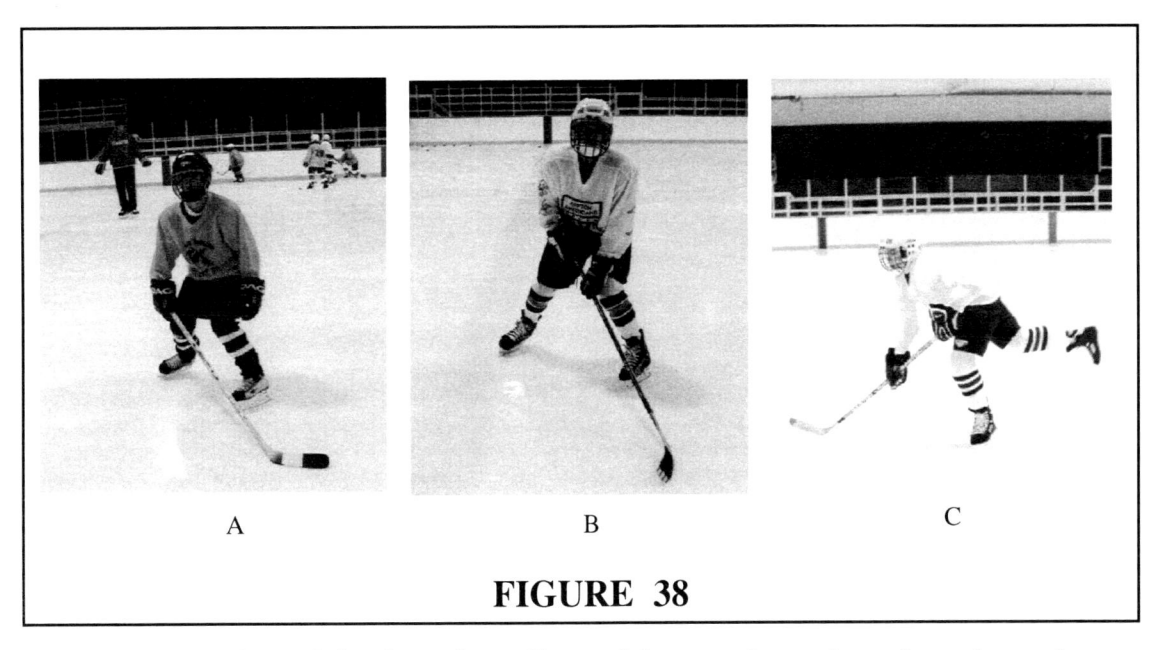

FIGURE 38

alternating back and forth action, first with one skate than the other, always keeping the weight over the striding leg. In other words it's not a stride-recover-stride action, but more like a stride-glide and recover, then another stride- glide and recover action.

The "pivoting backward to forward" move is used when the player needs to turn around from going backwards, and start going forward again. Since this is a turning type move, players need to learn to turn in either direction. This is also going to be hard to teach the little kids. Don't give up on them though they can learn how to do this. Have them start out by skating backwards. When they want to turn to their left, the skater first transfers their weight to the right foot. Next they rotate their left shoulder backward. The body and the hips will follow. After that they lift the left foot up off the ice or floor surface, then they turn it 180 degrees to their left *(SEE FIGURE 38-A)*. Then they glide straight backward on the right foot. Next they transfer their weight to the left foot as it comes down on the ice or floor. At that same moment they dig in the right skate and push down hard as the right leg is fully extended *(SEE FIGURE 38-B)*. This will cause them to turn left. What they do next is swing the right leg on around, crossing over the left leg. At that point they begin to stride forward *(SEE FIGURE 38-C)*. Turning to the right is just flip flopped or opposite for the moves.

For the "backward crossover stride" technique (sometimes called cross-unders), have them start by moving backward in the ready position *(SEE FIGURE 28)* with their weight evenly distributed on both feet. Next to turn to the left, have them step way out wide with the inside (left) leg *(SEE FIGURE 39-A)*. Tell them to reach out as far as possible. Then they grip the ice or floor with the front inside edge of the left skate, and pull the skate under their body. Next shift

A   B   C
FIGURE 39

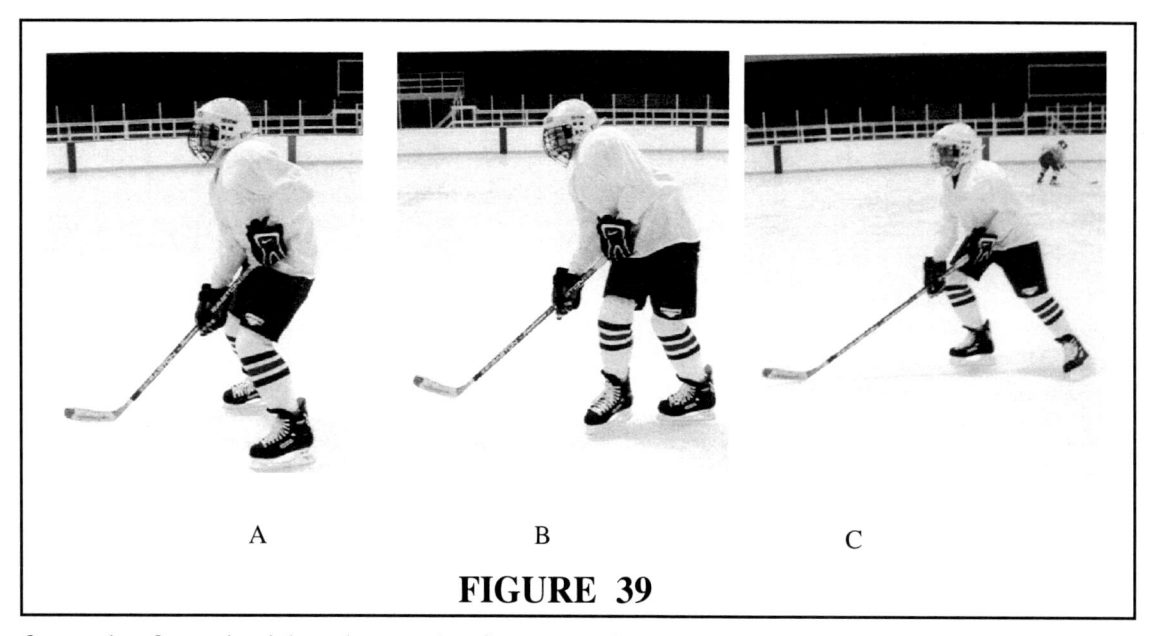

from the front inside edge to the front outside edge of the same skate, then push or drive it hard into ice or floor, and fully extend your leg *(SEE FIGURE 39-B)*. Then reach inward again with left leg, grip the ice or floor, keep stepping and repeat the process until you get slowed down, and are ready to start moving forward *(SEE FIGURE 39-C)*. All the time this process is taking place, the right foot stays over the top and on the ice or floor. One direction will probably be easier for them than the other, but keep trying to teach them to turn both ways. If you like, you can flip flop everything and try starting out to the right first. In that case every movement is with the opposite skate. If they can't seem to be able to go to the other side, then stick with the way that is easiest for them until they get older. Eventually though teach them to both sides.

A   B   C
FIGURE 40

50

For the "backward one foot stop and T-push" technique, have them start by skating backward in the ready position *(SEE FIGURE 28)*. Then have them extend their right leg and shift their weight to the left leg *(SEE FIGURE 40-A)*. Next they start to move the right leg back in behind the left leg, then the shoulders, hips, and legs, turn right as the right foot turns and pivots to the right, and uses the inside edge of the skate for breaking *(SEE FIGURE 40-B)*. At the same time the player bends the right knee and shifts their weight from the left leg to the right leg. The stopping action comes from the right skate as it digs in the ice or floor. Then the left skate and knee move under the body and get into position for a T-push start in a forward direction *(SEE FIGURE 40-C)*.

Practice:
Some of these backward skating techniques can be practiced out in the street, or on a flat driveway if you are using the in line roller skates. You will have to find an available ice rink though to practice the ice hockey techniques. What you want to do is put a cone down where they start, then get another cone and place it out ahead of your son or daughter about 20 yards. Have them practice each technique until they have mastered it. I would suggest having them work at least 15 minutes on each technique, especially "defensemen". There are 5 techniques to learn, and that is 1 hour and 15 minutes each day just to work on their backward skating. It's a lot of work but it is important.

Drill no. 23- Skating to the Side
The Basics are:
Start off by getting a hockey stick. Not only do you have to get used to skating around with a hockey stick, but it does give you some support as you are standing up on your skates learning to go side ways. It's not used very often, but it's still a good technique to know in certain situations. Have them start out standing up in the ready position *(SEE FIGURE 28)*.

FIGURE 41

To go to the left have them step straight out to the left and extend the left leg as far as they can. At the same time they have to push left using the front inside edge of the right skate while facing the front *(SEE FIGURE 41-A)*. The next step is to recover by shifting the weight to their left foot, then lifting up the right foot and bringing it up next to the left foot while still facing front *(SEE FIGURE 41-B)*. Then momentarily shift their weight so it is in the middle of both feet. The next move is to step out to the left again with the left foot, and the whole process starts over again. You could call this a "stride left- recover", "stride left- recover" type move, sort of like sliding over to cover a dribbling player in basketball. Going to the right is just the opposite, you step right with the right skate, then recover.

Practice:

This technique can be practiced out in the street, or on a flat driveway if you are using the in line roller skates. You will have to find an available ice rink though to practice for ice hockey. All skaters should know how to go to the side. Goalkeepers can especially benefit from working on this technique. Have them practice half of the time going to the left, and the other half to the right. They should work on this technique at least 10 minutes at a session.

Drills for Communicating

Teaching kids on a team how to communicate with each other is very important, especially in ice or roller hockey. It's not being used much, or taught, as a skill in youth hockey today. In fact I don't notice it being used in most youth sports at all as I go around and observe teams. According to the "American Sport Education Program" (ASEP), it's the key to a teams ability to play together. And I personally think communicating with each other could help us adults. Maybe then we would not have some of the problems we have in the world today. When I am talking about "communicating", I mean on and off the rink. I am told that there is a particular practice used by some kids, called "banging the stick on the ice or floor". The reason they do this is, to have the other player with the puck pass it to them. And if they don't get the pass, they bang the stick harder on the ice or floor. I don't know what your thoughts are, but this sounds like a selfish "I-me" practice to me. Hockey is a team sport. Now I realize that some teams have one very good player and shooter. However, all kids need to get involved with the game, not just the best player all the time. And if they never get the chance, they won't learn.

Drill No. 24- Communicating Techniques
The Basics are:

Verbal Communicating
     Probably the easiest way to communicate is to *talk*. But you have to be careful how you do it though because the other team will hear to. There are some verbal messages that the NHL players use to communicate with each other. When a player wants their team mate to execute a play or move, they will use terms like "Turn up", Wheel", "Over", "Ring", and "Reverse". "Turn up" means turn up the ice towards the boards on the side the puck is on. "Wheel" means carry the puck behind the net to the other side. "Over" means a defenseman to defenseman pass behind the net. "Ring" means shoot the puck hard along the boards to the weak side. "Reverse" means carry the puck behind the net and then drop it back to the area they just came from so that their team mate can retrieve it. These can work with kids because the other team may not know what they mean even if they do hear them.

     Players should be taught to talk to each other during the breaks, when they are on the bench. As an example if you notice you are open a lot on one side of the rink, let the other players know about it. Then if they pass it to you, it might mean a clear shot on goal for you. If you mention it to the other players on the team and they don't pass it to you when you are open, then wait until after practice and privately let the coach know. Kids and coaches on youth teams catch on real quick that a team has only one or two good players. So what the opponents do is have most of their players surround them so they can't get a shot on goal. And that means some of the other players must be wide open for a shot.

     There is another good time to communicate, and that is when your son or daughters line comes off a shift change. Explain to them that this is the time for them to quickly talk over the strategy on the last shift, and what will be the strategy plan for the next shift. There is a NHL saying that says, "You were born with two ears and one mouth. Listen twice as much as you speak, and you will have an illustrious hockey career". Teach this to your son or daughter.

     All through the game, players should listen to their goalkeeper. They have a very good wide view of the rink, and they can see which one of your team mates is open, and whether the other team might be setting up on the weak side or the strong side. If your son or daughter wants to be a goalkeeper, teach them to recognize what is happening in front of them on the rink, then let their team mates know this as they are starting to set up play out of the defensive end of the rink.

Nonverbal Communicating

There is also nonverbal communication techniques for players to use. Kids need to learn how to fake (deak) opposing players. What I mean by this is pretending to go in one direction with the puck, then actually going the other way. Your eyes are a good way to signal a team mate. As an example, try to make eye contact with a team mate before passing them the puck. When you get older and are a professional, then you can make no look passes because you know where your team mate will be. Since it is hard sometimes to make eye contact through the cage that players wear on their helmet, make sure your son or daughter does not remove their helmet to make eye contact. Nodding the head between players is an effective substitute if players are unable to make eye contact. The stick can also be used to let a team mate know where you want them to go, or where you want to go. Explain to them that when they get to their first team, to make sure they read the message to them accurately, by checking with the coach. Some coaches like to use false indicators for confusing the opposing players. As an example, they might have a player point in one direction for a pass when what they really mean is the pass is going in the opposite direction.

Practice:

To practice this skill, you can use two methods with your son or daughter. One, sit down and explain to them about verbal and nonverbal communicating. Two, play the communication game with them and have them use as many of the different techniques as they can, to help them score points.

Drill No. 25- Passing Communication Game
The Basics are:

Here is a little game you can set up at home with your son or daughter and 2 friends out in the back yard, using only the stick and a rubber ball or a tennis ball. You will need a small goal, or cone markers, so you can tell when the ball gets past the goalkeeper. However, make sure that whoever is playing the goalkeeper has on a helmet with a face mask, and uses hockey gloves for their protection and stopping the ball. The object of the game is for the player and team mate to set up signals, either with their eyes or the stick, then fool the goal keeper by passing and shooting the ball into the goal.

How you can set this up is have one friend play the goalkeeper, and the other friend is a team mate. Remember though this game is for a player to practice their non verbal communication skills, not for goalkeeping. The only reason to have a goalkeeper is to have someone in front of the goal to try and fake or deak.

How you can set up the rules are, 1 point for fooling the goalkeeper and getting the puck into the goal. However, every time the goalkeeper stops a shot, 1 point is taken away. This will give the goalkeeper some incentive to not be fooled. Mom or dad, get a note pad and keep track of each game, with dates and scores, to use for progress comparison later on.

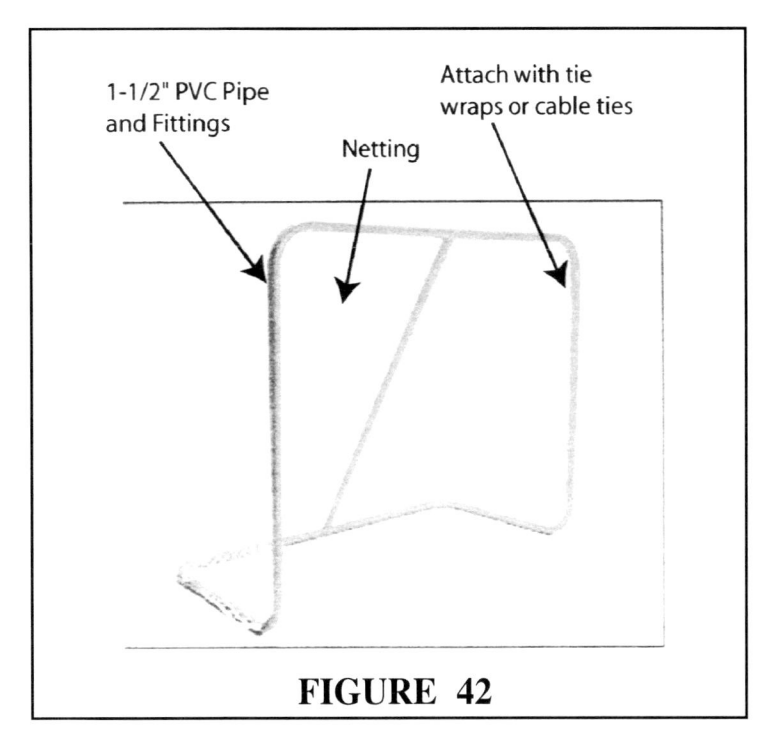

FIGURE 42

Practice:

To practice out in the back yard you can make a goal out of 1-1/2 inch PVC fittings, some netting, and cable ties. Your goal should be at least 6 feet wide by 4 feet high (regulation size), with netting on the back, and sides *(SEE FIGURE 42)*. It will probably cost under $20 to make. Or you can just go out and buy a net for under $40. And if that is to much work for you, or too costly, you can put out two cones to mark boundaries for the goal sides. The size of your backyard game field can be 85 to 100 feet wide (regulation size), or the width of your backyard if it is smaller. You can set a time limit for the game, or you can set a point limit. I would suggest a time limit of 30 minutes.

Drills for Puck/ Ball Handling

Puck or ball handling, as it is sometimes called, is the next most important thing for young kids to learn. If they do not know how to handle the puck or a ball using a hockey stick, they will not be successful playing ice hockey or roller hockey. Puck/ ball handling breaks down into stationary techniques, and moving techniques.

Drill No. 26- Puck/ Ball Handling Techniques
The Basics are:

Hand Position and Grip

The first thing you must teach them is how to hold, and grip, the hockey stick. To correctly grip the hockey stick, the top hand has to be located at the end of the stick, just before the end or butt of the stick. The lower hand should be located about 1-1/2 to 2 feet (shoulder width) down the shaft for the little kids *(SEE FIGURE 43)*. To actually make sure their distance apart of the hands is correct, use this technique. Have them grab the stick with the top hand at the top butt end of the stick, then place the elbow of the lower arm on top of the thumb of the top hand. Next have them lay the lower arm down along the shaft. Then they grab the shaft with the fingers of the lower hand, where ever that point is *(SEE FIGURE 44-A)*. That will be the correct distance between hands. Both hand grips should form a "V" with the thumb and forefinger, with the thumb of the top hand pointing down the shaft *(SEE FIGURE 44-B)*.

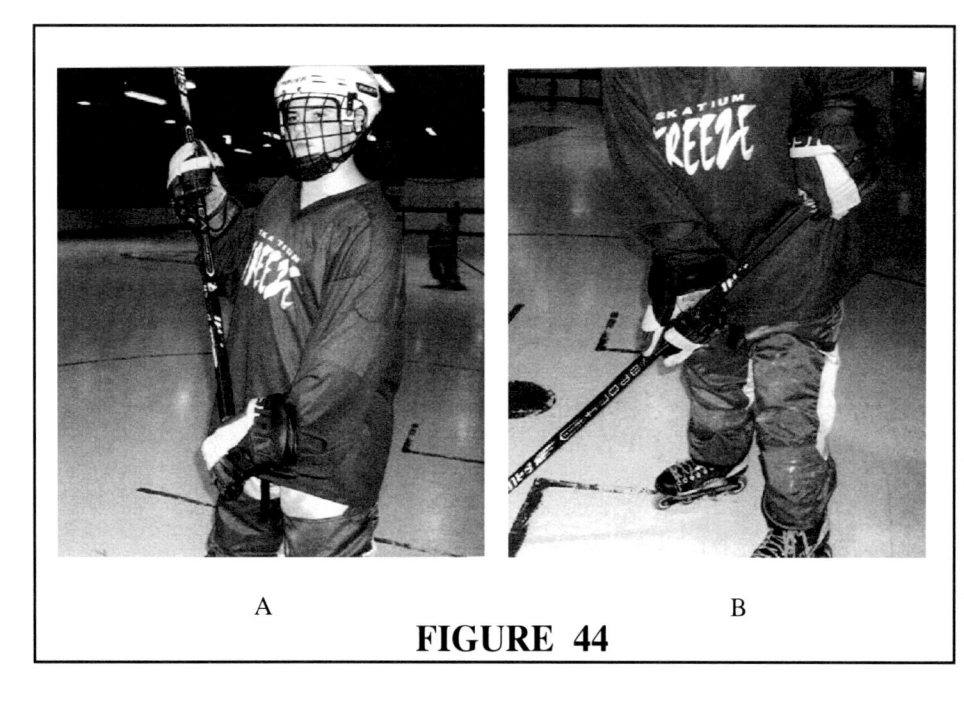

FIGURE 43

FIGURE 44

Stationary Puck/ Ballhandling

When you think of puck or ball handling in hockey, you think of players flying down the ice or floor and dribbling a

56

puck or ball. But young kids need to start out in a stationary position first before they graduate to the moving techniques. When they are stationary, it's easier to concentrate on what they are doing with the puck or ball. Otherwise they

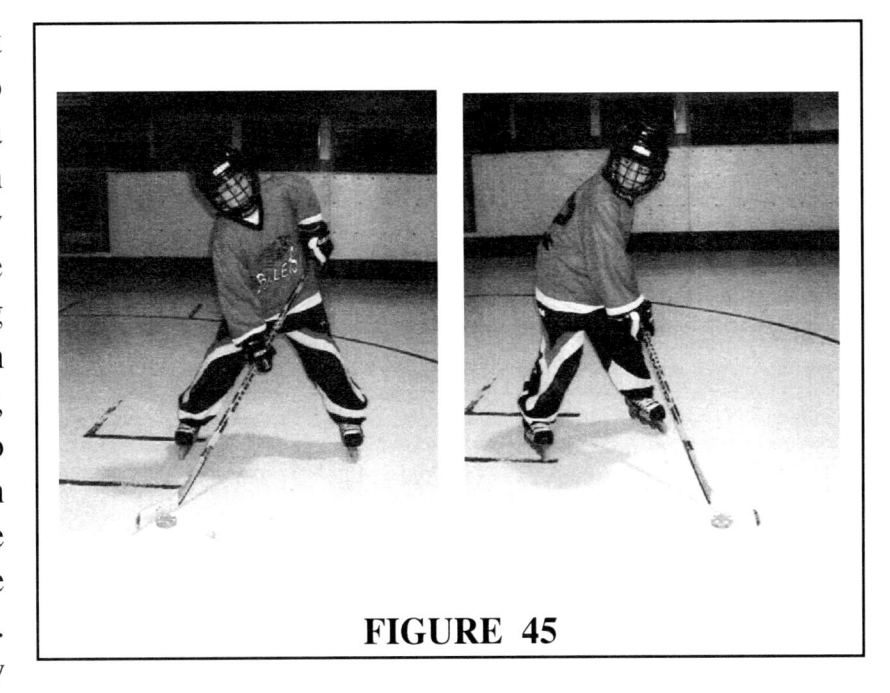

FIGURE 45

have a tendency to concentrate more on the skating, and less on the handling. Start out by having them get into the ready position *(SEE FIGURE 28)*. Then with both hands on the stick, and the blade on the ice or floor, have them move a puck or ball from side to side. They do this by rolling their wrists, and shifting their weight to the same side the puck or ball is on. They catch the puck or ball in the middle of the stick blade, first on the forehand side then the backhand side *(SEE FIGURE 45)*. This rolling the wrists, dribbling, kind of action is accomplished by turning the forehand side of the blade slightly downward *(SEE FIGURE 46-A)*, and the backhand side of the blade slightly upward *(SEE FIGURE 46-B)*. While doing this exercise, have them keep the arms out away from the upper body and relaxed. Watch and listen for their stick blade banging on

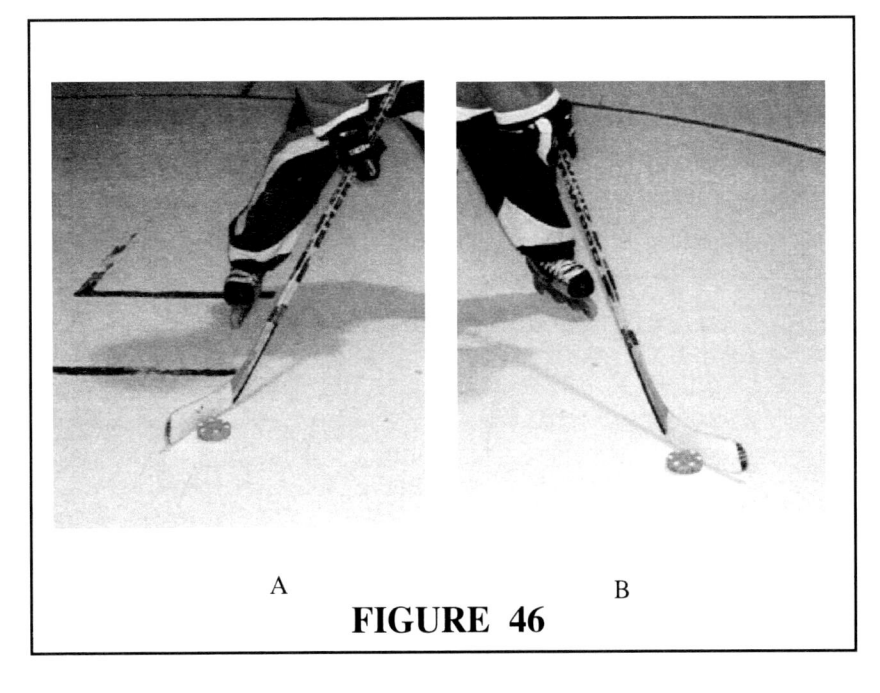

FIGURE 46

57

the surface because this is a sign they are not controlling the stick correctly. If they are doing this, check their hand placement. The exercise should be quiet, smooth, and sort of rhythmic as they go through it.

Moving Puck/ Ballhandling
To start out working on the moving puck or ball handling, have them get into the ready position again *(SEE FIGURE 28)*. Now have them go through the same side to side exercise as in the stationary position, except this time they are going to turn the stick blade at a slight angle so that the puck or ball moves forward instead of side to side in the stationary position. Your son or daughter will have to use a trial and error method of finding a comfortable angle to turn the blade to that lets them move the puck or ball forward. They also have to learn how to skate forward at different speeds while moving the puck or ball from side to side. The forehand and backhand action with the stick, except for the angle, will be the same as in the stationary position *(SEE FIGURE 45 & 46)*.

Practice:
These techniques can be practiced out in the street, or on a flat driveway if you are using the in line roller skates. You will have to find an available ice rink though to practice for ice hockey. Or they can practice this out in the back yard, without skates, using a rubber ball or a tennis ball. However, eventually they are going to have to practice this skill with skates on. All skaters should know how to do both of these drills. I suggest having them work on the stationary, and the moving, technique for at least 15 minutes each at a practice session. They may have to work on this longer if they are little kids or beginners.

Drill No. 27- King of the Circle Game
The Basics are:
This is a clever little puck/ ballhandling game to help them learn the techniques in a confined circle. This game is usually played on a rink in one of the face off circles. These circles are 30 feet in diameter. How this game works is, you send each player inside of the circle, each one with a puck or ball. The object of the game is for each player to keep control of their puck or ball while staying inside of the circle. In addition to keeping control of their own puck or ball, each player tries to knock the puck or ball off the other players stick causing it to leave the circle. If a players own puck or ball leaves the circle, they have to skate around the circle twice before they can reenter the circle. When they do reenter the circle it is <u>without</u> a puck or ball. What they have to try to do then is

steal the puck or ball from one of the players still inside of the circle. If they do manage to steal a puck or ball, then lose control of it, they have to go out and skate around the circle 2 times again before they can reenter. The last player alone inside of the circle, with their own puck or ball, wins the game. What this game does is, force them to become a very good puck/ballhandlers, in order to stay inside of the circle *(SEE FIGURE 47)*.

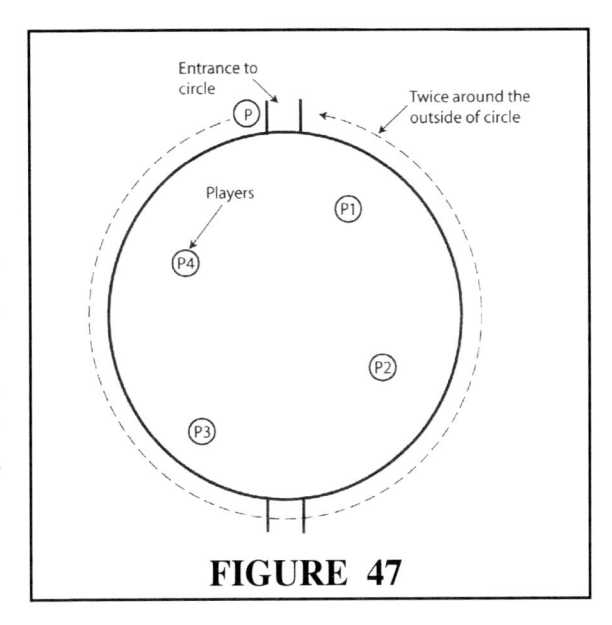

FIGURE 47

Practice:

So if you have access to a hockey rink, you could play this game there in one of the face off circles. Or you could set up a 30 foot diameter circle in your back yard by marking the boundary with chalk, or use heavy twine spray painted orange so it can be seen in the grass. And you could use "U" shaped pieces of heavy wire to hold it down. Your son or daughter will need to find 3 or 4 of their friends to come over and play the game with them. To make the game easier, reduce the number of players. To make the game harder, increase the number of players, and give each player 2 pucks or balls to control. And mom or dad, you are probably going to have to referee this game in order to make them play fair. Kids will be kids. My suggestion is start with 3 players inside of the circle for the little kids and beginners, then increase the number from there.

Drills for Passing/ Receiving the Puck or Ball

Passing and receiving the puck or ball is a specialized form of ballhandling. It is a method, or technique, to get the puck or ball quickly down the rink into scoring position. Passing and receiving can be accomplished while in a stationary or a moving position. There are several different types of passes. They are, the "forehand sweep pass", the "backhand sweep pass", and the "flip pass". The sweep type passes are the most common. These passes get their name from the sweeping type motion of the hockey stick which looks like sweeping the floor with a broom.

Receiving is the technique of catching the puck or ball with the blade part of the hockey stick. Players need to learn the correct methods for receiving the puck or ball.

59

Drill No. 28- Passing Techniques
The Basics are:

The Forehand Sweep Pass
Have them start by getting in the ready position *(SEE FIGURE 28)*. First they put the puck or ball down on the ice or floor surface. Next they place the middle of the blade of the hockey stick, pointing down behind the puck or ball, and at a right angle to the target, then move it outside away from the body and slightly back of the rear skate *(SEE FIGURE 48-A)*. At this point their weight should be on the back leg, their eyes on the target, and the head up *(SEE FIGURE 48-B)*. Pushing with the bottom hand and pulling with the top hand, the player shoots the puck or ball towards the target using a sweeping motion with their hands *(SEE FIGURE 48-C)*. At this point the player starts to shift their weight from the back foot to the front foot. The stick follows through and points toward the target *(SEE FIGURE 48-D)*. Try to keep follow through low if possible.

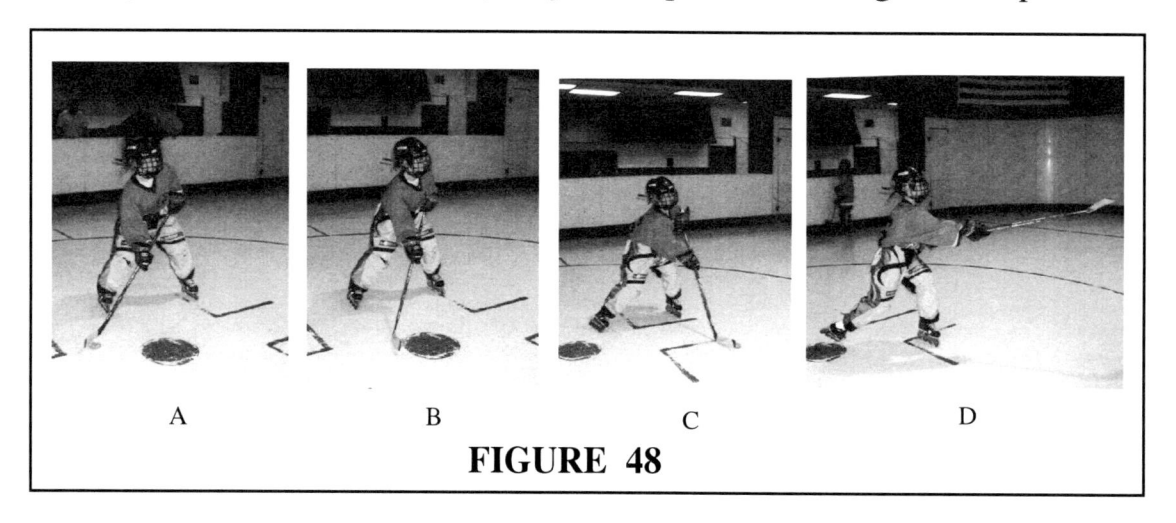

FIGURE 48

They immediately go back to the ready position in case they get a return pass right back at them.

The Backhand Sweep Pass
This is similar to the forehand pass, with the hands out away from the body. Except the puck or ball is placed slightly in back of the rear skate, and out to the side. The stick blade is pointed up and the puck or ball is located in front of the blade, and more on the back part (heel) where the shaft starts to come up *(SEE FIGURE 49-A)*. At this point their weight should be on their back leg, their eyes on the target, and the head up. Next they shift their weight from the back foot to the front foot as they sweep the stick across their body, to shoot the

FIGURE 49

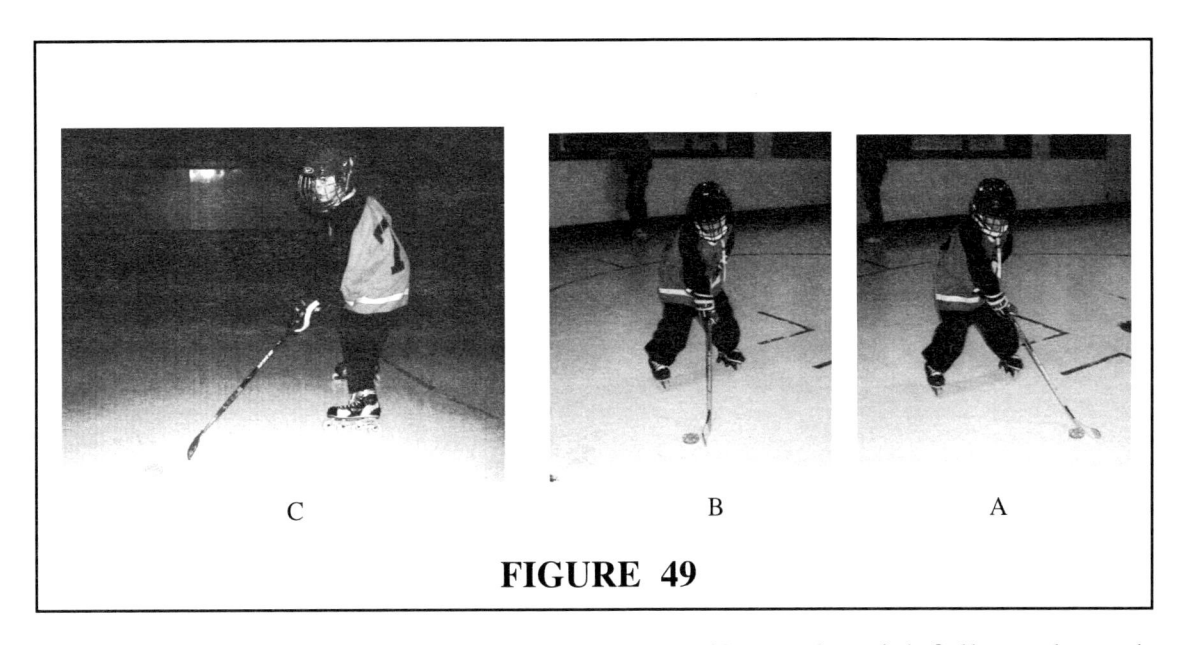

puck or ball towards the target *(SEE FIGURE 49-B)*. The stick follows through low and points toward the target *(SEE FIGURE 49-C)*. They immediately go back to the ready position in case they get a return pass right back at them.

The Flip Pass

The flip pass is a technique to get the puck or ball over an object, like an opponents leg or stick, and on it's way to the target. This is sometimes called a saucer pass. To start have them place the puck or ball on the heel of the stick, either on the forehand side or the backhand side while they hold the stick right in front of their body *(SEE FIGURE 50-A)*. To use the forehand method, they slide the puck or ball off the blade, from the heel to the toe part of the blade using

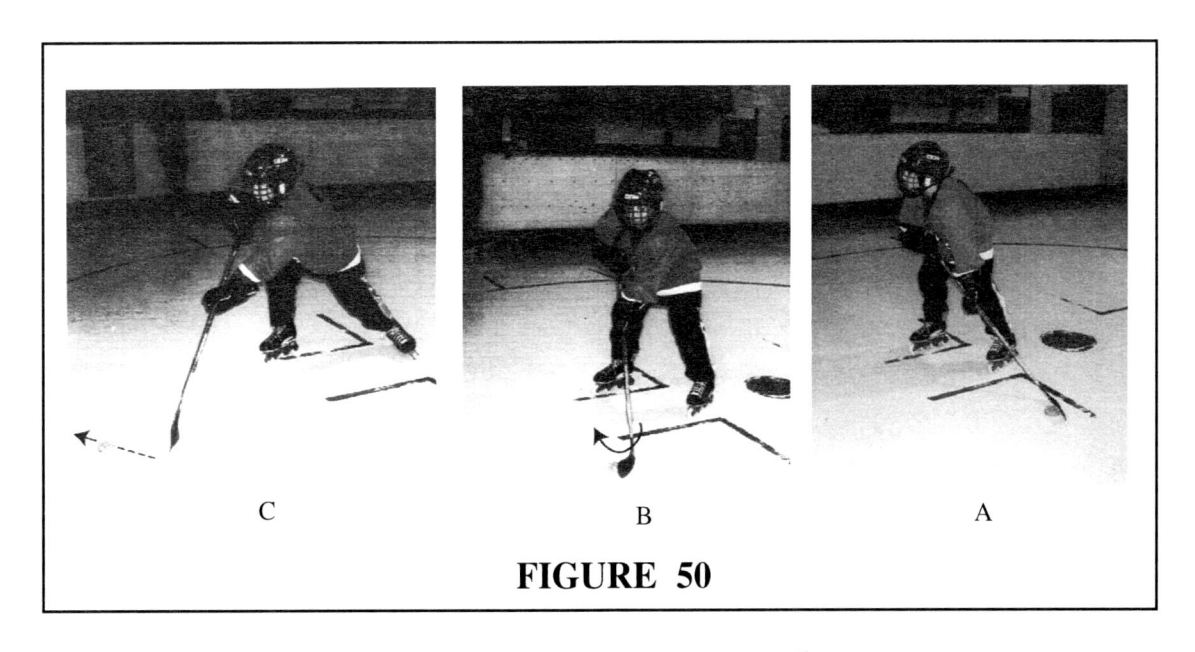

FIGURE 50

61

a little wrist twisting flip up action (this is where it get it's name) *(SEE FIGURE 50-B)*. The follow through is an upward motion, which causes a puck to spin and fly like a saucer (where it gets the other name) in the air while it is flying over the obstacle and toward the target *(SEE FIGURE 50-C)*. With a ball, this action causes it to spin like a top.

The backhand flip pass is a little harder to master. It works the same way in that you want to make the puck or ball spin, except from the backhand position *(SEE FIGURE 49)*. But you kind of have to pull the stick toward you, with a little wrist flip, to get the puck or ball to spin. The forehand way is easier for most players to learn. If they want to try the backhand technique though, it's probably going to take some trial and error attempts to get the knack of it.

Practice:

These techniques can be practiced out in the street, or on a flat driveway if you are using the in line roller skates. You will have to find an available ice rink though to practice for ice hockey. Or they can practice them out in the back yard, without skates, using a rubber ball or a tennis ball. However, eventually they are going to have to practice this skill with skates on if they are playing ice hockey. All skaters should know how to do all of these passing drills. I suggest having them work on them from a stationary stance some of the time, and a slow moving position some of the time. They should work on each technique for at least 10 minutes each at a practice session. They may have to work on this for a longer period of time if they are little kids or beginners.

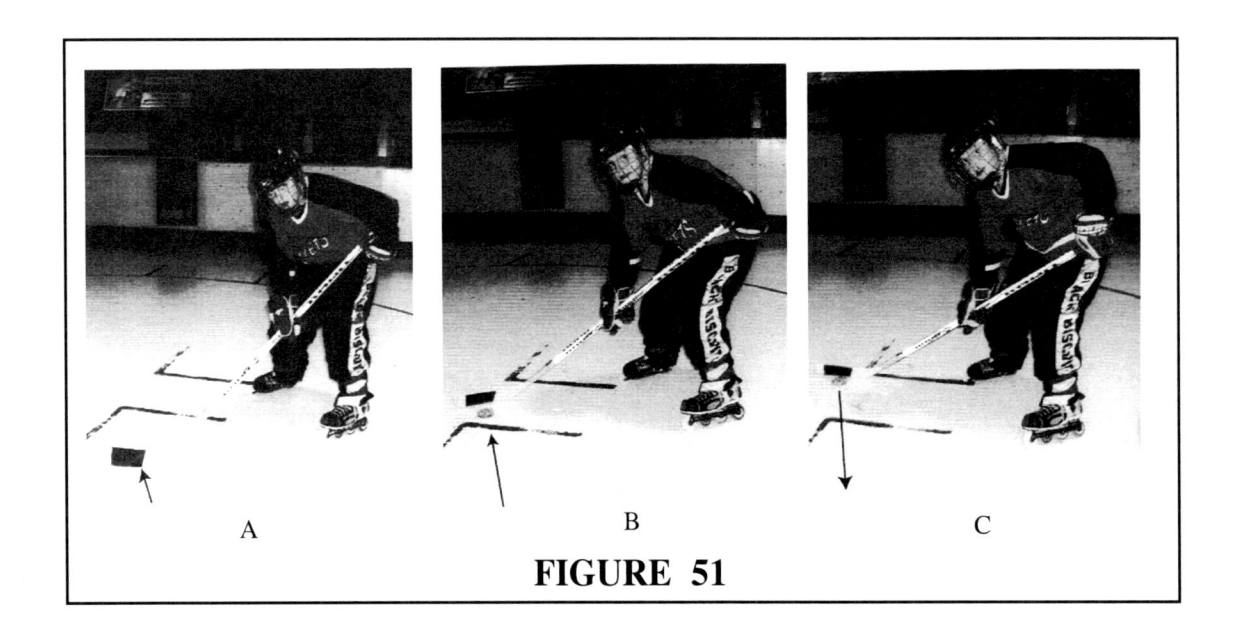

FIGURE 51

Drill no. 29- Receiving Techniques
The Basics are:

Receiving on the Forehand
      Have them start by getting in the ready position *(SEE FIGURE 28)*. The first thing they have to learn is to keep their head up, and their eyes on the puck or ball carrier. The next thing they have to learn is, put the stick blade down on the surface and keep it there *(SEE FIGURE 51-A)*. Then they watch for the puck or ball when the puck or ball carrier releases it. When they determine the direction it is coming from, they turn the stick blade so it is 90 degrees to that direction *(SEE FIGURE 51-B)*. Another important lesson they have to learn is, watch the incoming puck or ball all the way onto their stick blade. If they take their eyes off of the puck or ball, they may miss catching the pass. Just as the puck or ball hits the blade, they have to bring the blade backwards a little bit to provide a cushioning effect, and keep the puck or ball on the blade so it doesn't bounce or skid off. If they do this correctly, the blade should be in position to immediately send a pass *(SEE FIGURE 51-C)*. As they receive the puck or ball, they have to stay in the ready position so they are ready to make a relay pass back to the team mate it came from, or another team mate if necessary.

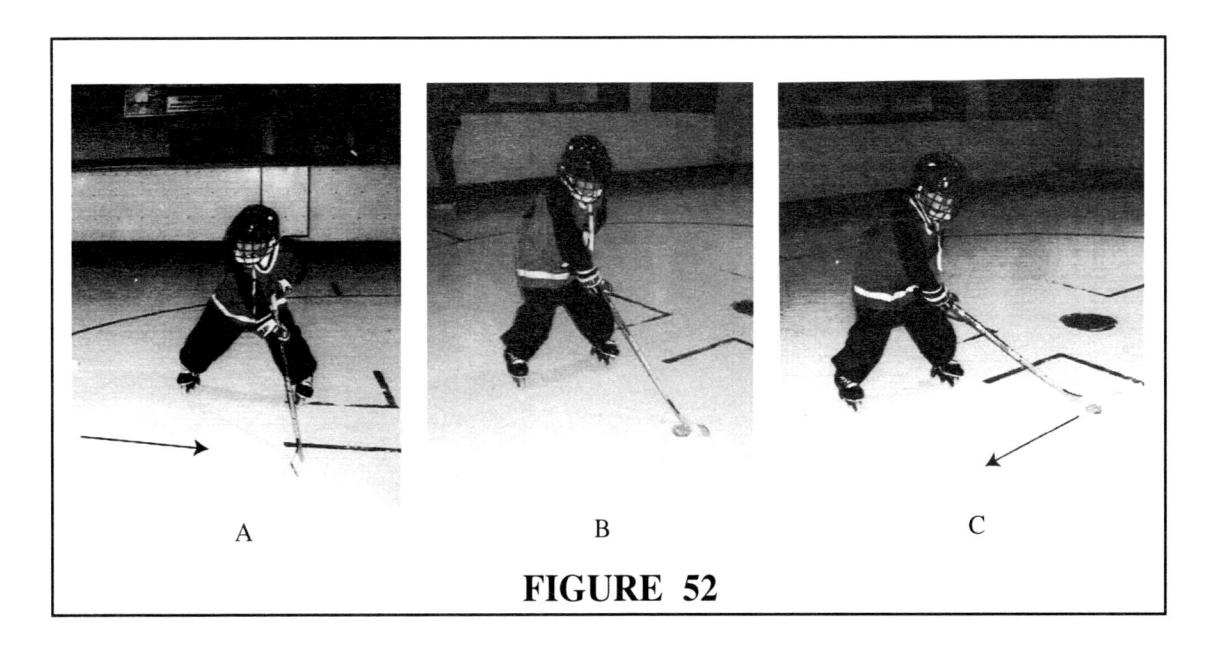

Receiving on the Backhand
      Have them start by getting in the ready position *(SEE FIGURE 28)*. The first thing they have to learn is to keep their head up, and their eyes on the puck or ball carrier. The next thing they have to learn is, put the stick blade down on

FIGURE 52

the surface and keep it there *(SEE FIGURE 52-A)*. Then they watch for the puck or ball when the puck or ball carrier releases it. When they determine the direction it is coming from, they turn the backhand side of the stick blade so it is 90 degrees to that direction *(SEE FIGURE 52-B)*. The only difference between backhand and forehand receiving is, the blade is in the backhand position when the puck or ball comes in. Another important lesson they have to learn is, watch the incoming puck or ball all the way onto their stick blade. If they take their eyes off of the puck or ball, they may miss catching the pass. Make sure they catch the puck or ball before they start to look around for a team mate to pass to. Just as the puck or ball hits the blade, they have to bring the blade backwards a little bit to provide a cushioning effect, and keep the puck or ball on the blade so it doesn't bounce or skid off. If they do this correctly, the blade should be in position to immediately send a backhand pass *(SEE FIGURE 52-C)*. As they receive the puck or ball, they have to stay in the ready position so they are ready to immediately make a relay pass back to a team mate if necessary.

Practice:

    These techniques can be practiced out in the street, or on a flat driveway if you are using the in line roller skates. You will have to find an available ice rink though to practice on for ice hockey. Or they can practice them out in the back yard, without skates, using a rubber ball or a tennis ball. However, eventually they are going to have to practice this skill with skates on if they are playing ice hockey. All skaters should know how to do all of these receiving drills. I suggest having them work on them from a stationary stance some of the time, and from a slow moving position some of the time. They should work on all three techniques for at least 10 minutes each at a practice session. They may have to work on this for a longer period of time if they are little kids or beginners.

Drill No. 30- Monkey in the Middle Passing Game
The Basics are:

    This is a game your son or daughter can play to help them develop their passing and decision making skills. This game is usually played on a rink in one of the face off circles. These circles are 30 feet in diameter. How this game works is, you have one player (the monkey) get into the middle of the circle. Then your son or daughter goes to the outside of the circle, and another player goes to the opposite side of the circle and faces them. The object of this game is the two players try to pass the puck or ball to each other, back and forth across the circle, without the monkey in the middle intercepting it. If the monkey intercepts the pass or it leaves the circle, the player making the pass becomes the monkey, then the former monkey goes to the outside of the circle and becomes a passer. The players on the outside of the circle are allowed to move anywhere they want on the outside of the circle. The monkey has to stay in the middle of the circle, within an approximate 8 foot diameter circle *(SEE FIGURE 53)*. This game can be played with two teams, or on an individual player basis. It can also be played based on a time period, or points awarded.

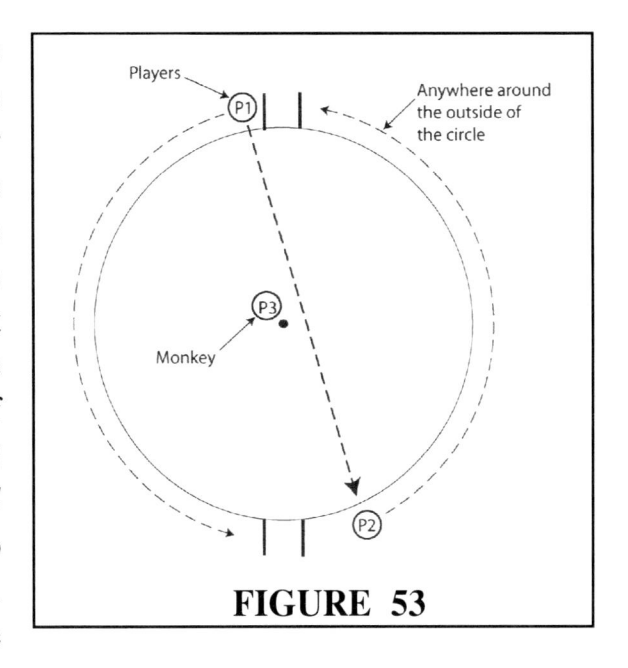

FIGURE 53

The rules are: For a time game the team, or player, that keeps the puck or ball away from the monkey for the longest time period wins the game. You can set a time period for the drill to last about half an hour to an hour. And you will have to have a pad of paper, and a watch, to keep track of the time. This method works out better on a rink because you can play the game in 5 different face off circles at the same time. The other way to play the game is when points are awarded to the individual players.

A points awarded game is probably going to work out better for parents training their son or daughter at home. If a player completes a forehand pass across the circle successfully, award 1 point. If a player completes a backhand pass across the circle sucessfully, award 2 points. If a player completes a flip pass across the circle sucessfully, award 3 points. If the monkey intercepts the pass, award the monkey with 2 points. If the pass misses the other player and goes out of the circle past them, award 1 point to the monkey. You can play this game to a time limit of one half hour or one hour. Whoever has the most points at the end of the time period wins the game. Or you can play to say 15 or 21 points. Whoever gets to the point limit first wins the game.

Practice:

So if you have access to a hockey rink, you could play this game there in one of the face off circles. Or you could set up a 30 foot diameter circle in your back yard by marking the boundary with chalk, or use heavy twine spray painted orange so it can be seen in the grass. And you could use "U" shaped pieces of heavy wire to hold it down. It will probably be easier to use a tennis ball out in the back yard grass. Your son or daughter will need to have 3 or 5 of their friends come over and play the game with them.

To make the game easier:
    1. Play the game with 3 players vs 1, or 4 players vs 1.
    2. Allow the monkey to move anywhere inside of the 30 foot circle.

To make the game harder:
    1. Increase the number of players in the game to 2 players vs 2 players.
    2. Require all passes to be only one of the 3 types, such as all backhand.

And mom or dad, you are probably going to have to referee this game in order to make them play fair. Kids will be kids. My suggestion is start with 2 players on the outside of the circle for the little kids and beginners, and one monkey in the center of the circle. Then adjust from there, depending on whether it's too easy or too hard for them. You can try the time period game or the total points game, and see which works best. Remember though this game is for your son or daughter to practice the 3 different types of passes. You may have to rotate the monkey player (friend) at some fair period of time or they will lose interest, especially if they are not very good at handling a stick to stop the puck or ball. No friends, no game. Well you know what I mean.

Drill No. 31- Monkey in the middle Receiving Game
The Basics are:

This game is to help your son or daughter develop their receiving skills. This game is usually played on a rink in one of the face off circles. These circles are 30 feet in diameter. Play this game almost like the passing game in drill 30, except change the object and the rules a little for practicing receiving. The object of this game is, have the players on the outside of the circle receive the puck or ball correctly and get points for it. The other player can always make a forehand pass to their partner on the other side of the circle *(SEE FIGURE 53)*. It will be easier that way for the little kids and beginners. Award the player receiving the pass 1 point if they receive on the forehand. Award the player receiving the pass 2 points if they receive on the backhand. The same points as in the passing game can be awarded the monkey for intercepting the puck or ball (2 points).

And you can make the game easier or harder, using the same rules as in the passing game. You will have to have a pad of paper, and a watch, to keep track of the time, or points.

Practice:
Practice this game the same as the passing game, except for the slight change of rules for receiving the puck or ball.

Drills for Shooting

Shooting is a method of getting the puck or ball into the goal or net for a score. In hockey if you don't shoot you don't score points. Players must understand the basic concepts of shooting. They have to learn the correct form techniques, regardless of what type of shot they take. This is the most important concept. The next most important concept is shooting accuracy. You don't always get lots of shots on goal, so when you do they have to be accurate. Next most important concept is quickness. Don't give the defenders or goalkeeper any extra time to set up a defense against you. Last most important concept is shot variety. If the defense knows you take the same type of shot every time, it makes it easier for them because they can over compensate to stop or block your shot. There are basically four different techniques for young kids to learn for shooting the puck or ball.

They are: The forehand sweep wrist shot, the backhand wrist shot, the flip shot, and the snap shot. We agree with the "American Sport Education Program" (ASEP) that the "Slap Shot" for the little kids is probably to hard to learn. They can learn how to do slap shots when they get older (12 and up), and have enough upper body and lower body strength to make an accurate shot.

Drill No. 32- The Forehand Sweep Wrist Shot Technique
The Basics are:
This is very similar to the forehand passing technique *(SEE DRILL NO. 28)*. The main difference is, this has to be a hard fast shot because you will usually be farther away from the goal. Also the wrist snap at the end of the sweep, gives the puck or ball a little extra speed as it comes off the hockey stick. The grip on the stick is the same as for passing *(SEE DRILL NO. 26)*. The puck or ball is brought back behind the plane of the body *(SEE FIGURE 48-A)*. At this point they shift their weight to the back foot, head up, and keep their eyes on the goal *(SEE FIGURE 48-B)*. Pushing with the bottom hand and pulling with the top hand, you use a sweeping motion to shoot the puck or ball towards the goal *(SEE FIGURE 48-C)*. While the puck or ball is being swept forward, the weight is shifted to the front foot. Bend the knee on the front foot to make sure you get more power on the shot. Then as the puck or ball is released, you snap

and roll the wrists. Until that point you keep the wrists cocked. The aim and the follow through has to be in line with the goal. Follow through low for a low shot, and follow through high for a high shot *(SEE FIGURE 48-D)*. Make sure they keep their eyes on the goal, all the way through the shot and follow through. This helps the accuracy.

Practice:

This technique can be practiced out in the street, or on a flat driveway if you are using the in line roller skates. You will have to find an available ice rink though to practice for ice hockey. Or they can even practice this technique out in the back yard, without skates, using a rubber ball or a tennis ball. However, eventually they are going to have to practice this skill with skates on if they are going to play ice or roller hockey. You will need a small goal or some cones for them to use as a target to shoot at *(SEE FIGURE 42)*. All skaters except the goalkeeper need to learn how to shoot. The little kids and beginners can start out about 10 yards away from the goal. Then as they get better at shooting, they can move out to 30 yards away or more. I suggest having them work on this shot from a stationary stance to start with, then as they get better at shooting they can move to a slow moving glide position some of the time. If their shot is weak or slow, it's probably because they are not putting their weight on the back foot, then transferring it to the front foot with the knee bent. They should work on this technique for at least 15 minutes at a practice session. They may have to work on this for a longer period of time if they are little kids or beginners.

Drill No. 33- Backhand Sweep Wrist Shot Technique
The Basics are:

This is very similar to the backhand passing technique *(SEE DRILL NO. 28)*. The main difference is, this has to be a hard fast shot because you will usually be farther away from the goal. The wrist snap at the end of the sweep, gives the puck or ball that little extra speed as it comes off the hockey stick. The grip on the stick is the same as for passing *(SEE DRILL NO. 26)*. The puck or ball is located slightly in back of the rear foot, and in front of the heel of the stick *(SEE FIGURE 49-A)*. At this point their weight is on the back foot, head up, and keep their eyes on the goal *(SEE FIGURE 49-B)*. Pulling with the bottom hand and pushing with the top hand, you use a sweeping motion to shoot the puck or ball towards the goal *(SEE FIGURE 49-C)*. While the puck or ball is being swept forward, the weight is shifted to the front foot. Bend the knee on the front foot to make sure you get more power on the shot. Then as the puck or ball is released, you snap and roll the wrists. Until that point you keep the wrists cocked. The aim and the follow through has to be in line with the goal. Follow through low for a low shot, and follow through high for a high shot. Make sure they keep their eyes on the goal, all the way through the shot and follow through. This helps the accuracy.

Practice:
    Practice this technique the same as you would for the forehand technique, except use your backhand.

Drill No. 34- Flip Shot Technique
The Basics are:
    This is very similar to the flip shot passing technique *(SEE DRILL NO. 28)*. The main difference is, sometimes this has to be a hard fast shot compared to a little short flip. If the goalkeeper comes way out in front of the goal, you could use the technique to flip the puck or ball up and over their head. Mainly though this technique is used to clear the puck or ball out of the area around the zone. This shot can be made forehand or backhand, but I suspect it will be easier for the little kids and beginners to use the forehand shot method. They have to concentrate more on learning to loft (lift) the puck or ball over the head of the opponent, and not so much on accuracy to get it into a net.

Practice:
    Practice this technique the same as you would for the forehand technique, except use the flip shot technique.

Drill No. 35- Snapshot Technique
The Basics are:
    This has been described as a wrist shot *(SEE DRILL NO. 28)* with a little extra snap at the end. You use the same techniques as with the forehand and backhand, except just before you release the puck or ball. Your motion needs to snap right through the puck or ball (where it gets it's name). This shot can be made forehand or backhand, but I suspect it will be easier for the little kids and beginners to use the forehand shot method until they get 12 years or older. Instead of placing the puck or ball on the stick, you bring the stick back a little so it strikes the floor or ice about 2 inches behind the puck or ball as you snap through on your swing. The hand position, body position, weight transfer, and follow through are the same as the forehand and backhand wrist shots.

Practice:

Practice this technique the same as you would for the forehand technique, except use the snap shot technique. Have them work on this shot at least 15 minutes at a session. All players except the goalkeeper need to work on this technique.

Drill No. 36- Coaches Choice Shooting Game
The Basics are:

This is a game, mostly for the little kids, to improve on their skills for each of the different shots. The game is played on each end of the rink, cross court, down near the goal and face off circles. If you are a coach of a team, you can get two games going at one time. How this works is, you place two goals, each one in 10 feet from the side boards, or about at the edge of the face off circles *(SEE FIGURE 54)*. The game is usually played with one 3 player team vs another 3 player team. The object of this game is for players to try all the different shots, and being awarded points when they make them. The game can be played by setting a time limit, or a point total limit. Whichever team is leading with points at the end of the time limit, or gets to the point limit first wins the game. The whole game has to be played trying to make a particular called for shot, such as a forehand sweep wrist shot. When they make that particular shot, bonus points are awarded. Getting off the called for shot towards the goal is awarded 1 point, if they score a goal using the called for shot it is worth 2 points. All other shots or goals, except for the called for shot, are not counted. To get them to work on the harder shots, award more points for backhand or snapshots. Award 2 points for getting the shot off toward the goal, and 3 points for scoring a goal.

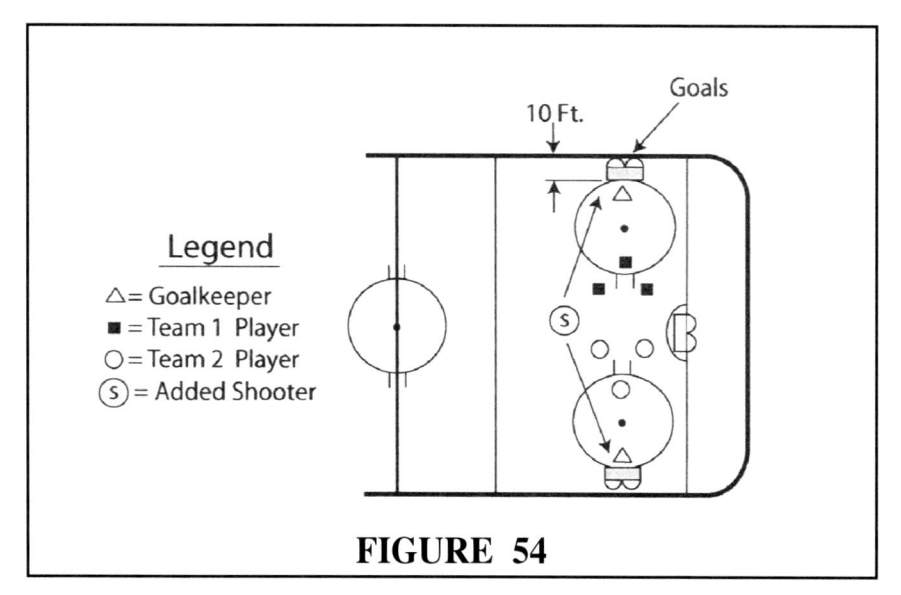

FIGURE 54

Legend
△ = Goalkeeper
■ = Team 1 Player
○ = Team 2 Player
Ⓢ = Added Shooter

To make the game harder for the older kids, add an additional player called "the shooter" (S). Have the shooter stand halfway between the nets *(SEE FIGURE 54)*. The shooter will make shots on goal for the team on offense. The shooter gets the pass from an offensive player, and makes the called for shot towards their goal. The shooter always stays right in the center court area and must not be guarded. This is so they can get off the called for shot. Award 2 points for a tipped shot or a goal by the offensive team. Award 1 point for a rebound goal. All other goals are not counted. Make sure each player gets to play the shooter position, by rotating the players.

Practice:
    To play this game you will have to have 4 to 7 of your son or daughters friends come over. And to play this game on ice, you will have to find a vacant ice rink in your area (not likely). Or you could set it up out in your street (with caution), if it's not heavily traveled, and use in line roller skates. Or you could also set it up in your back yard using regular sport shoes, a hockey stick, and a ball. Have them play the game to at least 15 points, or 45 minutes at a session. All players except the goalkeeper need to work on this technique.

Drills for Checking

    Checking in hockey means stopping or restraining your opponent. There are a number of ways to check an opponent. In youth hockey they are, body checking, stick checking, and covering the opponent. Many leagues for the little kids do not allow body checking because of the danger to young kids. However, where it is allowed you need to know how to learn each one of these checking fundamentals. We will also have some games for learning how to check.

Drill No. 37- Body Checking
The Basics are:
    Body checking involves giving a check and taking a check. Little kids need to start out by learning to keep the stick and elbows down when giving a check. The hard hip type slam check to the body is for the older kids to use, probably 12 years old and on up to high school age.
    To give a check first teach your son or daughter to focus on the puck carrier and not the puck. However, don't watch their eyes when they get close because they can fake you with their head and eyes. Concentrate on their belt or waist area. Where it goes, they will go. Teach them to keep both hands on the stick, and the blade on or near the ice ***(SEE FIGURE 55)***. Use angling, timing, and steering, to limit the opponents speed, direction, and space. Don't lunge at the puck carrier, don't contact them with your stick, and don't put your glove in

FIGURE 55

their face. By avoiding these infractions they will not get many penalties called on them.

You will also need to teach your son or daughter how to take a check. There are several ways to take a check. The first and most common way is to curl up and get your body into a very compact position, but keep your head up *(SEE FIGURE 56-A)*. If you are hit, use the shoulders and shoulder pads to absorb the impact against the boards, or of going down on the ice or floor. If possible have them cushion any collisions with the boards, glass or screen, by using their arms as a shock absorber *(SEE FIGURE 56-B)*. Another technique to use when they see they are about to be hit with a check is, have them reach out and place a hand on the player checking them. Sometimes this even lets the player slip away from the check *(SEE FIGURE 56-C)*. Also show them how to move one of their legs back to set themselves in a wide solid base with the feet, bend the knees just a little, then lean into the check if possible. This will help lessen the impact.

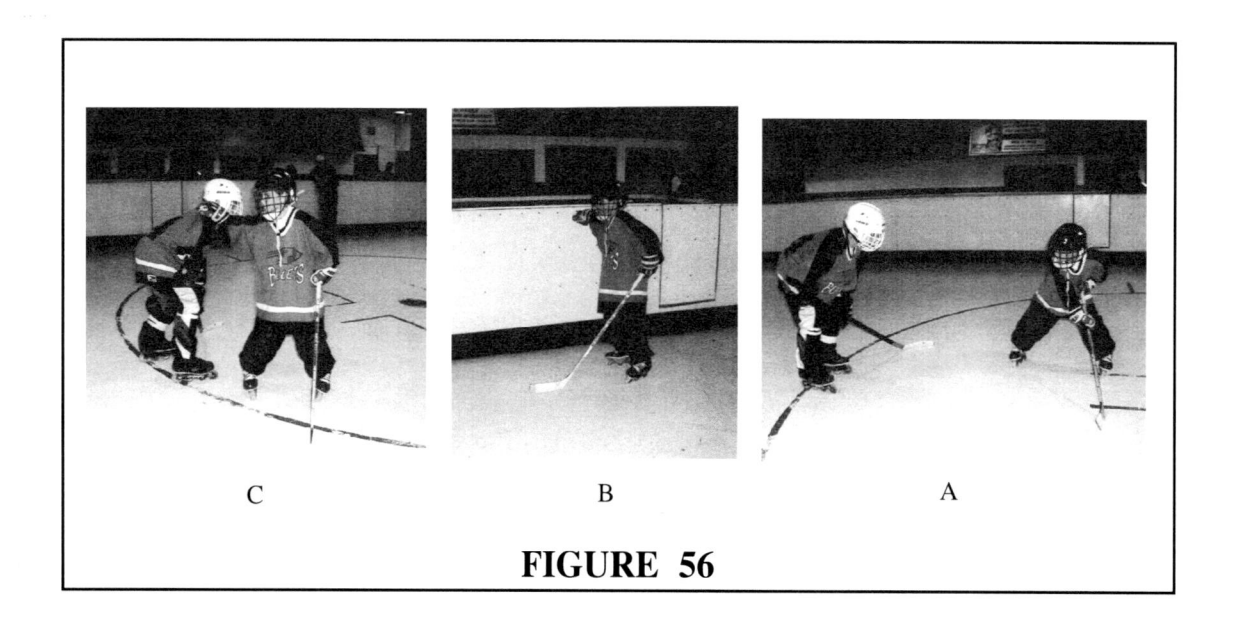

C   B   A

FIGURE 56

Practice:

This technique can be practiced out in the street, or on a flat driveway if you are using the in line roller skates. You will have to find an available ice rink though to practice for ice hockey (not likely). You will also need a small practice goal or 2 cones, to simulate a target area. Unless you mom or dad know how to skate, they will probably need to find a friend that can skate in order to work on this technique with them. Have the friend take the puck, or ball, and go out about 15 or 20 yards in front of the goal. Have your son or daughter move to a spot about 5 yards in front of the goal, to practice making a check. Then have the friend try to move a puck or ball towards the net. Your son or daughter has to get in front of them to block them from getting off a shot.

Next practice taking a check. Switch positions with your son or daughter and let them be the puck handler. First have them skate towards the goal and try for a shot on goal. When they get close, throw a soft shoulder body check into them. Not too hard though for the little kids. When they see you are going to collide with them, they need to get low and fold up their whole body into a compact shape. The knees should be bent, then they get ready to absorb the hit *(SEE FIGURE 56-A)*.

After working on "compacting", have them get knocked into the boards where they put one arm out to absorb the shock. Don't hit them into the boards to hard though until they get better at using this technique. Make sure they keep the arm somewhat flexible though and not too stiff. Otherwise they could possibly break a wrist *(SEE FIGURE 56-B)*.

Last have them practice putting one arm out on the shoulder area of the checker, to absorb the shock of the check hit. Same as above, have them keep the arm somewhat flexible though and not too stiff. When they have made contact with the checker, and held them off, they need to quickly break away, then skate around the checker towards the goal for a shot *(SEE FIGURE 56-C)*. All players except the goalkeeper should work on giving and taking checks. They should work on each of these techniques for at least 15 minutes at a session.

Drill No. 38- Stick Checking
The Basics are:

The "American Sport Education Program" (ASEP) is suggesting that roller hockey and the lower levels of ice hockey, only use this type of checking. This is probably mostly for the safety of the little kids. This breaks down into three different fundamental techniques. They are "stick checking", "lifting the hockey stick", and "guarding a player".

Stick Checking

This is where a player uses the stick blade to poke or hit an opponents stick blade, the puck, or the ball (sometimes referred to as poke checking) in order to keep them from advancing or getting off a shot on goal. This is usually accomplished using one hand, the top hand holding the stick.

FIGURE 57

When they get close to the opponent, they extend their arm and stick towards the opponents stick blade, the puck, or the ball. While doing this, their stick blade should remain in contact with the ice or the floor (no high sticking). Also teach them to not lunge at the target, so they will be in control and in a good skating position to recover from the move *(SEE FIGURE 57)*.

Lifting the Hockey Stick

This is a technique where the player comes up behind an opponent carrying the puck or ball *(SEE FIGURE 58-A)*, and in a kind of sneaky move, then slides their stick blade under the opponents stick. Next they lift up the opponents stick

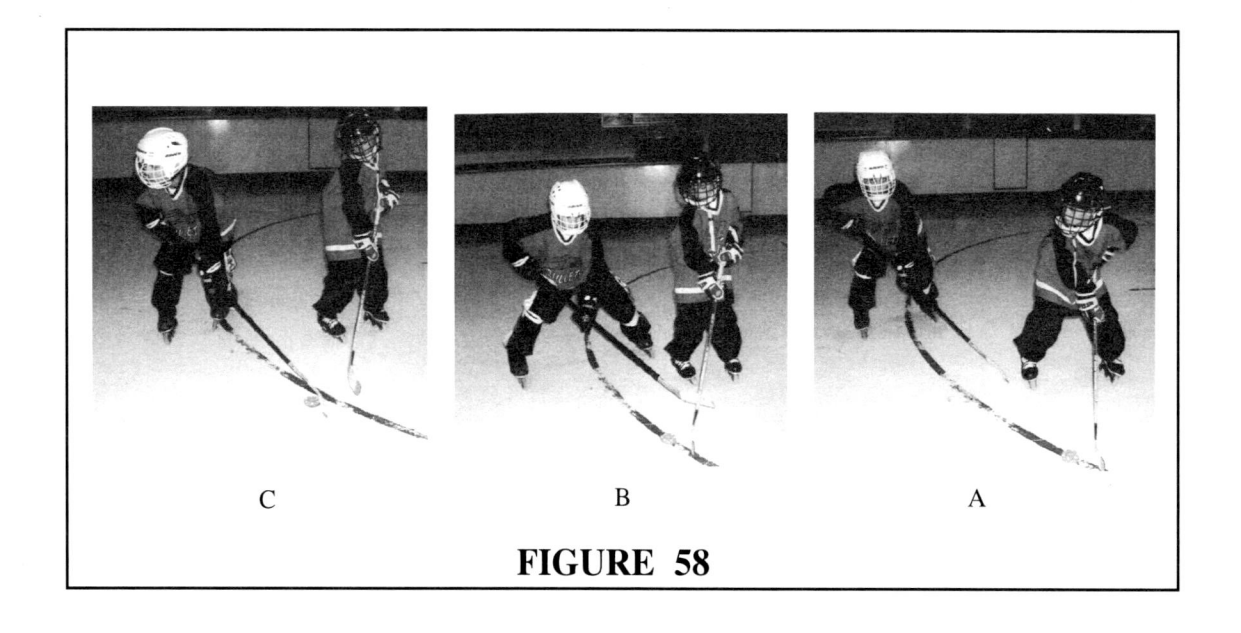

C   B   A

FIGURE 58

74

quickly, then put their stick back down quickly, on the ice or floor *(SEE FIGURE 58-B)*, so they can steal the puck or ball away. If they succeed in stealing the puck or ball, they should quickly skate away from the opponent or pass the puck or ball to a team mate *(SEE FIGURE 58-C)*.

Guarding a Player

This is a technique very similar to the non-contact body check *(SEE FIGURE 55)*. It's a little different though because it depends on whether the opponent has the puck or ball or not. If the opponent has the puck or ball, they should try to get within one to two stick lengths away from them. Next they should try to force the opponent to the outside along the boards, staying between the opponent and the goal *(SEE FIGURE 59)*. If they block them off correctly, the opponent will run out of room and have to stop. However when the opponent gets close enough, they should use either one of the other two techniques to get the puck or ball away from them, instead of just backing up.

FIGURE 59

If the opponent does not have the puck or ball, they position themselves about one to two stick lengths away from them, and between the opponent and the puck or ball. In other words they block the opponent from getting the puck or ball on a pass.

Practice:

These techniques can be practiced out in the street, or on a flat driveway if you are using the in line roller skates. You will have to find an available ice rink though to practice for ice hockey (not likely). You will also need a small practice goal or 2 cones, to simulate a target area. Unless you mom or dad know how to skate, they will probably need to find a friend that can skate in order to work on this technique with them. Have the friend take the puck, or ball, and go out about 15 or 20 yards in front of the goal. Have your son or daughter move to a spot about 5 yards in front of the goal, to practice making the different stick checks. Then have the friend try to move a puck or ball towards the net. Your son or daughter has to work on "guarding" them first, then "poke checking", and last "lifting the stick". Learning to lift the stick will be harder for the real little kids to learn. What I suggest doing is get a stick yourself mom or dad, then show them how to do it by first walking them through the moves. All players except the goalkeeper should work on all 3 stick checks. They should work on each of these techniques for at least 15 minutes at a session

Drill No. 39- The Tight Checking Game
The Basics are:

This is a game they can play to work on the different checking techniques. This game lets them practice in more of a game type situation. It can be played one on one, but it's probably better, and more fun being played 2 on 2. How this works is, a 20 x 40 foot area is set up using cones to mark the boundaries and end lines. One end is designated as the endline to defend *(SEE FIGURE 60)*. One player or team is designated as the offense (the team with the puck or ball). Since this is defensive training, it is the defense that will be awarded points. After every 5 to 10 minutes switch players, then have the offensive player or team become the defensive team, so all the players get a chance to score points. The object of the game is for the defender(s) to keep the offense player(s) from advancing the puck or ball to the end line. The defender(s) are awarded 1 point, by not letting the offensive player(s) carry or pass the puck or ball behind them. However, award 1 point to the offensive player(s) if they can carry or pass the puck or ball behind the defender(s). Award 2 points to a defender(s) if they can take the puck or ball away, and cause a turnover. Either by lifting up the puck or ball, or by poke checking it away

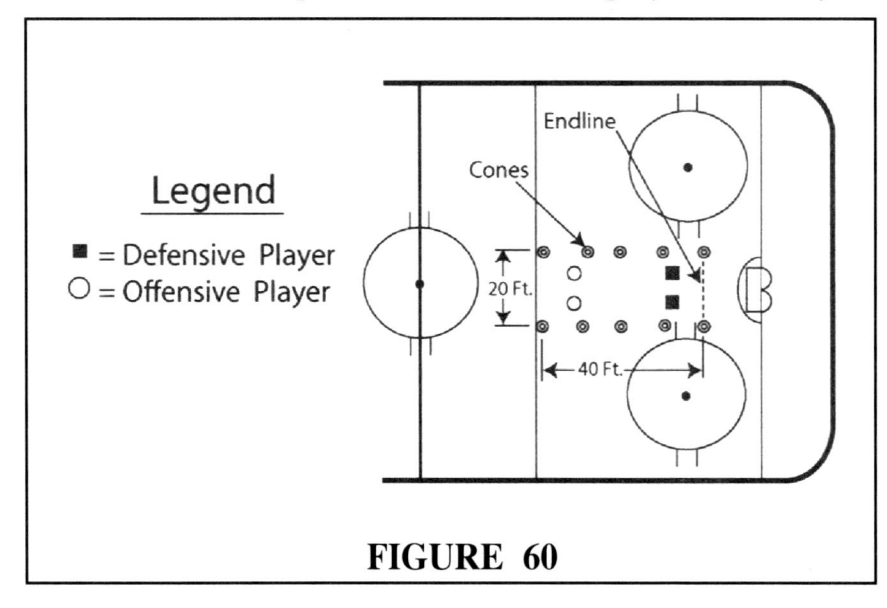

FIGURE 60

from the offensive player(s). The player or team with the most points wins the game.

To make the game easier, play 2 vs 1, or 3 vs 2 players. Or you can decrease the width from sideline to sideline. To make the game harder, play 2 vs 3, or 2 vs 4 players. Or you can increase the width from sideline to sideline to give the offensive player(s) more room to skate in. Also you can move the end lines closer together to make it harder. Remember to switch roles with the players every 5 to 10 minutes, so they get a chance to be a defender.

Practice:
To play this game you will have to have 1 to 5 of your son or daughters friends come over. And to play this game on ice, you will have to find a vacant ice rink in your area (not likely). Or you could set it up out in your street (with caution), if it's not heavily traveled, and use in line roller skates. Or you could also set it up in your back yard using regular sport shoes, a hockey stick, and a ball. All players except goalkeepers need to play this game to practice their checking techniques. I would suggest keeping the game to around 40 minutes, so you have time for other types of training.

Drills for Carrying the Puck or Ball

This is a little different than puck or ball handling. What we mean here is the open surface carry for long distances. This is a technique to use when a player is moving fast down the rink unchallenged, possibly on a breakaway.

Drill No. 40- The Open Surface Carry
The Basics are:
The player should try to use the top hand only to control the hockey stick if possible. The puck or ball is pushed just slightly ahead of them using the bottom edge of the stick blade. The arm is straightened at the elbow after you begin to push the puck, making sure to keep in contact with the stick blade. The top hand that is controlling the stick needs to be on the top portion of the stick handle, and

FIGURE 61

away from the upper part of the body *(SEE FIGURE 61)*. This technique can be used on the forehand side or the backhand side. Players need to learn how to carry the puck or ball this way while skating at top speed down the ice or floor. The skating part is really just "power skating". Some of the NHL stars say when you get to your top speed, "Stride out as far as you can and relax. Then nice and slow long strides". For the basic skating techniques *SEE DRILL NO. 19*.

Practice:
    This technique can be practiced out in the street, or on a flat driveway if you are using the in line roller skates, but you really need a length of 100 feet to simulate a carry from face off circle to face off circle. You will have to find an available ice rink though to practice on for ice hockey. If you can't find an open rink, the street or even a long enough back yard might work. If you have a long enough back yard, you could use regular sport shoes on the grass, with a stick and a ball. If they play ice hockey though, you eventually need to get them on the ice, in a rink, for them to get the real feel of the technique.

Drills for Faking

Faking is the art of fooling, or making, the opponent into thinking you are going to do one thing, then doing another. Or making them think you are going one way, then going the other way. Faking can many times be an "equalizing" factor when the opponent is bigger, faster, and maybe has more skills than you. There can be head fakes, eye fakes, and body lean fakes. I never hear people talk about faking too much in hockey. In the youth leagues, it can be a useful skill.

Drill No. 41- Faking in Hockey
The Basics are:
    Lets look at the basic 3 ways to fool an opponent. They are "head fakes", "eye fakes", and "body fakes".

<u>Head fakes</u>
    When you see the opponent looking you in the eyes, you can sometimes fool them by turning, or swiveling, your head in one direction when you actually want to go in the other direction. Most of the time they will take the fake, and you can skate around them in the opposite direction. One turn is a "single" fake. Turning it back and forth two times is a "double" fake. The double head fake is like when you turn the head quickly to the right, then back to the left, then quickly back to the right. Head fakes can work really well on opposing players

that want to get an edge on you, by thinking they know what direction you are going in. "Double" head fakes work really well on an opposing player you have used the "single" fake on once already. This is because the next time they won't go for the first head turn because they expect you to go the other way again. But what you are really going to do is keep going in the same direction, even though the head is doing all this turning, and swiveling. What sometimes happens is the opposing player gets all messed up trying to figure out which direction you are going. So what they will do is almost stop in front of you to see what you are going to do. And then you may be able to sprint around them for a break away. Also when you do change directions, you will have to learn how to sometimes switch from a forehand carry to a backhand carry,to get around them.

<u>Eye Fakes</u>

Eye fakes are generally when you look one way with your eyes then pass the puck or ball in the other direction. As with head fakes you can have "single", or "multiple", back and forth, left and right, eye movements. And the same as with the head if you can make the opponent think you are going right with your eyes, then go left around them. The same with the double eyes shift, if they think you are going to go the other way again on the second shift of the eyes, then keep going the same way.

Another eye fake move is look in one direction, then pass or shoot the puck or ball in the opposite direction. Again this all depends on the opponent watching your eyes. This is why you <u>should not</u> watch the players eyes when you get close (6 or 8 feet away) to them. Keep your eyes on the puck or ball, or on their waist, for location and direction changes.

<u>Body Fakes</u>

Body fakes are usually when you twist or turn your body or shoulders in one direction, then go in the opposite direction. Twisting and leaning to the right, then dipping the right shoulder down a little, will usually fool the opponent into thinking you are going to right when you really are going to go to your left. And as with the other two type of fakes, you can also have "single" twisting and dipping, or "double" twisting and dipping.

Practice:

You can practice faking anywhere, in the house, out in the yard, or on the ice. You can try them on your friends when you are out playing with them. Faking is usually self taught, by using trial and error methods. The first thing to determine is, which opponents, or friends, always seem to be making eye contact with you. They are the ones that can usually be faked. Faking is also sometimes referred to by coaches as "feinting" or "feint", this way or that way. Feint just means pretend to do something. In football this is sometimes referred to as "juking". Train for this by trying it out on people, or other kids, to see how they react. This is how you learn.

When you are out on the floor or ice with a hockey stick, learn to shift quickly from forehand stick handling to backhand stick handling. This will help you quickly change your direction, with or without the puck or ball. The first rule is "fake", but don't get "faked". The second rule is, when you determine that a certain player *can't* be easily faked, don't keep trying, play it straight up. All players, including the goalkeeper, should work on faking. They should work on each of these techniques for at least 10 minutes at a session.

Drills for Rebounding

Rebounding is when a shot on goal does not go in the net, and instead bounces or deflects off the goalkeeper, or another player. Also sometimes a shot deflects off another players skate. This is when a player hanging around close to the goal tries to tip, flip, or flick, the shot into the goal for a score. Rebounding is a special fundamental skill. To be good rebounders, players need to be very alert, smart, and quick with their stick and hands.

Drill No. 42- Rebounding the Puck or Ball
The Basics are:

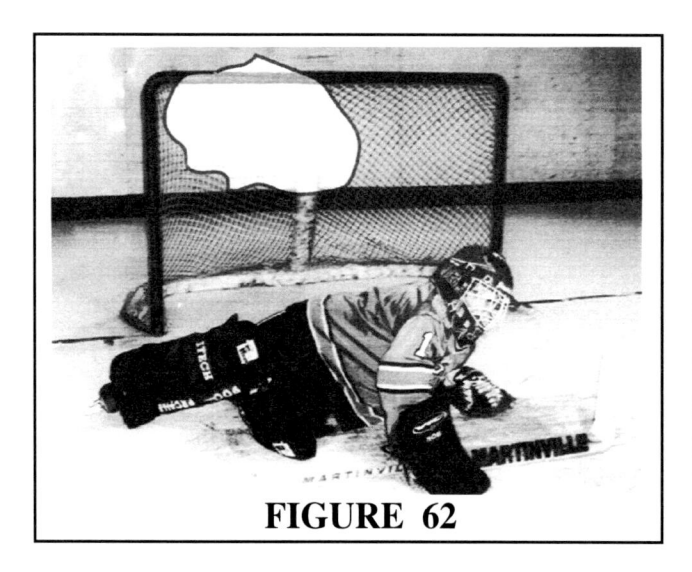

FIGURE 62

When you see a rebound opportunity, look beyond the goalkeeper for lots of white net *(SEE FIGURE 62)*. If you see lots of white net, take the shot in that direction, especially in the low area. Release the shot quickly before the goalkeeper can get set. If you give the goalkeeper lots of time to set up, they will probably make the save. If you see the goal keeper go down on the ice, take the shot up in the top part of the net *(SEE FIGURE 62)*. Sometimes just bringing the stick back, as if to shoot, then faking a shot will get the goalkeeper to go down on the ice or floor, giving you more room above them to score a goal. This is where the practice on "flip shots", and "faking" becomes useful. Take the puck or ball to the net whenever you can. Don't hang around on the outside perimeter. Most of the time goals are scored within just a few feet of the goal. When you see the play is headed toward the goal, go to the goal without the puck or ball as hard and fast as you can. Then stop right in front of the net, and get ready for a deflection or to make a rebound shot on goal *(SEE FIGURE 63)*.

Practice:

This technique can be practiced out in the street, or on a flat driveway if you are using the in line roller skates. You will have to find an available ice rink though to practice for ice hockey (not likely). Or they can practice this technique out in the back yard, without skates, using a rubber ball or a tennis ball. However, eventually they are going to have to practice this skill with skates on, and a puck or ball, if they are playing ice or roller hockey. You will also need a small goal for them to use as a target to shoot at. And mom or dad, you will need to have them find 1 or 2 of their friends to help out on this drill. If your son or daughter is friends with a goalkeeper on their team, they can put on all of the equipment and come over to help, to make it more like a game situation. However, *do not* let anyone get in front of the net, without all of the pads and goalkeeper equipment on. They could get seriously hurt.

Your son or daughter can still practice their rebounding with an open net. They need to just practice making the short shot go into the upper part of the net.

FIGURE 63

What you mom or dad can do is, stand out about 20 or 30 feet in front of the net, then make little shots to the side of them *(SEE FIGURE 63)*. They then go to the puck or ball, get it on their stick, turn around, and make little flip shots into the upper part of the net. After they get better at rebounding, you can add a friend with a stick between them and the net. The friend can then lightly bump them, and slash at their stick to make it harder for them to get a shot off. Because this is what will happen in an actual game situation. All wingers, forwards, and centers need to work on this drill. They should work on the drill at least 30 minutes at a session.

Drills for Protecting the Puck or Ball

Puck protection is really just keeping your body between the puck or ball, and the opponent (checker). Your son or daughter needs to stay on the inside edges of the skates as much as possible for maximum strength and balance. The experts say there is a 3 step progression of 1 vs 1 techniques to learn, to become effective in puck or ball protection. Remember this is a step by step progression sequence to follow.

Drill No. 43- Protecting the Puck or Ball
The Basics are:
Step No. 1

Your son or daughter has to stay in a stationary position, with the puck or ball in front of them, out on the open floor or ice. Start with the feet shoulder width, or slightly wider, apart. The knees and ankles have to be loose and flexible. A player (checker) stands behind them, with your son or daughter between them and the puck or ball. The puck protector (your son or daughter) is not allowed to touch the puck or ball with their stick. What they have to do is use their stick, and their body, to keep the checker from stealing the puck or ball away from them. They use the inside edges of their skates to spin, and to keep

FIGURE 64

themselves between the checker and the puck or ball.

Step No.2

Your son or daughter next stays in the same position as in step No. 1, except now they can use their stick to control the puck or ball while trying to maintain their body position on the checker. Whenever they feel the checker is moving in towards the puck or ball or reaching in for it, they can spin around and push the puck or ball to a new position. Or they can use their stick to hit the checkers stick. All of this has to be generally accomplished, in a stationary position, by spinning around using the inside edges of their skates *(SEE FIGURE 64)*.

FIGURE 65

Step No. 3

The last step has to come over to the edge of the boards, with the puck or ball up against it. Same rules as in step No. 2, except your son or daughter has to keep the puck or ball up against the board *(SEE FIGURE 65)*. They will have to swing their body around with their back to the checker if the checker tries to get around them. Then they use the inside edge of the skate, and turn back and forth to keep their back facing the checker, to keep them away from the puck or ball.

Practice:

Step No. 1 and 2 can be practiced out in the street, or on a flat driveway if you are using the in line roller skates. You will have to find an available rink though (not likely) to practice for ice hockey, or roller hockey. This because step 3 requires boards, to practice against. Or they could practice these techniques out in a back yard with a fence, without skates, using a rubber ball or a tennis ball. However, eventually they are going to have to practice this skill with skates on, and a puck or ball, if they are playing ice or roller hockey.

Mom or dad, you will have to work real hard with the little kids, on their skating, to perfect their technique for spinning and turning on the inside edges of the skate. It might be a good idea to work with them on this outside in the back yard first, by walking them through the moves. Then have them put on the skates and move into the rink. Don't give up on them though, they can learn how to do this. All players except the goalkeeper should work on all 3 steps. They should work on each one of these steps for at least 15 minutes at a session

Drills for Pressuring the Puck or Ball

The minute your team loses the puck or ball, at least one member of your team should quickly cover the puck or ball carrier. The closest player to the puck or ball carrier needs put pressure on them. This is called pressuring. The best advice is keep the puck or ball carrier as close to the boards as possible. For the little kids this technique is basically the same as body checking *(SEE DRILL NO. 37)*.

Practice:
Practice this technique the same as for ***DRILL NO. 37***.

Drills for Blocking, Catching, Stopping the Puck or Ball

"Blocking" the puck or ball is just what it says, getting the stick or body in front of a moving puck or ball. This is to block it, stop it, or deflect it, from going into the net, or sliding on a pass to an opponent. "Catching", and "stopping", the puck or ball use the same basic techniques, except the object is to recover and keep it. To accomplish this players need to always be reading, then quickly reacting to play around them.

Drill No. 44- Block, Catch, and Stop the Puck or Ball
The Basics are:
Always be ready to get your stick blade out to make a block, catch, stop and recovery, or a deflection of a puck or ball. When you attempt to stop a *long* hard hit puck or ball, always try to keep the flat part of the stick blade straight up, or close to 90 degrees to the surface. This gives you a better chance of dead stopping, or at least having the puck bounce off in front of you where you can control it *(SEE FIGURE 66)*. Otherwise it might skip off the blade, and on past you. Also just when the puck or ball makes contact with the blade, bring the blade back a little bit to absorb the force so that it has less of a chance to bounce way off.

On shorter puck or ball passes, just watch and focus on the puck or ball off the opponents stick, not the opponent. That will help your eye to hand coordination for getting the stick blade quickly in front of the puck or ball. Also see the section on "receiving" for similar tips and techniques.

Practice:

These techniques can be practiced out in the street, or on a flat driveway if you are using the in line roller skates. You will have to find an available ice rink though to practice for ice hockey (not likely). Or they can practice them out in the back yard, without skates, using a rubber ball or a tennis ball. However, eventually they are going to have to practice this skill with skates on if they are playing ice, or roller, hockey. Walk through how to position their body and handle the stick before they do a run through. Then you, mom or dad, get a stick and go out in front of them about 20 or 30 yards. Then hit different speeds of shots towards them. All Players should know how to do all of these techniques, even goalkeepers can benefit from working on them. I suggest having them work on them from a stationary stance some of the time, and from a slow or fast moving position some of the time. This way they get a "game" type feel of the techniques. They should work on all three techniques for at least 10 minutes each at a practice session. They may have to work on this for a longer period of time if they are little kids or beginners.

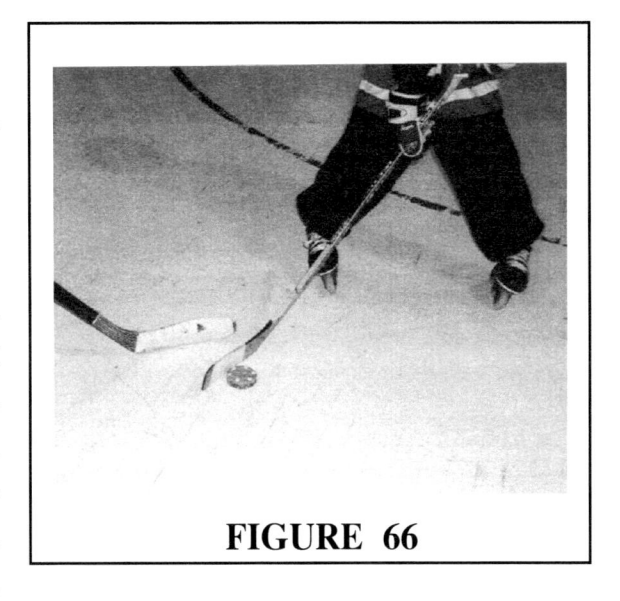

FIGURE 66

Drills for Reading & Reacting

Reading and reacting are two very special skills for hockey players to learn. This is because hockey is a fast pace game, and players have to react quickly to all the changes going on around them. Line changes, and quickly changing from offense to defense while on the move, are just a few of them. Then there are tactics and strategies they have to be aware of.

Reading is sort of like the old phrase "know thy enemy", except it is the opponent you have to read. What this means is get an edge on them, by knowing what their tendencies are, and what their tactics are.

Drill No. 45- Reading the Opposition
The Basics are:
Reading is really noticing the players around and close to you. Especially if the same players always seem to be guarding or shadowing you, or attacking against you. Do they always move, with or without the puck or ball, on the same side. This means you can get away from them, more easily on the opposite side. And by shading them to their strong side, it will be easier to stop them. What are their tendencies.

Are they watching your eyes or the puck or ball. If they are watching your eyes, then you can probably use fakes on them. Are they slow and clumsy skaters, or are they quick fast and agile. If you see your opponent is better than you, use an "edge" to keep the playing field level so to speak.

Puck and ball carriers have to read the open floor or ice in front of them. Where are the opposing team players located, and where are their own team mates located. Is there defensive pressure on them, and what are their passing options. What are the opponents tendencies on offense. Players always have to be reading and reacting because transitions come very fast sometimes.

Defenders need to read the floor or ice in front of them also. Where are the wingers, forwards, and the center, located. Where is the puck or ball carrier located. Where are their team mates on defense located. Supporting team mates need to learn when to back up their puck or ball carrier, set screens, and create passing options for them.

Practice:
Practice for this drill is basically going to be you, mom or dad, sitting down with them, with some sketch paper and this book. Then going over the basic offensive and defensive reading tactics and strategies explained above. The real practice will come when they play the game, and practice the reading and reacting techniques we have described. By using trial and error methods, they can learn how to do this. All players including the goalkeeper should work on "reading". I would suggest spending at least 20 minutes with them on this per session.

Drill No. 46- Reacting to Play Around You
The Basics are:
Reacting is really is doing something about what you see happening, don't just stand there on the skates and watch. Help your son or daughter to react quickly to the different game situations as it goes on around them, by explaining

the different play scenarios to them. Puck and ball carriers have to react to what is going on in front of and next to them. Where are the opposing team players located, and where are their own team mates located. Is there defensive pressure on them, and what are their passing options. As an example if you see you are about to be double teamed, pass the puck or ball off quickly because a team mate is probably open. Don't wait until they are all over you, react quickly and pass off. Supporting team mates need to react quickly also, by setting screens, and creating a passing option for the puck or ball carrier.

When you are defending, keep the play in front of you and pinch the puck or ball carrier in towards the boards. Supporting team mates need to learn how to react quickly by backing up the play, and block passing options. As an example if you see a "break away", and you are the closest defender, react quickly and go after them, don't just stand there and let them go. Why let them have an unchallenged shot on goal. Who knows, you may catch up to them and stop a rebound.

Practice:
Practice for reacting to play around your son or daughter is going to be the same as for "reading", except explain to them how to react quickly to the above type scenarios.

Drills for Facing Off

Face-offs occur when play starts or resumes, either at the start of the game, or after a rules infraction has stopped the game. In other words this is a method for starting and restarting the game. Two opposing players are in front of each other, sticks down on the floor or ice, in one of the "face off circles or "spots". The referee drops a puck or ball between their sticks, and both players attempt to get control of the puck or ball, or hit it to one of their team mates.

Drill No. 47- Face Off Techniques
The Basics are:
Ice hockey games start in the center of the rink face-off circle. Offensive or defensive zone face-offs are in one of four different neutral zone locations, depending on whether the infraction was against the offensive team or the defensive team. It also depends on which side of the rink the infraction occurred on *(SEE FIGURE 67)*. Each player will face the opponents goal. They have to stand about one stick length apart, at the center of the face off circle or spot.

FIGURE 67

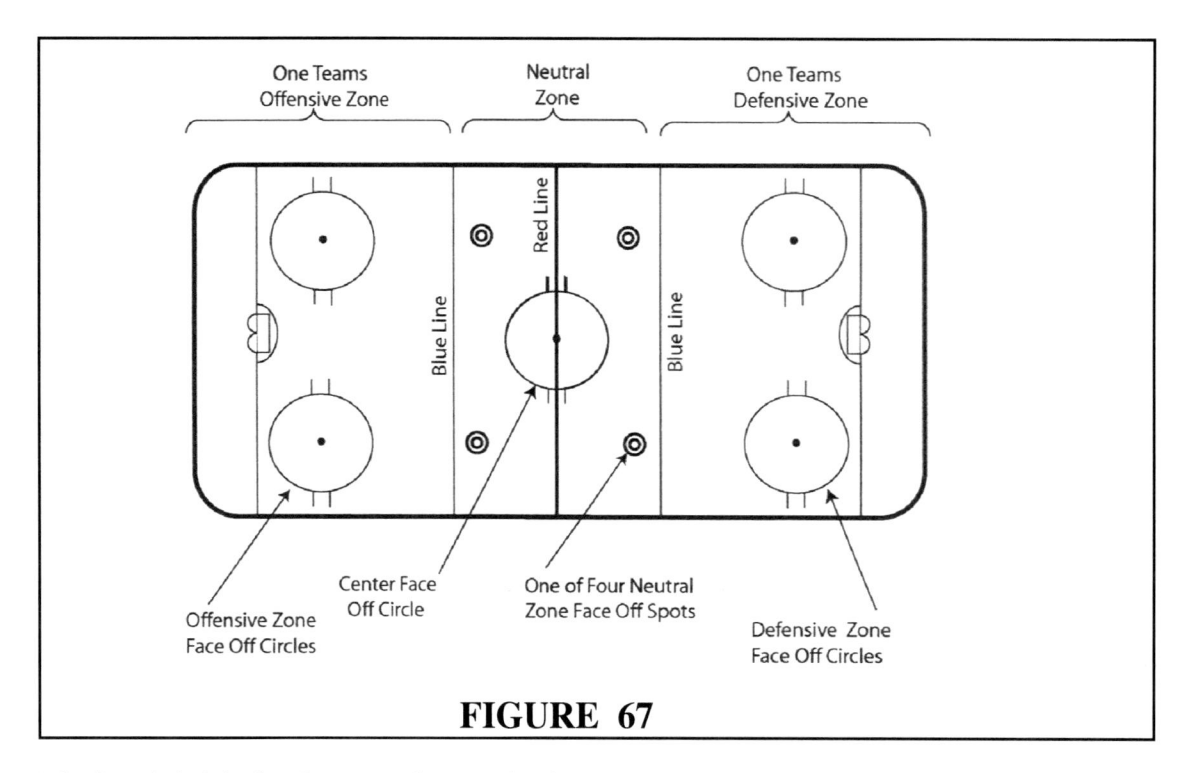

Their stick blades have to be on the ice, with the attacking team player putting their stick down first. For all face-offs on the red line only, the visiting team player puts their stick down first. All the players not facing off are not allowed to enter the circle, and they have to be at least 15 feet away from the players facing off.

At the conclusion or end of the "line change procedure", the players have 5 seconds after the referee blows the whistle to line up for a face off. Before the conclusion of the 5 seconds, the referee has to conduct a proper face-off. So make sure your son or daughter understands that after the line change they have to quickly line up and get ready for the face off. If any players, other than the players facing off, fails to maintain their proper position by the end of that 5 seconds, the "center" of that team will be ejected from the face off.

So what does this mean to your son or daughter. It means they have to focus and watch carefully when either they, or the opponent, puts their stick down. Then immediately after that, the next thing they have to do is watch the referee out of the corner of their eyes, so they can react just as the puck is dropped. Face-off players not paying attention are going to be left at the circle or spot, watching the opposing team skate off with the puck or ball. The object is to get your stick on the puck or ball quicker than the opponent. Kids that are not too coordinated, or quick, should not be facing off.

Face-offs in your teams offensive zone are particularly important, especially on "power plays". Since your team then has a player advantage, and your goal is very close, some teams will have a set play to try and score right off of the face-off. If the opposing (penalty killing) team gains possession of the puck or ball, it usually results in an icing call. Then your team has to skate all the way down to the other end of the rink and regroup, losing precious power play advantage minutes. So you can see, face-off techniques are very important for your son or daughter to learn.

Often, but not always, it is the "center" that lines up for face-offs. If your son or daughter is playing "center" a lot, then work with them on learning how to face-off. Probably the best way for them to learn how to face-off is, practicing it over and over again. And by trial and error they will learn the best ways to move their stick to gain control of the puck or ball. When they get to their first team, the coach will explain to them what plays, strategies, and tactics, he wants them to use on face-offs.

Practice:

If you can find a vacant rink to practice on, use it. I doubt you will find one though. So what you will probably have to do is create your own face off circle in the street, or out in the back yard. They don't have to be on their skates to learn the stick movements. Their are a number of ways to do it, but we will give you one way to do it that will work for you and your son or daughter.

Face-off circles are 30 feet in diameter. So what you can do is create one by getting an old tin can, dig a hole, and bury it in the ground out in the back yard to mark the center. Then holding a piece of string or twine at the center of the can, 15 feet long, walk around and mark a circle. You can put down powdered white chalk as you go, or you could use a heavy ply length of twine, jute, or cord, *painted orange*. Then hold it down with pieces of "U" shaped bent (using pliers) wire or coat hangers. Stick them in the ground every 6 or 12 inches. Either way it will give you a nice full size circle to practice in, and it won't hurt your grass. When hockey is over just pick it up if you like and use it again next year. If you use the chalk, the rain will eventually wash the lines away during the off season. You can also mark a face-off "plus" in the middle, so they will get used to where to put the stick down on the edges of the lines *(SEE FIGURE 68)*.

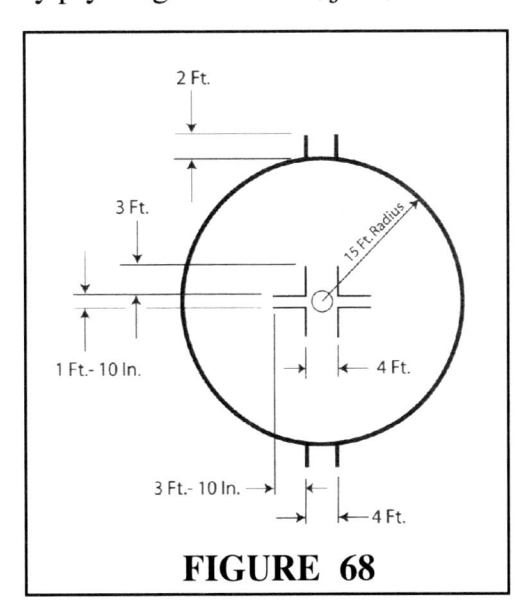

FIGURE 68

The neutral zone face-off "spots" are 2 feet in diameter if you want to practice for those face-offs. If the grass is short you might be able to use a puck and a stick, or you can use a ball. It still takes the same stick movement speed.

Now you will need to get a friend of your son or daughter, about the same size, to practice with. Have them first, one then the other, put their sticks down on the lines (not at the same time). Then you, mom or dad, drop the puck or ball between them. What you can do to help them learn, and make it less boring, is whisper to them which direction you want them to push or take the puck to. Right, left, or behind them. I can imagine there are a number of tricky ways to hold your stick, to gain an advantage. And they can probably get away with it against other little kids, but when they get older the opponents are going to see what they are trying to do, and have a better chance to stop them. Remember now, they are about one stick length apart. And you have to drop the puck right in middle of them (about 4 feet apart). So they are going to have to work on either sliding the stick blade over to the puck or ball, or picking it up and kind of chopping it between the opponents blade and the puck or ball. And this is going to have to be quick because the opponent is going to be trying to do the same thing. As I mentioned, the quick move towards the puck has to be explosive. If they are having trouble, stop and walk them through it until they can master the necessary moves. All young players except goalkeepers need to work on this. Have them practice this for at least 30 minutes at a session.

Drills for Goaltending

Goaltending is one of the hardest fundamental skills to learn. Most coaches in youth hockey probably don't spend near as much time as they should teaching goalkeepers. Probably the main reason is time. From what I can see, there is not enough rinks available, especially in ice hockey, to accommodate all the kids that want to play. So the coach has to get on to other things to work on, for the rest of the team. On most of the teams I have watched, goalkeepers don't have a special coach that works with them constantly on their skills. They wear more heavier equipment than the other players. This makes it harder for the little kids to move freely around. But they have to start someplace. So if you start helping them when they are 5 years old, they could be pretty good by high school age.

There is a big difference between ice hockey and roller hockey goaltending. Ice hockey goalkeepers can slide their skates to move from side to side where a roller hockey goalkeeper has to pick up their skates to move to the side. The little extra time it takes to do this makes it a little easier to score on a roller hockey goalkeeper. To cut down on the time it takes to make the move to the side, a roller hockey goalkeeper needs to learn how to do the T-push technique. There is a second big difference, ice hockey goalkeepers can do a two pad slide pretty easy. Where a roller hockey goalkeeper has to apply more force, depending on the floor surface, to move the same distance. So it takes them maybe a little longer, and maybe they don't move as far. Goalkeepers have to learn many fundamental techniques. They have to learn a ready stance, movements, save techniques, rebound techniques, and face-off techniques. There is a basic stance, so lets start there because that is where all the moves start.

Drill No. 48- The Basic Stance
The Basics are:
      The basic stance is what I like to call the "ready position". If the goalkeeper does not start from the ready position, it makes it harder for them to make the necessary moves. The legs need to be just a little wider than shoulder width apart, their weight needs to be distributed from the middle of the skates back to the heels, the knees should be slightly bent in the crouch position, the shoulders are back, your rear end slightly down, the hands and gloves are off your pads and out to the side, your stick is in front down on the ice between your skates, and your catch glove is open and located just above your hip *(SEE FIGURE 69)*.

Practice:
      To practice this you will first need to have your son or daughter get all of the equipment on. This is so they get used to, and get the feel of, the ready position. You can hollar "READY", and have them quickly take the ready position. Since this is the start for all the techniques, have beginners and the little kids work on this drill at least 15 minutes at a training session every day at first. Once you, mom or dad, see they are mastering the technique, then they only have to work on it once in awhile, or when you notice, during a session, they are not getting into the stance when they

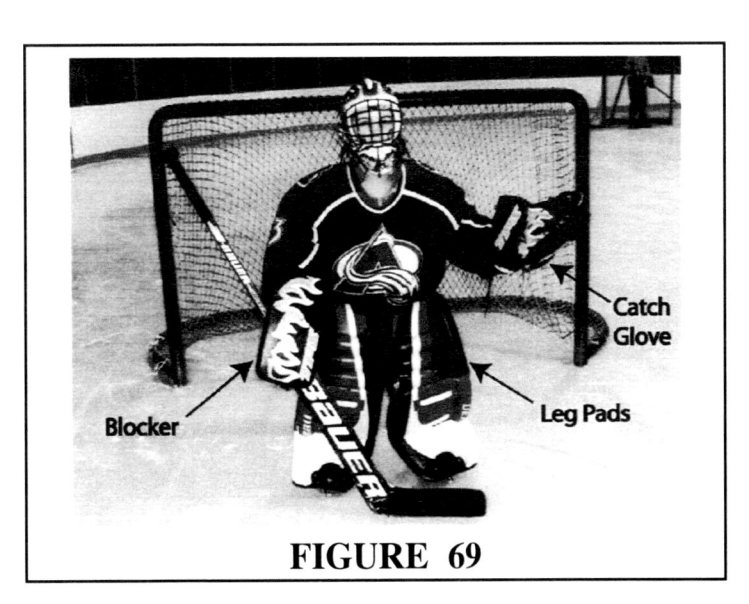

FIGURE 69

start. After they get into position and you check them, say "RELAX" and they stand back up straight. When they are beginners, check and see they are in the right position.

Drill No. 49- The Movements
The Basics are:
Good goaltending starts with quick movements. Teach them to have good movement equally from one side to the other side. There are long distance movements, and there are short distance movements. Some of these movements are related to one or the other. The fundamental movements they need to learn are, the shuffle step, the T-push, and telescoping.

The Shuffle Step
The shuffle step is best for short distance lateral moves. To make this move, they stay in the "ready" position and make short shuffle steps to the side (right or left) while keeping their back to net, and their shoulders squared to the front as they shuffle *(SEE FIGURE 70)*.

Practice:
Practice the shuffle almost like you would the "basic stance", except from the ready position say "GO", and have them step several short shuffle steps to the right, then stop. Then you hollar "GO" again, and they take 4 or 5 short shuffle steps back to their left. They do this by stepping sideways to their right about 8 to 12 inches with their right foot, then quickly bringing the left foot sideways up close to the right foot. Next they take another 8 to 12 inch step to their right again, then quickly bringing the left foot up close to the right foot again. Every time you step to the side, bring the other foot up towards it. Make sure they are keeping their shoulders squared to the front as they shuffle. They

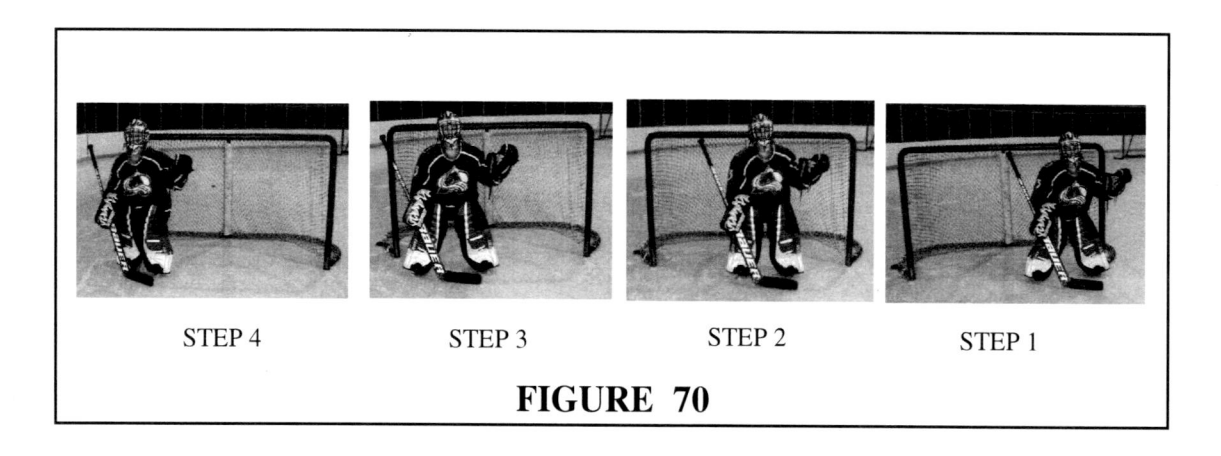

| STEP 4 | STEP 3 | STEP 2 | STEP 1 |

FIGURE 70

need to work at least 15 minutes on this drill per session. Half of the time to the right, and half of the time to the left.

The T- Push

The T-push step is better for long distance lateral movements. To make this move, they start out in the "ready" position, then have them turn the right foot 90 degrees pointing to their right, then they push off to the right sideways with the inside edge of the other leg (left skate). The next step is to bring the left foot back up close to the right foot *(SEE FIGURE 71)*. Then they step out again with the right foot, still pointing 90 degrees to the right, and push off again to the right using the left foot. The "T" name comes from the shape of the two feet making a "T" when they come together. They keep T-pushing until they get to where they want to go to the side. Then they quickly resume the "ready" position. Going to the left is just flip flopped, or opposite in steps and movements.

Practice:

Practice the T- push move almost like you would the "shuffle step". From the ready position on the left side of the goal, say "GO" and have them turn the right foot quickly to the right 90 degrees. Next they quickly make a big push off to the right with the left foot still pointing to the front. Then they bring the left foot up close to the right foot, and push off again with a big step to the right with the right foot. Since it is long steps, two steps is usually enough to get to the other goal side. After they practice going to their right two steps, then have them practice moving two steps to the left. Make sure they face as much front as possible while making the moves. They need to work at least 15 minutes on this drill per session. Half of the time to the right, and half of the time to the left. Roller hockey goalkeepers really need to work on the T- push move.

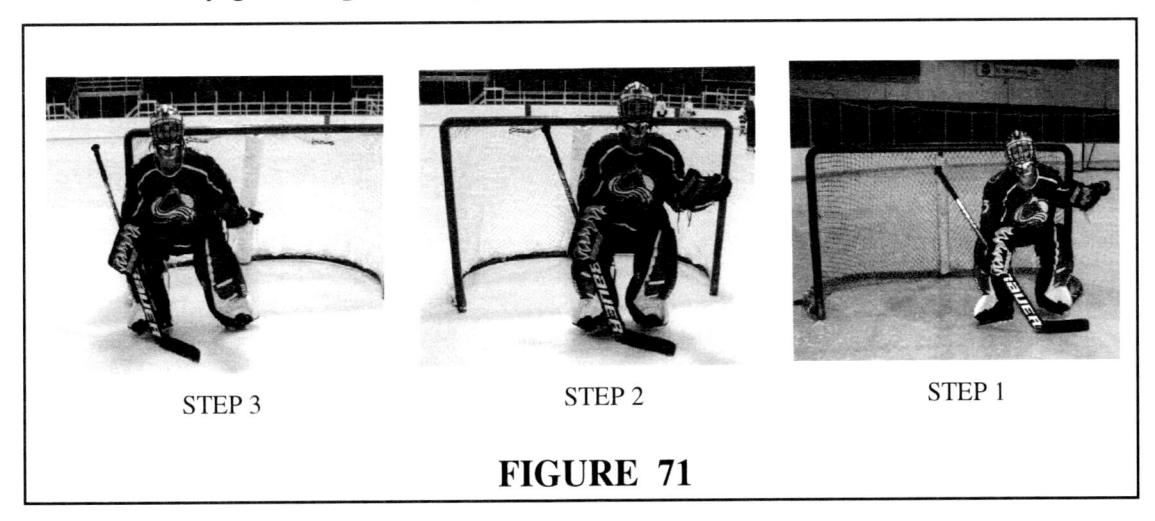

STEP 3   STEP 2   STEP 1

FIGURE 71

Telescoping Back and Forth

The telescoping moves are for going forward and backward from the goal. To make the move forward, they start out in the "ready" position in the middle of the goal. Then they push off to the front with either foot, using the inside edge of the skate. The push off is to get momentum going forward, then they glide forward in the "ready" position to the distance they want to go forward . They move backwards by drawing the letter "C", starting from the top to the bottom, on the ice or floor. They use the inside edge of either foot to make the "C". This starts momentum to the rear, then they just glide in the "ready" position to the distance they want to go to the rear *(SEE FIGURE 72)*.

Practice:

Practice the telescope move almost like you would the "shuffle step". From the ready position say "GO", and have them push off to the front, with either foot using the inside edge of the foot. Then when they get their forward momentum going, glide forward in the ready position about 2 feet and stop. Next they start to move backwards by making the letter "C" on the floor or ice, using either foot. Then when they get their backward momentum going, glide to the rear in the ready position about 2 feet and stop. They need to work at least 15 minutes on this drill per session. Half of the time to the front, and half of the time to the rear.

Drill No. 50- Fool the Goalkeeper Game
The Basics are:

This is a game they can play to help them work on their movements in a game type situation. This is a game they can easily play because it can be played with just your son or daughter, and two friends. It can be played at one end of a

| STEP 1 | STEP 2 | STEP 3 | STEP 4 |

FIGURE 72

rink in front of the goal, out in the street on in line roller skates, or out in the back yard with sports shoes, a stick, and puck or a ball. It's best for ice hockey players to be on ice because the blade works differently than roller skate wheels or shoes, and they get the feel of the ice better. Finding an open ice rink is almost impossible, so the street or back yard is better than not at all. By shuffling your feet in the same movements they would make on the ice, you will become familiar with the moves until you can get on the ice. Having them make calls like "T-PUSH" or "C-CUT", as they make the moves, will help their memory remember the moves.

How this works is, have your son or daughter get into their equipment and stand just in front of the goal. Next position the 2 shooters (friends) about 25 feet out in front of the net, and about 15 feet apart *(SEE FIGURE 73)*. The object of this game is to let the goalkeeper get quickly in position to stop shots. Points are awarded for both goal keepers and shooters. Award the goalkeeper 1 point for each save. Award the shooters (P1 & P2) 1 point for each goal they make. The shooters pass the puck or ball back and forth a predetermined number of times before they shoot. You mom or dad whisper to each friend how many passes to make. Make sure your son or daughter (the goalkeeper) does not know the number of passes before they shoot. This way they do not know when the shot is coming, and it keeps them alert and moving. When the pass goes to one side, your son or daughter has to move to that side of the goal. Keep the number of passes back and forth to 4 or less, to save time and be more like a game situation.

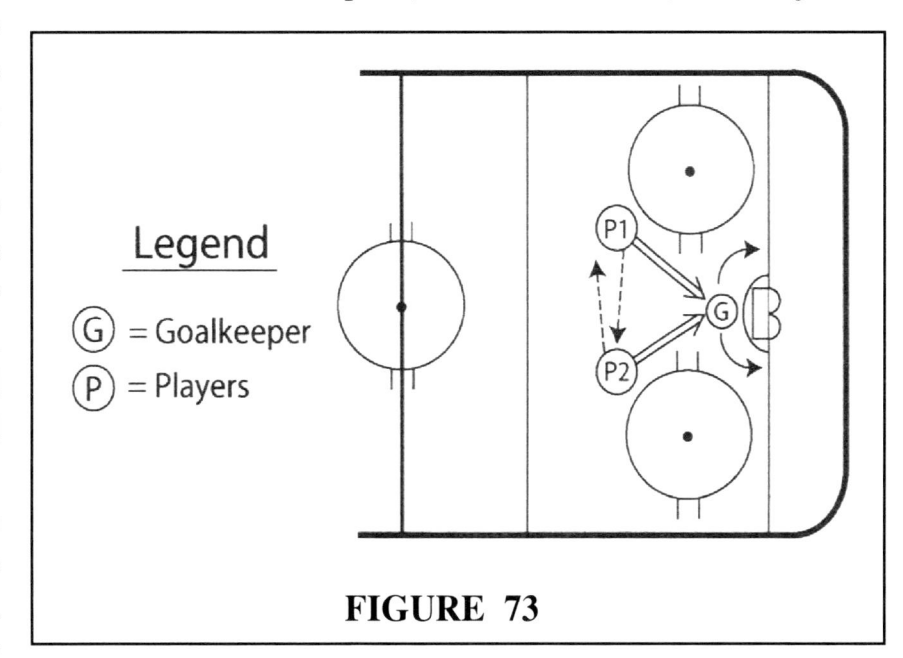

FIGURE 73

To make the game easier, increase the distance the shooters have to shoot from. Or you can tell all the players how many passes are to be made.

To make the game harder, and more like a game situation, have 3 vs 1 or 3 vs 2 players pass and attack the goal keeper, starting from the neutral zone.

The big problem with this will be finding enough friends to come over and play, or finding a big enough place to play in the street or back yard.

Practice:
To play this game you will have to have 2 to 5 of your son or daughters friends come over. And to play this game on ice, you will have to find a vacant ice rink in your area (not likely). Or you could set it up out in your street (with caution), if it's not heavily traveled, and use in line roller skates. Or you could also set it up in your back yard using regular sport shoes, a hockey stick, and a puck or ball. All goalkeepers need to play this game to practice their "moving" techniques in a game type situation. I would suggest keeping the game to around 60 minutes or less, so you have time for other types of training. Keep track of the score on a pad of paper, so you can compare your son or daughters progress later on.

Drill No. 51- Positioning Techniques
The Basics are:
Goalkeepers need to learn how to find the best position to be in, to make a save or stop shots. It's very important to get the best angle, without coming out of the crease too far. When the goalkeeper comes out of the crease to challenge an attacker, it leaves the shooter less open net to aim for. It improves the goalkeepers chance for a save or a stop. This is only true though if there is a single attacker. If there is several attackers, it makes it harder to move to a closer location if the puck or ball is passed. Here are some examples.

If the goalkeeper is playing inside of the net *(SEE FIGURE 74-A)*, it gives the shooter more open net to shoot at. If the goalkeeper is playing just 1 or 2 feet outside of the net *(SEE FIGURE 74-B)*, it cuts off some of the angle the

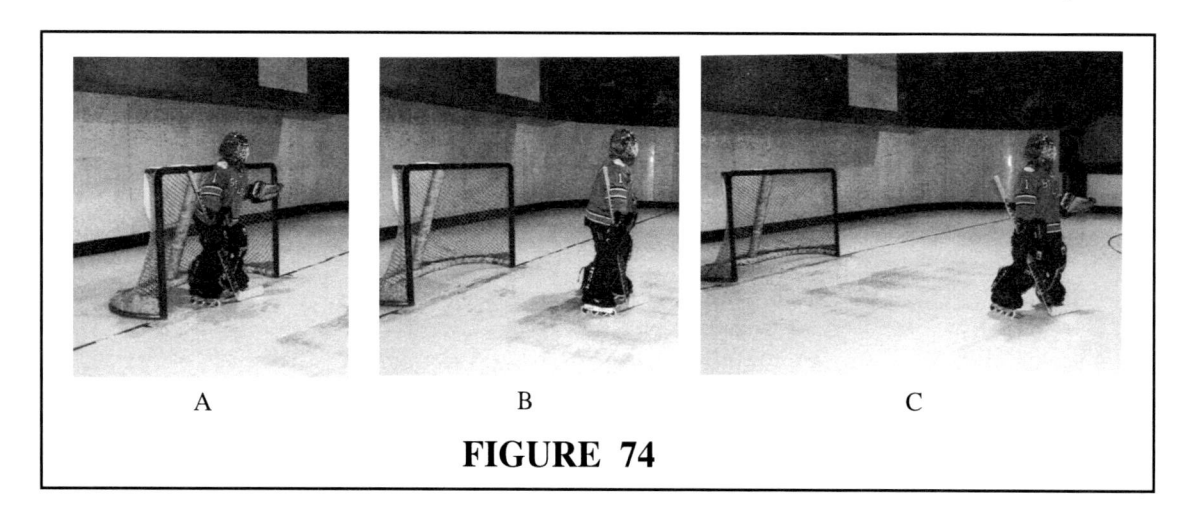

FIGURE 74

shooter has, and the goalkeeper still has time to move quickly to a new position to defend and save on passes (the best bet). If the goalkeeper comes out 6 to 8 feet out from the net *(SEE FIGURE 74-C)*, it's usually too far. The exception might be when a single attacker comes in on a break away. And that is only if the goalkeeper thinks they may shoot from far out (the exception).

Practice:

The first thing you need to do to practice these positions, mom or dad, is to sit down with them using this book and ***FIGURE 74*** and show them, as well as explain to them, where all 3 positions are located. The second thing is take them out to a net and have them get into all 3 positions. You can do this by calling out "NET", "FRONT NET", and "WAY OUT". Then they move to these positions as you call them out. Since this is practicing only learning the 3 positions, they don't need to wear all the equipment. Another way to practice these techniques is to play the "Fool the Goalkeeper Game" *(SEE DRILL NO.50)*. Then have them play at all 3 positions, just so they can see what happens when the shooters make their shots. Remember, they need to wear all the equipment for the game though.

I would suggest working with them at least 10 minutes at each position at a training session (30 minutes total). Just make sure you work with them often on their positioning, it's very important. Also be sure to explain to them the advantages, or disadvantages, of each position.

Drill No. 52- The 99 Percent Game
The Basics are:

This is a game, or almost a drill, used to teach goalkeepers just how far to come out of the net. This is kind of similar to the "Fool the Goalkeeper Game" *(SEE DRILL NO. 50)*. The idea is not to come away from the net any farther than is necessary. This involves having 2 players out on each wing area at the blue line *(SEE FIGURE 75)*. First one player from one side (P1) carries the puck or ball down toward the net, and takes a shot. They follow their shot in toward the net and if their is a rebound possibility around the net, they try to shoot it into the net. Right after player (P1) clears out of the way, and the goalkeeper is ready, the player from the other side (P2) carries the puck or ball down toward the net and does the same thing. Points are awarded to the goalkeeper, and the shooters.

When the goalkeeper (your son or daughter) makes a save they are awarded 1 point. If a shooter scores a goal, they are awarded 1 point. To make the game

FIGURE 75

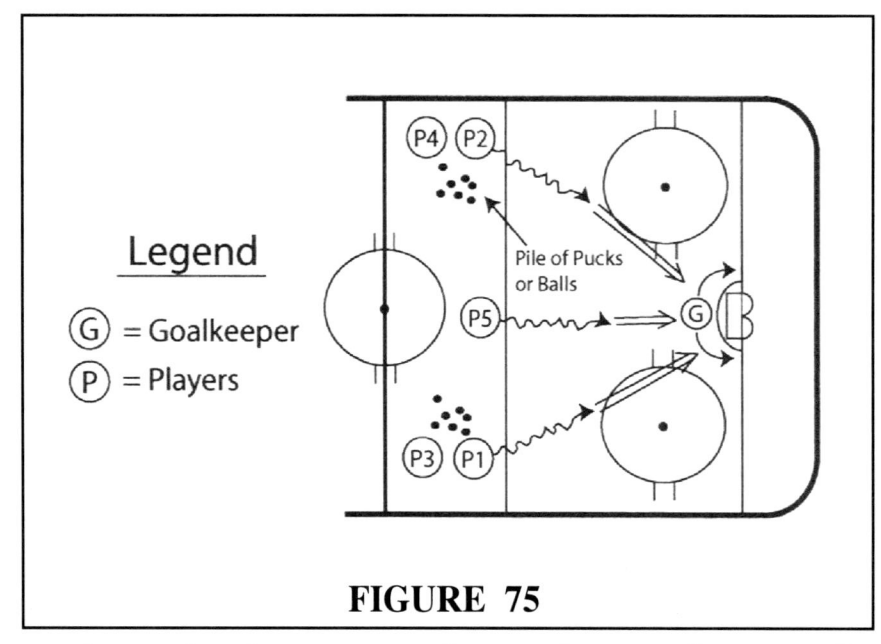

harder, add a second attacker (P5). When either of the wing puck or ball carriers move toward the net, they have the option of shooting or passing to the added attacker. Keep a pile of pucks or ball nearby so that the game can keep going at a fast pace. It will make a better goalkeeper out of you son or daughter. Tell your son or daughter to get into the best position they can, then get *set* in the "ready" position *(SEE FIGURE 69)*. And if they do not get to the ideal position in time before the shooter is winding up to shoot, they need to stop and get set anyway before the shooter gets the shot off. They will have a better chance of making a save or stop, if they are set than if they are still moving while making the attempt. Probably the best thing you can teach them is play no more than one foot out from the top of the 4 Ft. x 6 Ft. crease box if possible *(SEE FIGURE 76)*. If the goalkeeper performs correctly, they should not allow many, or hardly any, goals. This is where the name of "99 Percent" comes from.

Practice:

To play this game you will have to have at least 4 or 5 of your son or daughters friends, or team mates, come over. And to play this game on ice, you will have to find a vacant ice rink in your area (not likely). Or you could set it up out in your street (with caution), if it's not heavily traveled, and use in line roller skates. Or you could also set it up in your back yard (probably your best bet) using regular sport shoes, a hockey stick, and a puck or ball. All goalkeepers need to play this game to practice

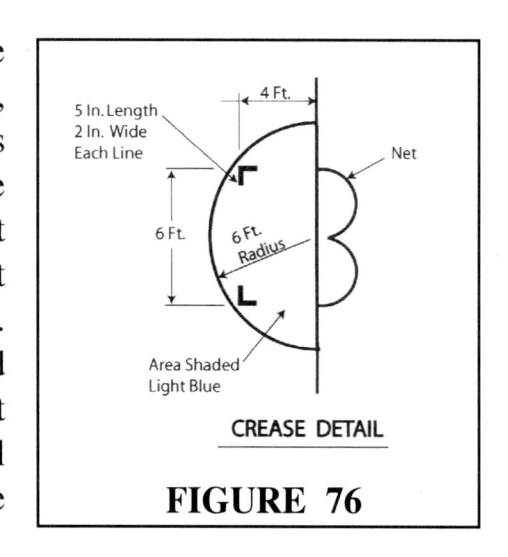

FIGURE 76

their "getting into position" techniques in a game type situation. I would suggest keeping the game to around 30 minutes or less for the real little kids, so they don't lose interest or get tired. And it will give you time then for other types of training, during the session. Keep track of the score on a pad of paper, so you can compare your son or daughters progress later on.

FIGURE 77

Drill No. 53- Save Techniques
The Basics are:

The next step after learning how to get set, move around, and position themselves, is how use their equipment to save, deflect, or stop, the puck or ball. There are many save techniques. We will go over stick saves, skate saves, pad saves, poke check saves, and glove saves. We will cover screen the shot saves, break away saves, playing the angle saves, covering up saves, behind the net saves, deflection saves, face-off saves, and 2 on 1 or 3 on 2 saves, as "*strategy saves*". There is a lot to go over for learning how to make saves. However, if you start them out young at 5 years and work on them a little each day or week, they will be pretty good by the time they get to their first team.

Stick Saves

The first thing they need to learn is have a firm grip on the stick with the blocker glove hand *(SEE FIGURE 77)*. They grab it just above the paddle, or widened portion of the stick shaft. Here is what makes stick saves work, make sure they always keep the stick blade in contact with the ice or floor surface. Don't let the stick blade rest on the front of the skates either. A blade always on the floor or ice almost always stops the low shot. When they make a low shot stick save, show them how to angle the stick to deflect the shot away from the front of the net, and towards one of the corners of the rink *(SEE FIGURE 78)*.

FIGURE 78

FIGURE 79

Bring the stick blade slightly back, to cushion shots that come directly at you from the front.

For high shots the stick can be used like a baseball ball bat, to deflect shots away. The flattened part of the stick below the glove, or paddle as it is referred to, is the part of the stick used for this. Goalkeepers need to learn to deflect the puck or ball away from the mouth of the goal when they bat it *(SEE FIGURE 79)*.

<u>Skate Saves</u>

There are basically two types of skate saves, standing, and on one knee saves. The rule is, if the goalkeeper can reach the puck or ball with a standing skate save, they can also reach it with their stick.

In the *"standing skate save"* the stick should always be used first if possible, using the skate only as a back up. To make a skate save correctly, the toe of the skate on the side where the save is to be made, should be pointed right at the incoming puck or ball. Then the opposite foot is turned so a push off on the front inside edge of the skate can be made to propel the goalkeeper forward (T-push). The weight is then shifted to the front glide foot. The knees should be flexed, which helps you stay in the normal crouched stance. It gives you better outward extension, and it helps you keep your stick on the ice. And it also helps you stop right where you want to. The stick is then placed in front of the leading foot *(SEE FIGURE 80)*. They should work on being able to go from post to post with the T-push move.

The *"one knee skate save"* is the other technique. This save is made by resting on the inside knee. When they go down, the weight is shifted to the inside knee, keep the

FIGURE 80

100

skate blade or roller wheel of the other leg on the ice or floor, then kick or snap the leg out, with the stick down and the glove up *(SEE FIGURE 81)*. When it gets down, the rear skate is tuned to stop any shots from going in behind you. While doing all this, have them make sure they don't fall backwards. Sometimes they will get a little out of balance on this move. Just point out to them to be aware of the falling. The other thing is have them try to keep from using the gloves, to push themselves up if they fall.

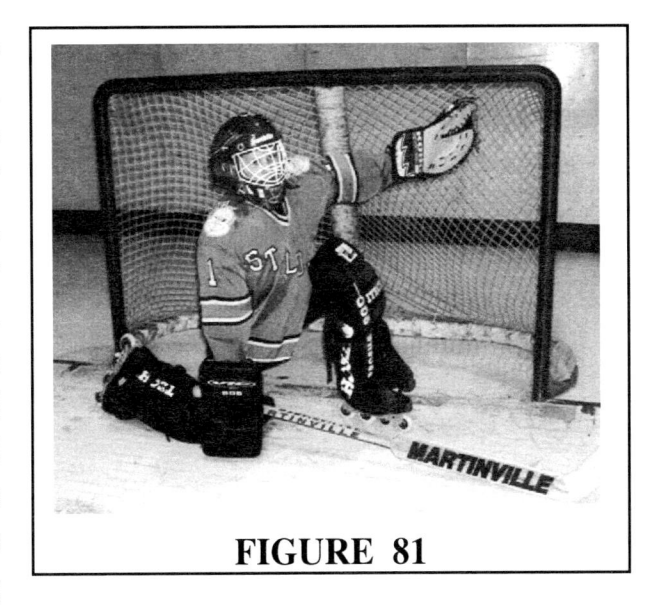

FIGURE 81

Pad Saves

There are many types of pad saves, and little variations of them. We will go over the 3 basic versions. First there is the coming straight in "butterfly" pad save, then the "stacked pads" save, and last the "Butterfly slide" save. Which save technique to use is going to depend on whether the shot is straight on, or from the sides.

The *"straight in butterfly"* save is used mostly when there is a lot of traffic right in front of the net, or the shot is coming in more or less almost straight at you. It's advantages are, it lets the goalkeeper cover more area, and they have better odds on making the save if they are guessing. The disadvantage is while making this type of save, they will probably give up more rebound goals in front of the net. This type of save does cover more of the upper part of the net though which is a good thing.

What your son or daughter has to do is start out in the "ready" position, face the front, then they drop down to their knees, next they kick their legs out to the rear and point their toes outward . As they go down they shift their weight to the knees and keep the upper part of their body upright. The front of the knees and the legs form a "V" *(SEE FIGURE 82)*. The object with the legs and knees is, cover as much of the ice or floor as possible. If their pads are not placed right, it's probably because they are not driving the knees down hard to keep the pads flat on the surface. Also make sure they are covering the slight opening between their knees correctly with their stick. They do this by keeping the stick flat and down on the floor or ice. Locate the stick about 3 inches in front of the pads. All

FIGURE 82

of this while keeping the upper body in the "ready" position. There is a variation of this technique, some goalkeepers like to use, where you drop down on only one knee and not two.

The *"stacked pads save"* is where the pads are stacked one on top of each other. Describing this save is sort of like a baseball players slide into second base. This type of save is used mostly on low quick shots right around the net area, and on break away shots. This save also works well when the goalkeeper is on one side of the net, and the pass goes to a receiver on the other side of the net. The disadvantage is once they go down on the ice or floor, they are vulnerable to a high shot into the upper part of the net. It's all in the timing, they don't go down from the T-push until they are reasonably sure the shot will come in low.

To start the move your son or daughter goes to one side of the net. Then they turn toward the opposite side of the net, and execute a T-push off with the foot farthest away from the direction they intend to slide *(SEE FIGURE 83-A)*. Then while gliding on the front foot, they drop down on the knee of the lower leg, kick out the other leg, and go into their slide *(SEE FIGURE 83-B)*. Next while sliding on the lower leg hip, they stack the pads of the upper leg right on

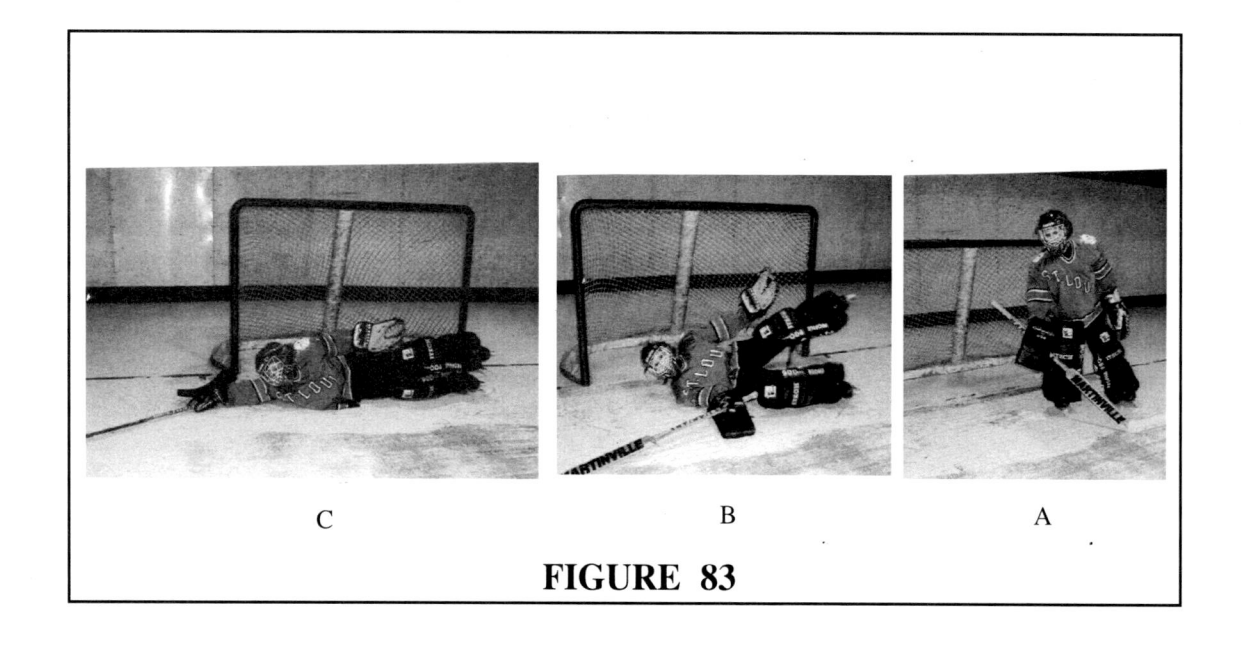

C   B   A

FIGURE 83

top, making a kind of wall to stop the puck or ball *(SEE FIGURE 83-C)*. After that they add the glove to the top of the stack to make it higher. Last they swing the stick out on the ice surface in front of their head, to protect the backside. I suspect this technique is going to be real hard for the little kids to perform. You can try it, but you may have to wait until the are 12 years or older.

The *"butterfly slide save"* is a technique that will take some strength and flexibility to perform. It's probably not for the real little kids either. You will probably have to wait until they are 12 years or older to work on this technique also. The bigger the goalkeeper is the more effective this save is. This save also works well when the goalkeeper is on one side of the net and the pass goes to a receiver on the other side of the net. This is also a quick way to get to the other side of the net in one move. Another advantage of this slide is, it's easier to keep your eyes on the puck or ball, when compared to the stacked pads technique.

To start the move your son or daughter goes to one side of the net. Then they turn toward the opposite side of the net and execute a hard T-push off with the foot farthest away from the direction they intend to slide *(SEE FIGURE 84-A)*. Then as they begin to glide on the front foot, they get the lead foot pad down quickly, and slide to the other side of the net. Next they bring the trailing leg pad down quickly to the ice or floor as they slide, with the stick down on the ice right between the legs, to stop any shots from going between their legs until the trailing pad closes the hole *(SEE FIGURE 84-B)*. Then the trailing leg pad is quickly brought up next to the lead pad to close the hole between the legs. The body along with the glove stays upright then, to stop any high shots from getting through *(SEE FIGURE 84-C)*. The stick stays blade down on the ice or floor to cover

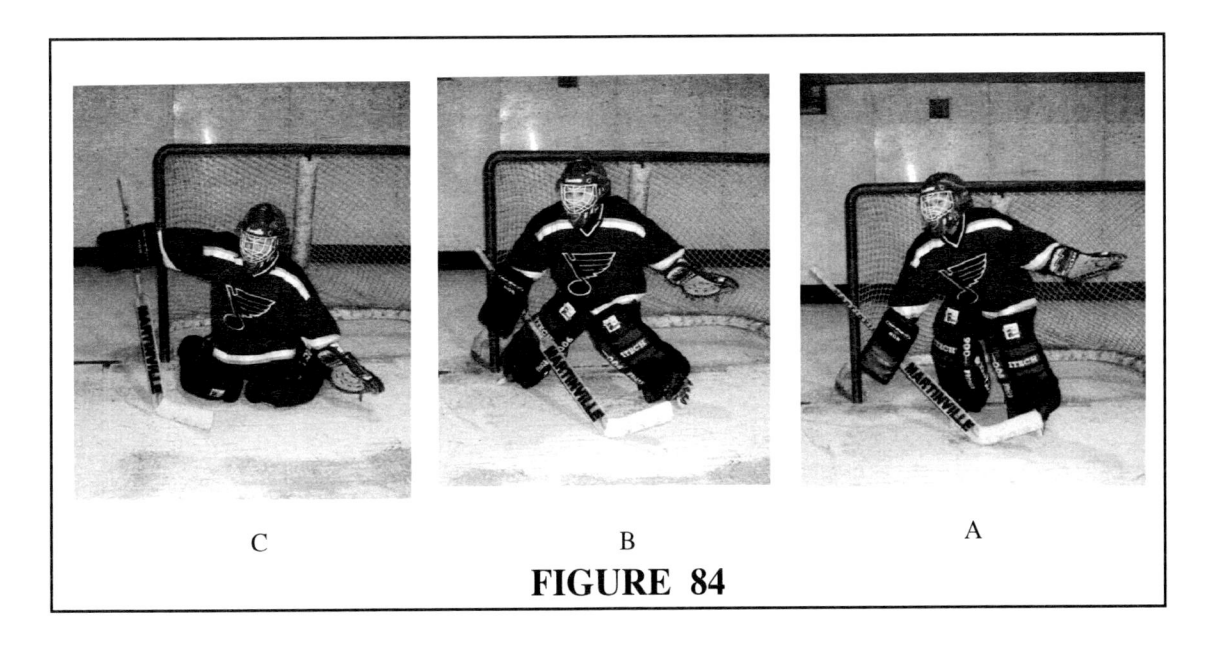

C   B   A
FIGURE 84

low shots. Also the stick can be moved all the way to paddle down, to cover more area of the ice or floor.

Poke Check Saves

The poke check save is made up of three different types of quick moves by the goalkeeper. They all basically use the stick blade, to reach out and push the puck or ball away from an attacking opponent. They only work though when the opponent is close to the net, or close enough to reach with an extended stick. The three types are, standing, diving, and power.

FIGURE 85

The *"standing poke check save"* is made by shooting the stick blade towards the puck or ball, and letting it extend out by slipping through the glove until it reaches the end, without the goalkeeper letting go of the shaft though *(SEE FIGURE 85)*. This is accomplished by taping the end of the shaft into a big knob, or wad of tape, which keeps it from leaving the glove. After poking, they quickly then draw the shaft back in, and resume the "ready" position.

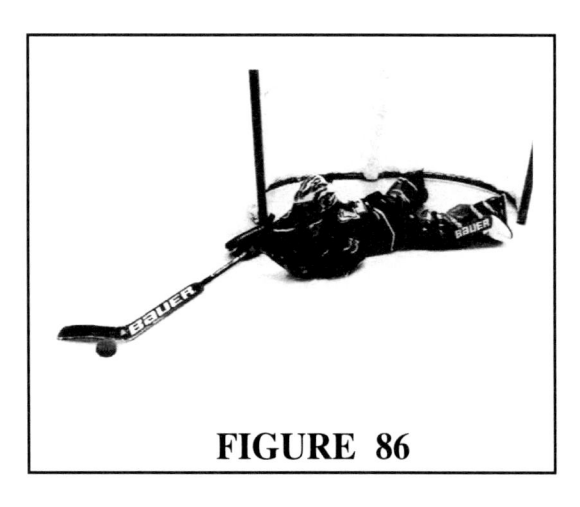

The *"diving poke check save"* is nearly the same, except the goalkeeper follows the stick out by diving and sliding on the ice or floor. And to cover as much ice or floor surface as possible, the goalkeeper while sliding spreads the legs out in a "V" shape, with the skates turned forward toward the direction they are sliding *(SEE FIGURE 86)*. The disadvantage of this technique is, when you go down on the ice, away from the net, you are vulnerable to being scored

FIGURE 86

upon by a rebound. When this technique is used the puck or ball has to be deflected away from the net towards a corner. This gives the goalkeeper at least a short time to try and recover back to a "ready" position in front of the net.

The *"power poke check save"* is similar to the "standing" technique, except the stick side knee goes down on the ice or floor as the stick is extended *(SEE FIGURE 87)*.

Glove Saves

Glove saves are mostly made with the *"catching glove"*. I suspect most goalkeepers like to save with the catching glove when possible. It's easier for them than using the skates or pads. Goalkeepers can protect the upper part of the net with the glove, without too much trouble, as long as they stay in the "ready" position. The other glove is the blocker glove, which is worn on the hand that holds the stick. Glove saves are made with the catching glove, by following the puck or ball all the way into the glove, then squeezing it tightly so the puck or ball does not come out *(SEE FIGURE 88)*. This is very similar to catching a baseball, except the puck is a different shape. And when it is flying through the air it is easier to roll right out the other side of the glove if not squeezed tightly and firmly. Coaches say one of the biggest mistakes an inexperienced goalkeeper makes is, catching too much with the glove. When they come across the body to make a catch on the stick side, they pull themselves out of the "ready" position. If there is a rebound, or a pass off the rebound, they are vulnerable on the glove side, for making a quick recovery. If they try to catch low shots down by their feet, it brings their head down, and they become vulnerable to high shots. And its also harder to see rebounds when the head is down.

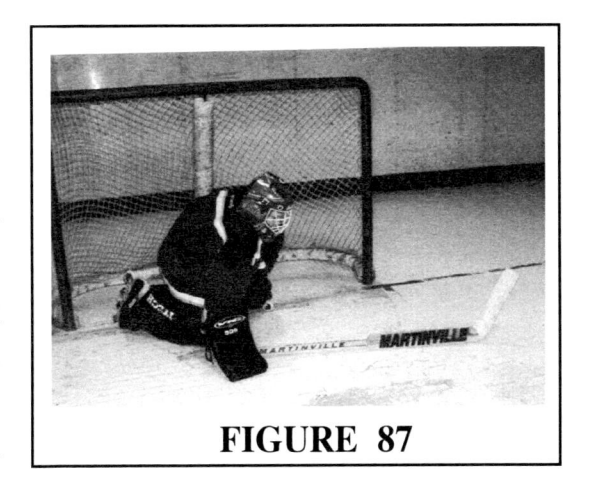

FIGURE 87

It's harder to learn how to use the *"blocker glove"*. It can be used very effectively though when you think of it as an extension of the stick. If a puck or ball comes in on the blocker glove side, the goalkeeper should follow it all the way in to the blocker glove, then deflect it away from the net into a corner. Do not swipe at the puck or ball with the blocker glove because it more than likely will bounce way out in front of the net. The angle of the blocker glove, with respect to the incoming puck or ball, is very important. If the up and down angle is too much, the puck or

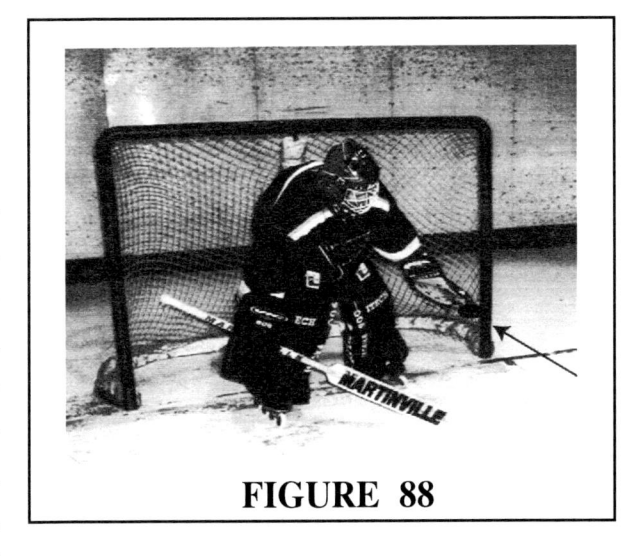

FIGURE 88

FIGURE 89

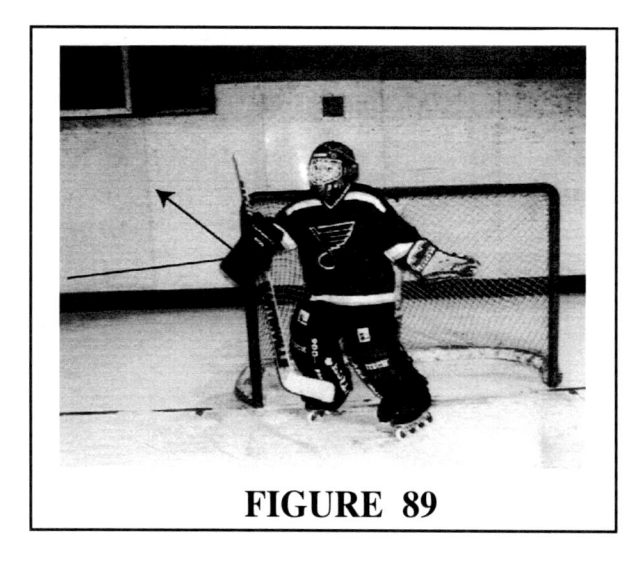

ball may pop up into the air *(SEE FIGURE 89)*. By changing the side to side angle (turning) of the blocker glove, the puck can be directed to the side away from the net. Goalkeepers should also learn how to trap the puck or ball, against the blocker, by bringing the catch glove over the top of the puck or ball the moment it makes contact with the blocker pad *(SEE FIGURE 90)*. This is very similar to bringing the other hand around when catching a baseball, to keep the ball from coming out.

Practice:

To practice all of these save techniques, you are definitely going to need a goal with a net. If you can find a vacant rink to practice on, use it. I doubt you will find one though. So what you will probably have to do is create your own goal area out in the street, driveway, or back yard. Your son or daughter does not have to necessarily be on their skates to learn these techniques. Their are a number of ways to do it. If you are in the street or driveway, you can use in line roller skates. If you go out in the back yard, they can be in tennis or sport shoes (no leather sole street shoes though). Then you use a stick and a ball. Eventually though they will have to practice on ice if they play ice hockey, and a floor if they are playing roller hockey, to get the real feel of the equipment and skates they have on. They can still get a lot of good practice in at home though.

The other thing is, they should be in *full equipment* so that they won't get injured or hurt. Then you mom or dad, or a friend, will have to get back about 10 to 20 yards away and shoot pucks or balls at them, from all different angles. Go over, and practice, each one of the five techniques with them for at least 10 to 15 minutes each at a training session. Watch their moves carefully, then stop and point out any

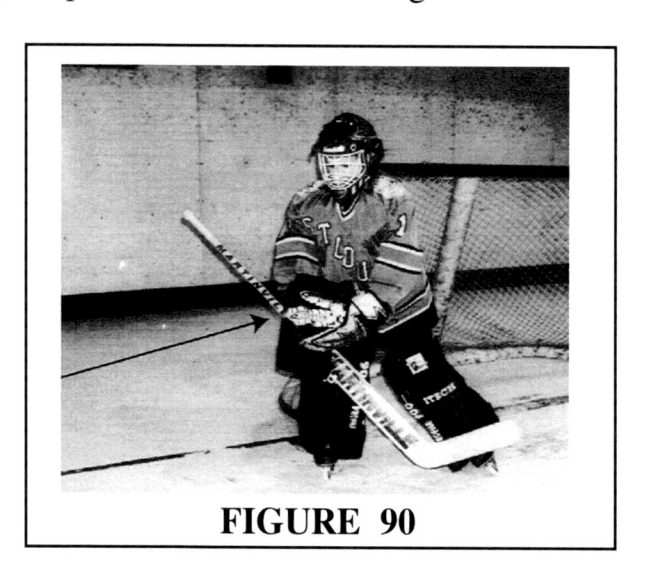

FIGURE 90

problems they are having. And if they still are having problems learning the technique, go back over the moves with them, then walk them slowly through it. Make sure they know all the moves to be a goalkeeper.

Drill No. 54- Save Strategies
The Basics are:
Here we will go over what I call the "save strategies" of the goalkeeper. These are some basic strategies your son or daughter need to learn. The strategies we will cover are, "screen the shot saves", "playing the angle saves", "covering up saves", "break away saves", "deflection saves", "behind the net saves", "face-off saves", and "3 on 2 or 2 on 1 saves".

<u>Screen the Shot Strategy</u>
When the opponents are running a screen out the goalkeeper shot technique in front of the goal, your son or daughter has to stay low and fight getting screened out of view of the incoming shot. The best technique to use for this is the "straight in butterfly" ***(SEE FIGURE 82)***.

Practice:
To practice this save strategy, you are definitely going to need a goal with a net. If you can find a vacant rink to practice on, use it. I doubt you will find one though. So what you will probably have to do is create your own goal area out in the street, driveway, or back yard. Your son or daughter does not have to necessarily be on their skates to learn this strategy. The "American Sport Education Program" (ASEP) is recommending you use a screen the shot board as they call it. What you would do is make a board frame out of maybe 2 x 4's and plywood, then hang a bed sheet on the bottom part so that the puck or ball slides under it ***(SEE FIGURE 91)***. Then you, mom or dad, go on the away side of the screen board and shoot pucks or balls under the bottom of the hanging sheet. To even add more of a game feel to the

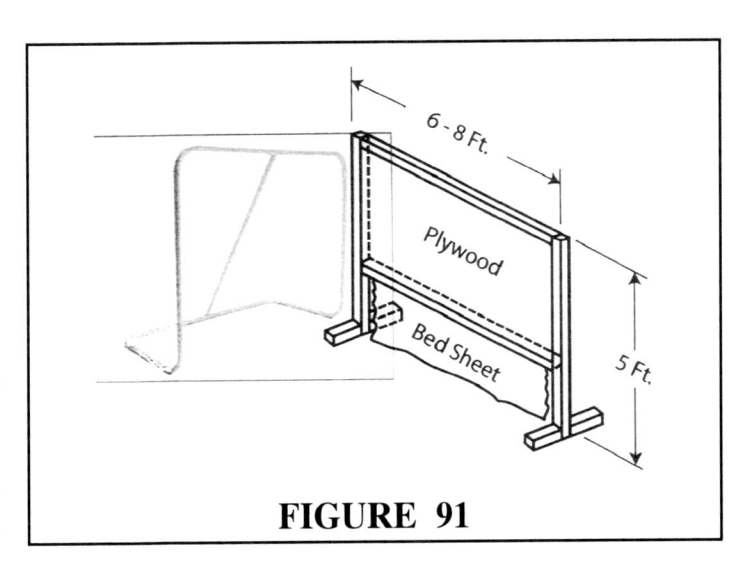

FIGURE 91

107

drill, have one of their friends come over and stand in front of them where a screener would be positioned. If you are shooting pucks at them, make sure the friend has the necessary protective gear on . Shoot pucks or balls at them for about 10 minutes per side, at each training session.

Playing the Angle Strategy

Coaches say that one of the most important save skills for a goalkeeper to learn is, the technique of playing the angles. What this amounts to is, blocking how much of the net a shooter can see. Another strategy is, don't set up back at the net in the middle between sides. If it's a regular shot, they can come out a little distance, then stay squared up to the shooter. Explain to them they always should play the puck or ball, not the shooter. As long as the puck or ball is out in front of the net, they can come out from the net. They must stay right in the net if the puck or ball is behind or to the side of the net.

Practice:

To practice this save strategy, you are definitely going to need a goal with a net. If you can find a vacant rink to practice on, use it. I doubt you will find one though. So what you will probably have to do is create your own goal area out in the street, driveway, or back yard. Your son or daughter does not have to necessarily be on their skates to learn this strategy. When you are practicing with them, make sure they have protective gear on if you are using pucks. Then you mom or dad, or a friend, will have to get back about 10 to 20 yards away and shoot pucks or balls at them, from all different angles. Also make some shots from each side, and behind the net. Make sure they are getting the right angles, and that they are going to the side of the net when necessary. Shoot pucks or balls at them for about 10 minutes per side, and behind the net, at each training session.

Covering Up Strategy

Covering up basically means falling on the puck or ball and covering it with your body. When it comes right in front of the net, the goalkeeper has to kind of pounce on, or smother the puck or ball so it doesn't come out from under their body. Tell them to keep their head up at all times. They use only the catch glove to cover up the puck or ball. Once the puck or ball is covered, they place their stick and blocker in front of the catch glove. This is to protect their glove hand from players hacking at them with their sticks.

Practice:
To practice this save strategy, you are definitely going to need a goal with a net. If you can find a vacant rink to practice on, use it. I doubt you will find one though. So what you will probably have to do is create your own goal area out in the street, driveway, or back yard. Then you mom or dad, will have to get back about 10 to 20 yards away and shoot pucks or balls at them. When you are practicing with them, make sure they have protective gear on if you are using pucks. Have them fall on the puck or ball, and try to keep it under their body. Shoot pucks or balls at them for about 10 minutes per side, at each training session.

Breakaway Shot Strategy
There are three basic save strategies against breakaway shots.
1. Come out far from the net.
2. Back up when the shooter is no deeper than the top of the crease.
3. Try for a save with a two pad slide.

Tell them to wait until the shooter makes the first move before they make their move. Explain to them that they have to time their backward movements, to react to the shooters movements.

Practice:
To practice this save strategy, you are definitely going to need a goal with a net. If you can find a vacant rink to practice on, use it. I doubt you will find one though. So what you will probably have to do is create your own goal area out in the street, driveway, or back yard. Then you mom or dad, will have to get back about 20 to 30 yards away, skate or run right at them, and make shots with either a puck or ball. When you are practicing with them, make sure they have protective gear on if you are using pucks. Adjust your distances to shoot way out, and up closer approximately where the crease would be. Make sure they are adjusting their position, with how far you are away from them. Also try to shoot around them, and see if they are using a "two pad slide' type save technique. Shoot pucks or balls at them for about 10 minutes per side, at each training session.

Deflection Save Strategy
If a goalkeeper thinks their only save chance is a deflection, they should move toward the flight of the puck or ball, and try to keep a good angle with the shot release point. Next they turn, and square off, to the direction they intend to deflect the puck or ball toward.

Practice:

To practice this save strategy, you are definitely going to need a goal with a net. If you can find a vacant rink to practice on, use it. I doubt you will find one though. So what you will probably have to do is create your own goal area out in the street, driveway, or back yard. Then you mom or dad, will have to get back about 10 to 20 yards away and shoot pucks or balls at them. When you are practicing with them, make sure they have protective gear on if you are using pucks. Make sure they are getting a good angle with you as you skate up. Then make sure they square away to the direction they are going to deflect toward. Shoot pucks or balls at them for about 10 minutes per side, at each training session.

Behind the Net Save Strategy

When the shooter goes behind the net, the goalkeeper has to move to the side post of the net closest to where the shooter is positioned. Next they square up to that side, turn their head towards the shooter to watch them. What they have to do here is prevent a wraparound shot, or a pass out to another shooter on that side of the net. If the shooter is waiting behind the middle of the net, they have to be ready to quickly turn, and T-push, or shuffle, over to the other side of the net post if the shooter reverses and goes back to the opposite side of the net.

Practice:

To practice this save strategy, you are definitely going to need a goal with a net. If you can find a vacant rink to practice on, use it. I doubt you will find one though. So what you will probably have to do is create your own goal area out in the street, driveway, or back yard. Then you mom or dad will have to go behind the net, try to fool your son or daughter, and make a wrap around shot into the net. Do this by curling the stick around the corner of the net post. To make the drill more like a game situation, have a friend come over and position themselves out on the side wing area for a pass. Then some of the time pass the puck or ball over to the friend, for a shot on goal. When you are practicing with them, make sure they have protective gear on if you are using pucks. Make sure they are tracking the puck or ball wherever it is, and not watching only you. Shoot pucks or balls at them for about 10 minutes per side, from back behind the net, at each training session.

Face-off Strategy

If the shooter is on their forehand off of the Face-off, the goalkeeper should face the Face-off circle. If the shooter is on their backhand off of the Face-off, it usually means a pass, the goalkeeper should always know where the opponents "gunners" are positioned. That is where the shot will be coming from. Then they have to be ready to quickly change positions in the net, to line up with the gunner.

Practice:

To practice this save strategy, you are definitely going to need a goal with a net. If you can find a vacant rink to practice on, use it. I doubt you will find one though. So what you will probably have to do is create your own goal area out in the street, driveway, or back yard. Then you mom or dad, will have to go to the Face-off circle, or about where it would be located. Then you shoot pucks or balls at them, using your forehand. Then switch to the backhand and fake a shot, then a pass. Watch their reaction and make sure they are moving towards the direction you are passing to, or faking to. To make it more like a game situation, get a friend to come over and position themselves on the side opposite of the Face-off circle where you are located. Then some of the time, backhand a pass over to the friend. When you are practicing with them, make sure they have protective gear on if you are using pucks. Shoot pucks or balls at them for about 10 minutes per side, from each Face-off circle, at each training session.

3 on 2 and 2 on 1 Save Strategy

On more than one player rush attacks on goal, the goalkeeper's first responsibility is line up with the puck carrier. If a pass is made to the open player, and they shoot, a 2 pad slide save technique should be used. Some coaches say, to make the goalkeeper's decision making a little easier, they should make a mark out on the ice or floor at their maximum reach poke checking point. This is so that when a shooter gets real close, then they know how far out from the net they can come. When a goalkeeper does poke check, they need to be sure and not go down, or lunge forward at the shooter with their shoulders. The reason is, when they do this it cuts down on their ability to move laterally if necessary.

When the shooters approach, the goalkeeper needs to come out of the net, but not too far, force them to take more time to make their shot decision. Generally speaking shooters coming in on the forehand are vulnerable to the poke check. Shooters coming in on the backhand can shield the puck easier, and they are less vulnerable to the poke check. Occasionally, using a fake poke check will force a shooter away from the net.

On 2 on 1 straight on rushes, the goalkeeper's first responsibility is to take away the short side angle. When the 2 on 1 is coming in from out of either corner of the rink, the puck or ball carrier will many times pass rather than carry it in to the net. What the goalkeeper should do is, be ready for that. Then reach out as far as they can with their stick, and deflect those passes across and in front of them.

Practice:
  To practice this save strategy, you are definitely going to need a goal with a net. If you can find a vacant rink to practice on, use it. I doubt you will find one though. So what you will probably have to do is create your own goal area out in the street, driveway, or back yard. You will need to have 1 or 2 of your son or daughters friends come over and help out on this drill. Before you even start this practice, sit down and go over with them exactly what all they have to do. Then you mom or dad, and the friends, will have to go out to a spot about 20 to 30 yards away. When you are practicing with them, make sure they have protective gear on if you are using pucks. Then make your 3 on 2, or 2 on 1 rushes at the net. Some of the time pass the puck or ball to the friend for a shot, and some of the time shoot yourself. And some of the time all of you come out of the corners at them. Mom or dad, observe what they are doing. Make sure they do a 2 pad slide save when necessary, and make sure they know how far they can come out to poke check. Shoot pucks or balls at them for about 15 minutes per side, from straight on and from the corners, at each training session.

Drill No. 55- The Hot Shot Game
The Basics are:
  This is a game to help your son or daughter develop their save techniques. You can play this game in the back yard. You will need 2 goal nets, one for each end. You can play with 1 or 2 shooters going at one goal. Then at the same time, 1 or 2 shooters going at the opposite goal. They continually shoot at just the one goal. This way the goalkeepers have more save chances. When you are practicing with them, make sure both goalkeepers have protective gear on if you are using pucks. If you are on grass, you can use a ball. Place your nets about 80 feet apart. The object of this game is to have your son or daughter practice all the different save techniques. For the set up **SEE FIGURE 92.** First choose a particular technique that the goalkeepers have to use. You will have to tell the shooters exactly where you want them to shoot. It may be in different areas for different kind of saves.
  The goalkeeper is awarded 2 points for each save they make using the predetermined technique. Do not give them points for other types of saves. Whichever goalkeeper allows the fewest goals gets an additional 2 points. The

FIGURE 92

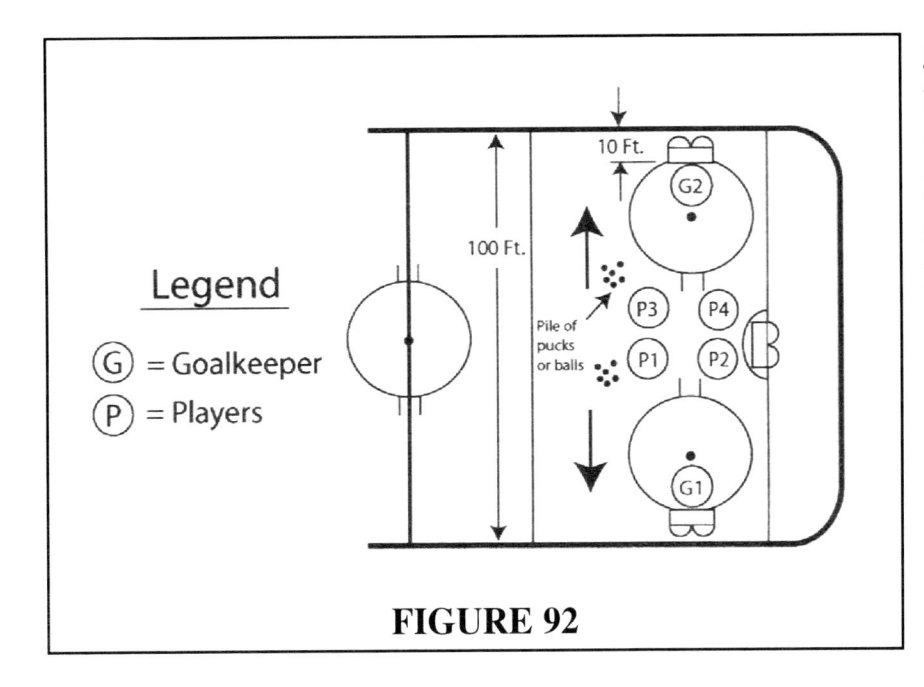

goalkeeper with the most points wins the game. Each game should last no longer than 10 minutes for each different technique used. I would suggest not playing the game longer than an hour. This should let them try at least 5 different techniques at a session. Wait a couple of days, work on other techniques, then come back to the game and use the rest of the techniques. This way they won't get tired of the game.

Practice:

They can have 3 or 5 of their friends come over, to play the game with them. That will make it more fun for them. To play this game on ice, you will have to find a vacant ice rink in your area (not likely). Or you could set it up out in your street (with caution), if it's not heavily traveled, and use in line roller skates. Or set it up in your back yard using regular sport shoes, a hockey stick, and a ball. All goalkeepers need to play this game to practice their techniques in a game type situation. Again I would suggest keeping the game to around 60 minutes or less, so you have time for other types of training. Keep track of the score on a pad of paper, so you can compare your son or daughters progress later on.

Drill No. 56- The Goalkeepers Magic 7 (Rules)

This is not really a drill. It is 7 rules you will have to teach them to follow:

>1. Have them make themselves look big. Tell them, they always have to try to cover up any open pieces (space) in the net.

2. Have them position themselves right in the middle of the shooters line of sight. Then they move out to the top of the crease, to take away more of the net that the shooter can see. Have them get set quickly and try to keep from moving too far.

3. Have them always face the puck or ball.

4. Have them line up with the puck or ball so that it hits them in the middle of the chest. Have them keep their shoulders square to the puck or ball. This way they only have to move half of their body to make the save.

5. Have them point their skates at the shooters, and try to move half a step behind the puck or ball as it gets to them.

6. Have them always control the puck or ball, and the play, so that they always know where the opponents are located. Have them play all four divided up segments of the net. They should read the shooter on all plays, including breakaways.

7. Have them force the shooter to shoot to the side of the net they are approaching, and not the side they are leaving.

Tactics and Strategies

Young kids should know some of the more basic tactics and strategies used in Hockey. We can't go over every possibility, but we will try to give you a good basic understanding of game tactics. Hockey is a team game. As many coaches have said, "There is no "I" in the word team". Individual tactics and strategies have been discussed all over the rest of this book. What we are going to talk about here is Team Tactics and Strategies. First you have communication, "verbal" and "nonverbal". Then you have the "offensive" game " tactics, and the "defensive" game tactics. After that you have the "transition" game, "power plays", and "penalty Killing".

Team Tactics
Communication

Verbal Communications

One of the best team tactics is communication between players. The best way to communicate with team mates is to talk. But you have to careful how you do it. The other team could be listening. The best way to communicate with team mates is during breaks or while on the bench. As an example, if you were open most of the time out on a wing, let your team mates know it. Or if you are being double teamed often, let them know about it. This means a team mate must be open somewhere else. Some hockey coaches tell their players, "You were born with two ears and one mouth. So listen twice as much as you speak".

Listen to your goalkeeper. When play is up on the other end of the rink, they have a good overall view of what is going on. And if they are doing their job of being observant as they stand around and wait, they should be able to let you know who is open and who is not. Also the goalkeeper should be able to notice if the opponents are setting up their defense on the strong side, or the weak side.

Nonverbal Communications

Another means of communicating is nonverbal, or body language. "Faking " or "deking" is an example of nonverbal communicating. By making a move with your head, puck, or ball, one way then going the opposite way, is sending a nonverbal message to the opponent. Using the eyes is a nonverbal communicating method. As an example, making eye contact with a team mate before making a pass is a nonverbal method. That way you can tell if the team mate is ready for the pass. There is a small problem sometimes with eye contact though. Making eye contact through the face cage on the helmet, might be hard for some players. For players that have that problem, another communicating method should be set up between them and team mates. Make sure they understand though that they do not remove the helmet to make eye contact. Nodding the head up and down is a good substitute for these players. Another method is, point their stick to indicate where they want to pass or skate. Tell them that they must interpret the message the same way as all their team mates. Sometimes a false message confuses their opponents. As an example, pointing the stick in one direction for a pass when actually you want the pass in the other direction.

Goalkeepers need to communicate to defensive players what is going on behind them. This is because they are moving backwards some of the time, and can't see what is going on behind them. Goalkeepers should learn how to keep track of the game time, and when the penalty time is winding down. Goalkeepers can see many things the rest of the team can not see. And because of that they need to communicate what they see. They should be a team leader and always be positive to motivate the team.

Offensive Strategies

Obviously, the object of the offensive game is to score points. But there is a lot more to it than just scoring points. Probably the first thing you will have to do, mom or dad, is sit down with your son or daughter in the evening or weekend and go over the basics. Use a chalkboard or a sketch pad, to illustrate your point.

Teach the following offensive concepts to your son or daughter:
    1. Have them learn to read and react to their team mates and opponents.
    2. Have them work on increasing their scoring productivity each game.
    3. Have them try to make the goalkeeper move, to open up more holes for shooting.
    4. Use one on one strategies and tactics.

Read and React
A puck or ball carrier must learn how to read defensive pressure, passing options, and open rink surface. They have to learn to execute counter tactics to what they read, then react to them. Team mates must decide whether to back up the puck or ball carrier, set up numerical advantages (double teams), set up screens, or create a passing option. These are all reactions after they make a read. Also mom or dad, you are going to have to teach your son or daughter which player position is responsible for each of the strategy options.

Increase Scoring Productivity
There are 6 basic rules for increasing scoring productivity:
1. When they are in traffic, players should learn to concentrate on shooting, or creating some kind of shooting opportunity. Teach your son or daughter not to shoot the puck or ball if a good scoring opportunity is not there (bad odds). When another player is more open for a scoring opportunity, your son or daughter needs to read that and get the puck or ball over to them quickly.
2. Players should anticipate then react by watching the goalkeepers position, puck or ball location, their own position, their team mates position, and the

opponents position. Your son or daughter needs to learn to look at the net before shooting. Then adjust their shot to the position of the goalkeeper, with respect to the open net areas.

3. Players need to learn how to become determined. They have to overcome any defensive efforts to keep them from driving to the net. They have to learn to be ready for rebounds, loose pucks or balls, and to not turn away from the net after taking a shot. If a player does not stay in front of the goal after the shot, and look for a rebound, they are giving the puck or ball right back to the opponents.

4. Players need to learn to release the puck or ball quickly after receiving a pass, or making fakes and dekes. If a player lets the goalkeeper and defenders set up and react after making a good fake, they may have wasted a great scoring opportunity.

5. During one on one tactics, all players should learn how to make different fakes and dekes, to be as unpredictable as they can to opponents. If players make the same moves each time, they make the defenders job easy. Teach your son or daughter to be creative when they come down the rink, they will have fun.

6. Player should try to position themselves so that they can move into an opening as soon as the pass arrives. This particular concept takes some creative skating and practice, for young kids to learn. Coaches say one on one reverses, and puck or ball races, are two good ways to practice and learn these skills.

<u>Making the Goalkeeper Move</u>

Moving the puck or ball around is the number one strategy, to force the goalkeeper to move around. One of the best ways to do this is set up on one side of the net, then pass the puck or ball to the other side of the net. Many times this gives a team mate, set up on the away side, a chance for a shot on goal. One way to set this up is, an "attack triangle" *(SEE FIGURE 93)*. If player P1 moves out to a "high position", they become the high support for players P2 an P3. This moves the point on the triangle *(SEE FIGURE 93)*. Movement of any player changes every players responsibilities. In 5 on 5 ice hockey, the last 2 players (P4 & P5) become the support of the initial triangle. Then they become a "secondary triangle" *(SEE FIGURE 94)*.

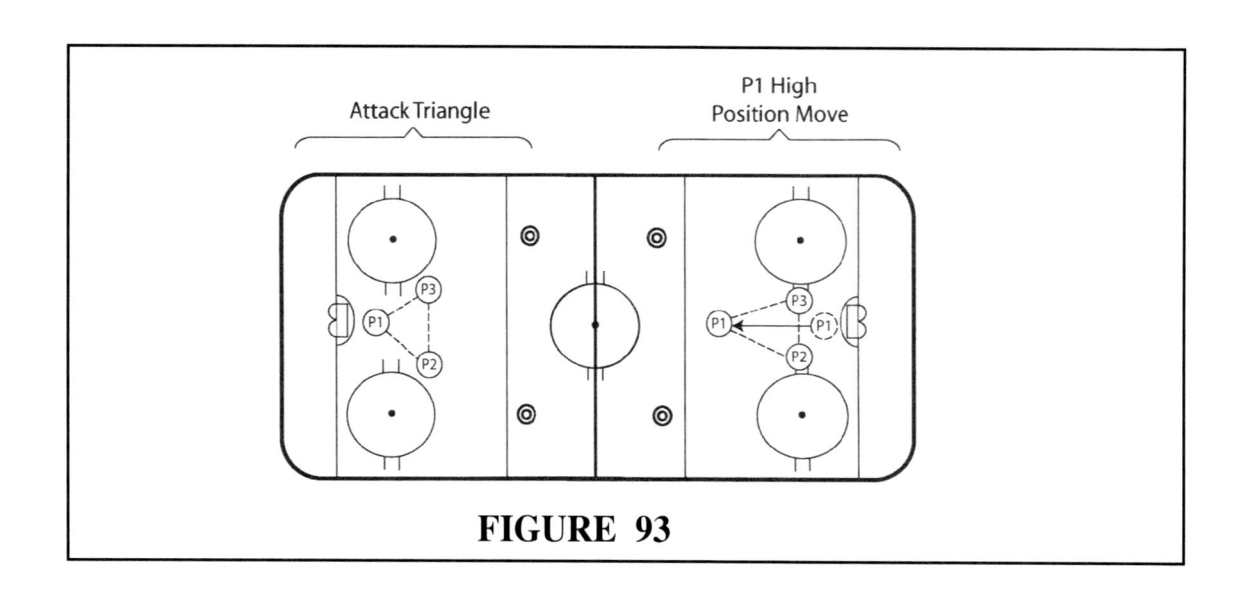

FIGURE 93

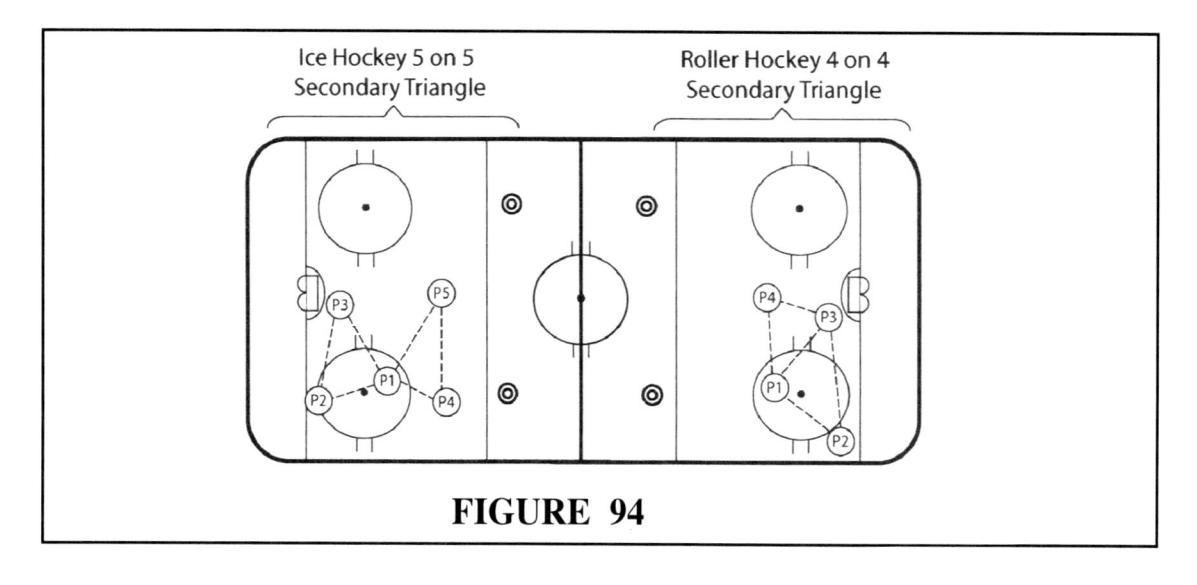

FIGURE 94

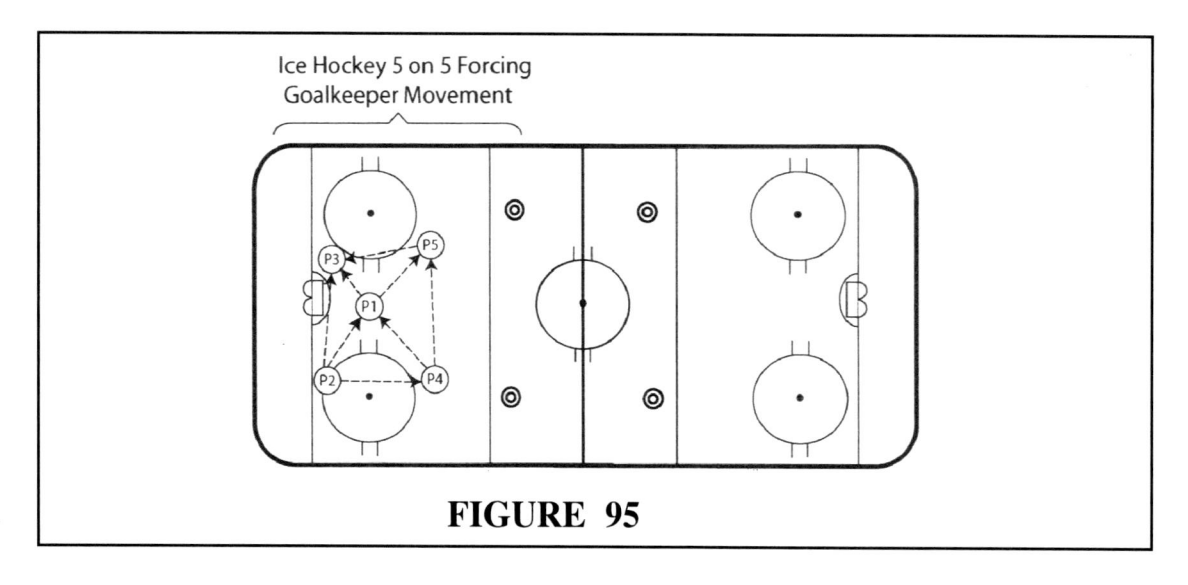

FIGURE 95

118

In 4 on 4 roller hockey, the last player in the zone becomes support. Then they become the "secondary triangle" to the initial triangle. Notice how the secondary triangle shifts to the opposite side rather than behind *(SEE FIGURE 94)*.

As the offensive players start to take control of the zone, they try to spread out at least one of the triangles. What they are trying to do, with all the movement, is keep the goalkeeper moving back and forth across the net. This creates more high percentage scoring opportunities for shooters *(SEE FIGURE 95)*. Tell your son or daughter to be creative with their passing. They will have fun, and it should create lots of scoring opportunities for their team mates.

One on One Strategies and Tactics

Players need to learn how to develop good one on one strategies and tactics. Tactics like change of pace skating, with or without the puck or ball. Inside and outside fakes. Fakes and dekes, using the head and the body. Fakes using their eyes before shooting or passing. Driving to the net before and after making a shot. Learn strategies like walkouts, and delaying. All of these one on one strategies and tactics will create offensive advantages. More goals will be scored.

Offensive Developmental Game

10 Yard WAR
The Basics are:

This is a game to help develop your son or daughters skills, for beating the opponent in tight spaces. This game is played with 2 players on each team. A 10 yard square area is marked off. Each team has an endzone behind them. The object of the game is to use fakes, dekes, picks, flip passes, and puck or ball protection, to get into the endzone. Each time a member of the team reaches or crosses the endzone with the puck or ball they are awarded 1 point.

To make the game easier, play one on one, or increase the size of the game area. To make the game harder, play 2 on 3. Require at least 2 passes be made before getting to the endzone. Or play the game along the boards, if you can find an open rink. When you play against the boards, emphasize using the boards as a third player *(SEE FIGURE 96)*.

FIGURE 96

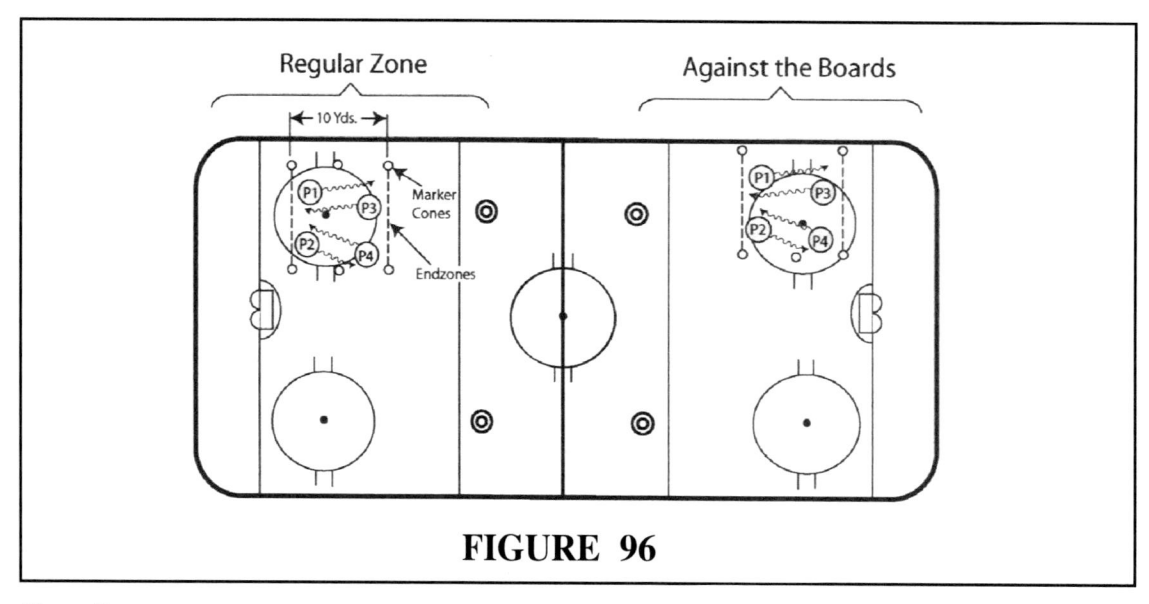

Practice:

To practice this game you will need to have 1 to 3 of your son or daughters friends come over. I suspect it will be more fun with 2 vs 2. Before you start, explain to all of them that this is going to be a rough and tuff game. Not to get mad and fight if they get roughed up a bit.

You don't have to have a rink to play this game. They can play out in the back yard. If you are using pucks, make sure to have the players wear protective gear. You can also play the game with a ball. This may be a little safer, and they are still learning the skills. To play this game on ice though you will have to find a vacant ice rink in your area (not likely). Or you could set it up out in your street (with caution), if it's not heavily traveled, and use in line roller skates. When you set it up in your back yard use regular sport shoes, a hockey stick, and a puck or ball. You can also set it up in the back yard against a fence. Although when they bang into your fence, it could be a problem for your fence (caves in). Use cones to mark the boundaries. I suggest you play this game for only 20 minutes at a session. For the little kids this will be enough. You can always come back to it on another day. Bigger kids may want to play a little longer. Get a pad of paper, or even better a small notebook. This is so you can keep track of the score, and measure their progress from game to game.

Defensive Strategies

The defensive strategy is obviously to stop the opponent from scoring. Defense is not as simple as it may look. There are a number of basic defensive concepts to prevent the opponents from even having scoring opportunities.

Teach the following defensive concepts to your son or daughter:
   1. Have them pressure the puck or ball.
   2. Have them always read then react.
   3. Have them always cover in front of the net.
   4. Have them always cover the point players in the offensive triangles.

Pressuring the Puck or Ball
   When your team loses the puck or ball, the closest player should immediately cover the puck or ball carrier. They accomplish this by cutting off the puck or ball carriers skating lanes, taking away their skating surface, forcing and angling them into the boards, and by forcing them to pass the puck or ball to a team mate. If body checking is allowed in your league, they can use this tactic to put pressure on the puck or ball carrier. If it's not allowed, they will probably have to use only stick checking.

Reading and Reacting
   When your team transitions into the defensive mode, players have to learn how to assess the situation then attack. Just like in pressuring, players have to attack the puck or ball carrier first. Second, they have to read and react to the other opponents, and to the opponents game plan. When they are sitting on the bench, they should be watching and observing what the opponents offensive game tactics appear to be. The closest player to the puck or ball carrier has to put pressure them, along with their team mates help. The next closest players have to read and follow the puck or ball, and anticipate intercepting any passes. If the puck or ball carrier reaches your defensive zone, players have to force the play to the outer edges of the zone. Teach them to especially keep the puck or ball carrier as close to the boards as possible.

Covering in front of the Net
   Offensive teams will many times have a player set up in front of your net. This is to help their team mates with tip ins and screens. One player from the defense has to stay right on this player, and cover them. They do this by placing their body between the net and the opponents body. Some coaches want their defender to stay in front of the net, even if there is no offensive player to guard. Also they want them to stay in front, and watch for passes, even if the offensive player in front moves to behind the goal. It will be your son or daughters coach that makes that decision. This is because many times this move is just to decoy the defender away from in front of the goal. Their real intention is to have the

front of the net clear, just so they can skate around the defender and get back out in front. Or maybe pass out to a shooter in front or out on the wings somewhere.

Covering the Point

The other important defensive zone coverage, especially in 5 on 5 hockey, is the points. This is the offensive player located at point of attack out on an attack triangles. A defender has to get on them quickly because they are usually a play maker. Remember the defense should be trying to get the puck or ball back if at all possible before your opponents gets into the defensive zone. Teach your son or daughter to expect the point player to attempt to fake and deke them, to get around them for a shot on goal. One way to counteract all the faking and deking is, don't watch the players head or eyes. When they get closer, just have them keep their eyes on the puck and not the player.

The Transition Strategy

The important thing to teach your son or daughter in the transition phase of the game is, learn how to quickly transfer their thoughts from offense to defense and then back to offense again. The better they become at focusing during transitions, the more success the team will have. Ice hockey transitions ideally occur in the neutral zone (in the center between bluelines). Roller hockey transitions ideally occur in the area between the tops of the Face-off circles. One way some coaches help young players visualize the transition process is, they tell them to picture the offense and defense as opposite ends of a light switch. Then they tell them to make the transition in the time it takes to flip the switch. Players have to make the transition mentally and physically. They do this by attacking the puck or ball carrier and quickly hurrying into a predetermined defensive position. Or they can try to move the puck or ball into the offensive end of the rink by scrambling into an attack triangle.

Teach the following transition concepts to you son or daughter:
    1. Have them learn about countering.
    2. Have them learn how to regroup.
    3. Neutral Zone offensive and defensive play.

Countering

Players need to learn how to counter faster than their opponent can get an attack organized. If your son or daughter can grasp this tactic, their team will have a good chance to regain control of the puck or ball very quickly. Countering is really the art of using surprise, and quickness, to catch your opponents off guard. In other words do something your opponent does not expect, then use your quickness to accomplish whatever it is you are trying to do. Countering can also be scoring a quick goal, right after your opponent has just scored. Or it can be just blocking or stopping an opponent, from driving down the rink.

Regrouping

When you have sucessfully regained the puck or ball on a counter play, the team must quickly regroup to get an offensive attack going. If players can regroup faster than the opponent can counter, it often can help you get an "odd player" rush going. And "odd player" rushes usually result in a goal being scored because of the man advantage.

Neutral Zone Play

The neutral zone is very important in transition hockey. Defensive strategy in the neutral zone includes "angling out", "trapping", "Face-offs", "forechecking and backchecking".

Angling Out

This is where the defender, or forward, forces the opponent to go to the side towards the boards.

Zone Trapping

This is where the defender or forward traps, or stops, the puck or ball handler from moving into their offensive zone. And they angle or loop around to stop the pass back to their team mate. This stops or slows down the advance of the offense. There are many other special trap techniques that we will not go into at this time.

Face-off Strategy

Gaining control of the puck or ball in the neutral zone is very important in stopping the offense from starting an attack.

Forechecking and Backchecking

The strategy of forechecking is to check, harass, and stop the opponents players as they try come out of their defensive zone into the neutral zone. The strategy of backchecking is to check, harass, and stop the opponents players from coming out after they go back and reenter their own defensive zone to regroup for an attack.

Offensive strategy in the neutral zone includes "speed", "rapid puck or ball movement", "counterattacking", and "regrouping".

Speed Strategy

Speed is the best offensive tactic to use against defenders going one on one. Players need to execute their skills as fast as they can.

Rapid Puck/ Ball Movement

Carrying the puck or ball too long gives the defender a better chance to cover or recover the puck or ball. Passing the puck or ball quickly as soon as they receive it, and changing the point of attack, confuses defenders and gives them a whole new set of problems to deal with.

Counterattacking (Attackers)

The strategy here is, push the puck or ball back towards the opponents net immediately after receiving it.

Regrouping Strategy

Immediately after regaining the puck or ball, players have to quickly regroup for an attack. Know your game plan, get into position, and get into it quickly.

Power Play Strategy

When your opponent is penalized it usually leaves your team with a numerical advantage. Its called a power play because with a 1 or 2 player advantage, your offensive team has a greater chance (the power) of scoring a goal. Most teams will have a special power play unit. Some youth teams will have their best shooters on this unit. Some coaches like to have a "quarterback" type of player on this unit. A player that is very good at reading the defense, so they can direct the attack. Players on the power play unit need to have good passing and receiving skills. If your son or daughter is on a power play unit, teach them to sharpen their skills for one touch passing, shooting the puck or ball, tip ins, and deflecting in shots.

The strategy for power play unit players is learn how to:
1. Spread out the defense, and find open spaces to move into when they don't have the puck or ball.
2. Create and master the 2 on 1 rush.
3. Address any problems as they occur.
4. Develop good individual skills.
5. Win face-offs.
6. Battle for pucks or ball in the offensive zone.
7. Properly manage the time limit.

8. Breakout strategy.
9. Regrouping Strategy.

The power play unit has to be able to read a defense, move the puck or ball along with opponents toward the net, and control the puck or ball (don't lose it). To sharpen their skills and get experience, some coaches practice by playing their power play unit against their penalty killing unit, during practice.

Spreading out a Defense

During a power play, your son or daughter has to learn to prevent one defensive player from covering two power play players. Teach them to spread out the defense, by quickly passing the puck or ball around the outside of the offensive zone. This will usually let your players have room to weave in and out of space between defenders. By doing this, players will find themselves open for a pass. And it should give them an easier chance to take a shot on goal.

Creating and Mastering the 2 on 1 Rush

When your team out numbers the defense 2 on 1, players have to read this and look for quality scoring opportunities. Teach your son or daughter to stagger themselves with their team mate. This makes it harder for the defense to cover them. Sometimes this even forces the goalkeeper to cover a player, which is usually the shooter. Shooters that are 1 on 1 with the goalkeeper should sometimes fake the shot, then pass off to a team mate that is probably wide open. And remember, the defense is trying to split the 2 players and force them to the outside. So teach your son or daughter to anticipate that movement, and look for a way to get around the defender on the inside lane. Sort of like maybe a spin move works in football.

Addressing Problems as they Occur

Standing still, and not moving the puck or ball, is one of the most common problems with power play units being ineffective. To be effective, power plays require almost constant motion. Standing still is also a big problem with players on the power play getting to loose pucks or balls. Having your better skilled players carry the puck or ball up the rink, and quarterbacking the unit, will usually avoid this problem. If your team can't win a Face-off, especially in the offensive end, this also causes problems. If you don't have the puck or ball, you can't score. Because lines are always changing, all players should learn good Face-off skills. Teach your son or daughter Face-off skills. At least one skilled player on each line should be designated as the Face-off player. This should help avoid that problem.

A big problem with young teams is, abandoning the "attack triangle" philosophy. This keeps them from exploiting 3 on 2's and other support techniques. There is another old saying, "Take what the opposition gives you". Take advantage of this and exploit their defense. Young players often have problems because they signal their intentions. This allows the defense time to prepare and get set up. Teach your son or daughter to read and react, and don't be too obvious with their movements and what they are doing.

Developing Good Individual Skills

If players on the power play do not develop their individual skills, they will not have much success even with a numerical advantage. These skills are accurately passing and shooting the puck or ball, shooting off direct passes, reading and reacting, making one touch passes, regrouping, and countering. The better a team gets at developing these skills, the more effective their power play will become.

Winning Neutral Zone Face-offs

Winning the face-off in the neutral zone is very important because it keeps the offensive attack going. See the section on "Facing Off", for the strategy of how to win the face-off.

Battle for Pucks or Balls

Players have to learn to keep battling for loose pucks or balls in all the zones. Player need to remember, they have the numerical advantage on power plays. Don't give up on a bad pass, keep battling to get it back.

Manage the Time Limit

Remember the numerical advantage only lasts for a short period of time. Players have to play "fast" and "smart" on a power play. Even in high school the power play is only successful about 30 percent of the time. Also remember "30" percent is better than "0" zero percent. Teach your son or daughter to have confidence. Their measure of success should be, did they do their job, as much as whether the team scored on the power play.

Breakout Strategy

Breakouts are very important on power plays. A good defensive zone breakout gets the puck or ball down the rink quickly. There are several patterns to use to accomplish this. There is the "3-2 formation", the "3-1-1 formation", the "1-2-2 deep double swing", and the "1-2-2 spread".

3-2 Formation

This pattern based on a 5 man power play team. There are 2 stretch players forward at the blue line. Two defensemen and a forward work together at the back of the zone. It is the job of the 2 stretch players at the blue line to pull the defenders back, and create space to help the rear players to get up rink quickly. When they see the puck is clear and coming up rink, the 2 stretch players slide towards the middle to make room for a controlled entry into the offensive zone or a ringed dump in *(SEE FIGURE 97)*.

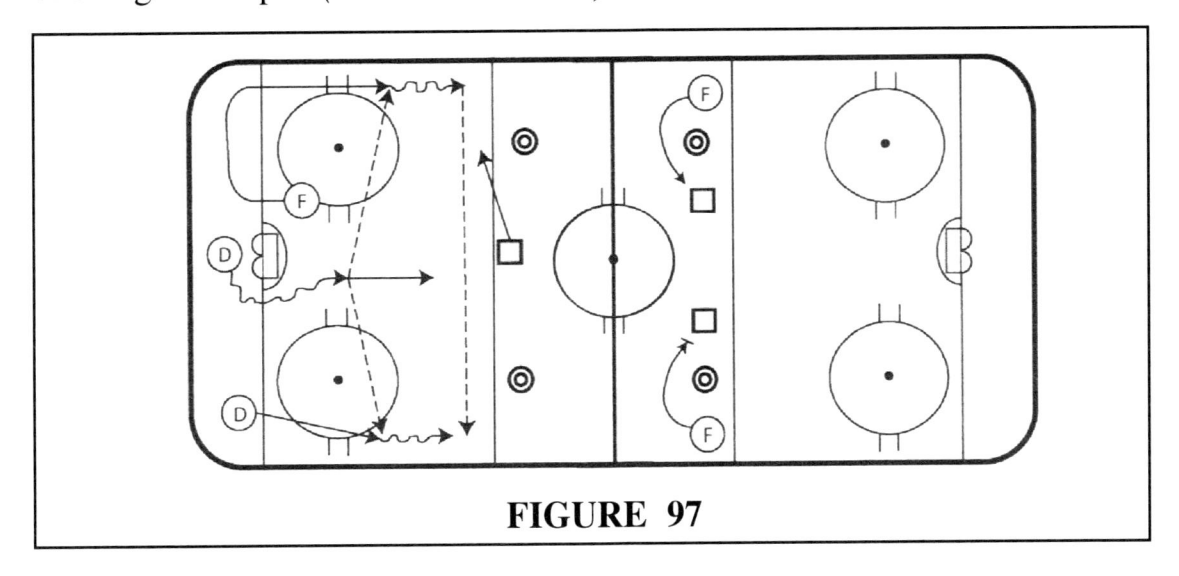

FIGURE 97

If the defensive team brings their forwards up to attack against this type of breakout, a second pass across the rink is made. The forward on the side of the pass moves in to check the defender on that side, to clear the way. If the receiver of the cross rink pass is too far ahead, the pass could be intercepted by a defender stepping up. The rear players have to all be advancing at the same depth. It is the job of the cross rink passer to read the defense as they skate up rink.

3-1-1 Formation

This pattern is also based on a 5 man power play team. There is 1 stretching forward at the red line. Two defensemen and a forward work together at the back of the zone. A third forward skates over to the middle to support the puck or ball carrier, by clearing space for them to move up the rink. The stretch player at the red line moves into the middle as the puck or ball reaches the neutral zone, to create a possible breakaway pass or clear a path for a ring dump in. For the first pass the puck or ball carrier has 3 options *(SEE FIGURE 98)*.

FIGURE 98

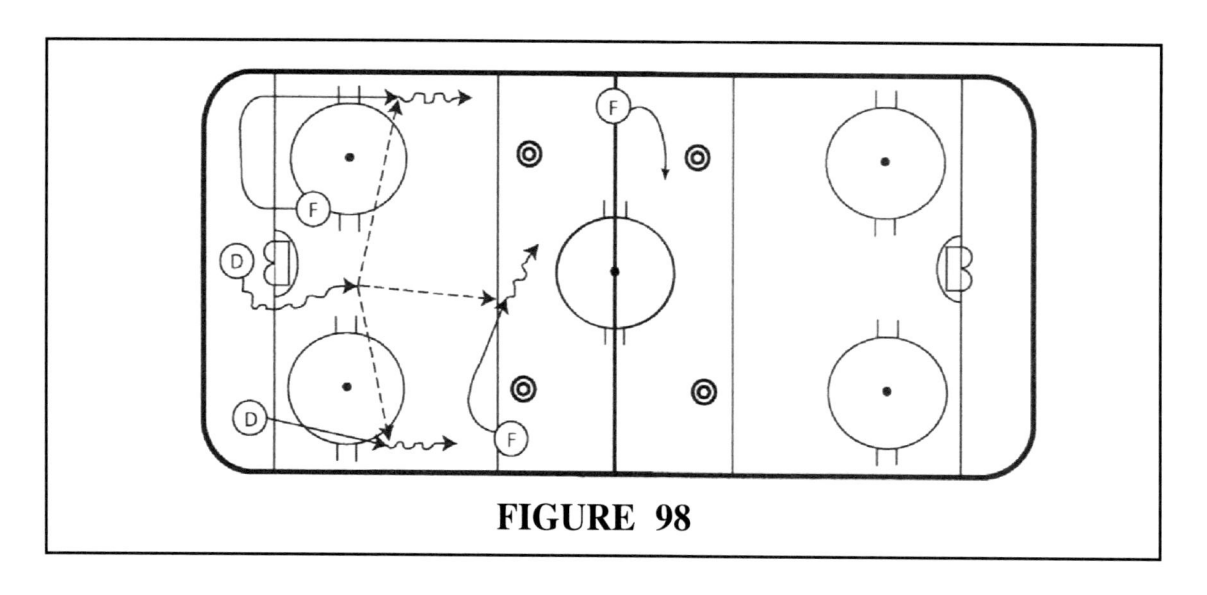

The next illustration shows the first of three options available after the first pass is completed. When the forward that is swinging around the left side corner gets the first pass, they have 5 options. They can pass back to the defenseman that made the first pass to them as they come over to support, pass across rink to the defenseman coming up on the weak side, pass to the forward supporting the middle lane, pass to the stretch player at the red line, or carry the puck or ball into the offensive zone themselves. All of these options depend on the opponents positioning *(SEE FIGURE 99)*.

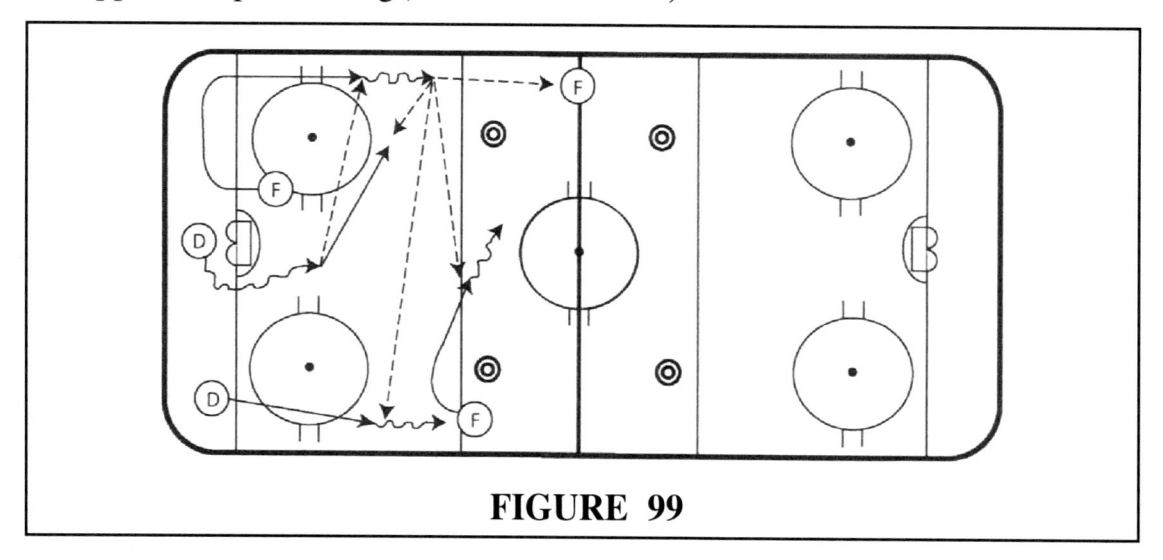

FIGURE 99

When the pass goes to the defenseman moving up the right side of the rink, they have 4 options. They can pass back to the defenseman that made the first pass to them, pass across rink to the forward looping around the left side of the rink corner, pass to the forward coming up the middle lane, or to the stretch

FIGURE 100

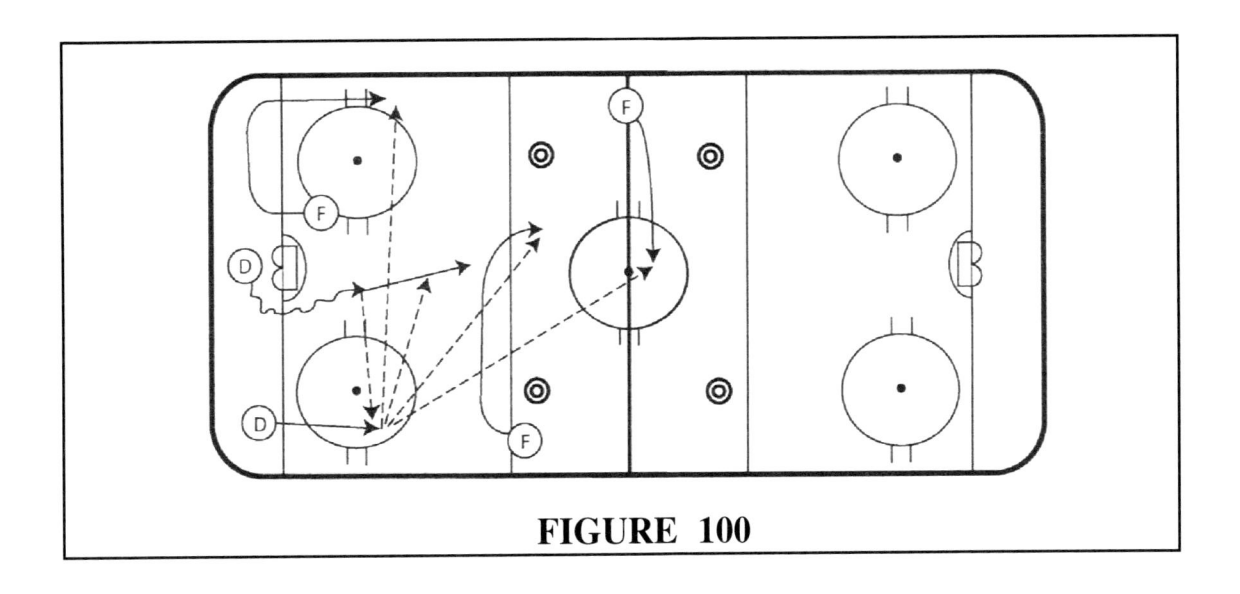

forward who has come over to the middle for support. All of these options depend on the opponents positioning *(SEE FIGURE 100)*.

If the opponents stay back and do not come up to pressure, the defenseman coming from behind the net up the middle has 4 options. They can carry the puck or ball all the way up to the red line, then they can then ring dump the puck or ball in wide at the offensive end, sending it around the rim of the rink. They can make a penetrating pass through the seam to the stretch player on a breakaway into the middle lane, pass to the forward looping around and coming up the left side of the rink, or last pass to the other rear defenseman coming up the right side of the rink. Again these are all options and depend on the opponents positioning *(SEE FIGURE 101)*.

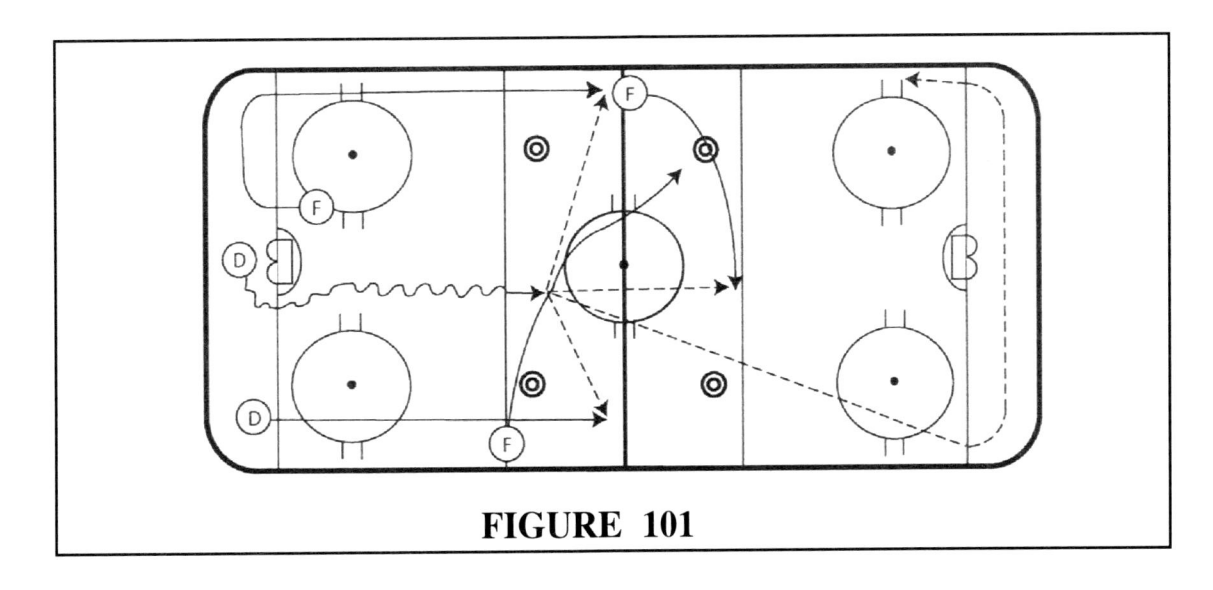

FIGURE 101

1-2-2 Deep Double Swing Formation

This pattern is based on a 5 man power play team. There are 2 defensemen that work together at the back of the zone. There are 2 forwards that will swing around the corner on one side of the net. Another forward, along with the defenseman on that side, will swing around and move up the opposite side of the rink. This formation uses speed, timing, and surprise as their main weapons. The puck or ball carrying defenseman coming up the middle has 3 options. The first option of the puck or ball carrier is, to pass to the first swinging forward coming up the right side of the rink. The second option is, to pass to defenseman coming up the behind the swinging forward on the left side of the rink. The third option is, to pass to the second swinging forward coming up the right side of the rink and cutting to the middle. All of these options depend on the opponents positioning *(SEE FIGURE 102)*.

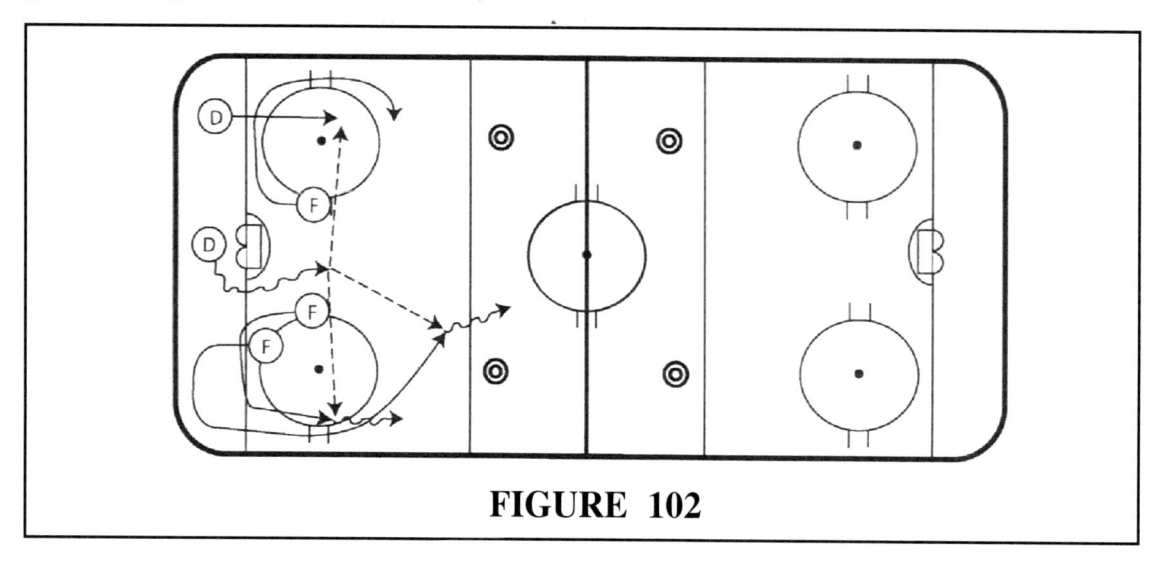

FIGURE 102

The second option of the puck or ball carrier is to do a delay. This is to establish the right timing. All looping swing players should come around and be in line with each other at the same time, across the front of the net. The other defenseman, without the puck, holds until they are in line with the 3 forwards. The puck or ball carrying defenseman behind the net has to wait until the other players make their swing and start to come forward before the carrier starts to come out from behind the net. The leading 2 players on each side of the rink start to advance up the rink, then at a predetermined moment they suddenly make their breaks. Either one may break into the middle lane, or criss-cross in the middle and continue on to opposite sides of the rink. If this is done with a lot of speed, it can be very confusing to young hockey players. Again all of these options are going to depend on the opponents positioning *(SEE FIGURE 103)*.

FIGURE 103

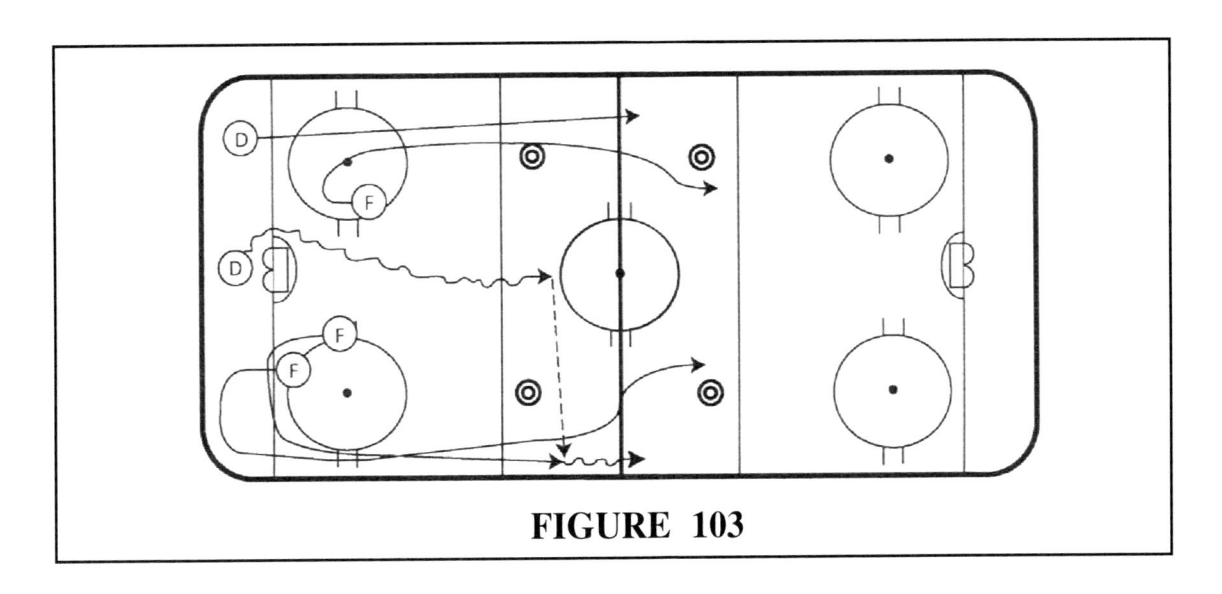

1-2-2 Spread Formation

This particular pattern can work on teams that have their penalty killers play deeply in your zone, and aggressively pursue the power player going back for a puck or ball that has been dumped in or cleared. This pattern is based on a 5 man power play team. There is one defenseman back to dig out the puck or ball that has been dumped in. Then there are 2 forwards on each side of the rink at the blue lines. As quickly as they can, the defenseman gets the puck and passes it to one of the two forwards at the first blue line. This quick outlet pass usually traps the opponents first forechecker back in the zone. This also usually leaves you with a 4 on 3 in the neutral zone. The forward receiving the first pass at the blue line, passes it on ahead to the second forward in front of them. Or they can make an across the rink pass to the forward parallel with them on the other side of the rink. Either on of these forwards can pass to the leading forward

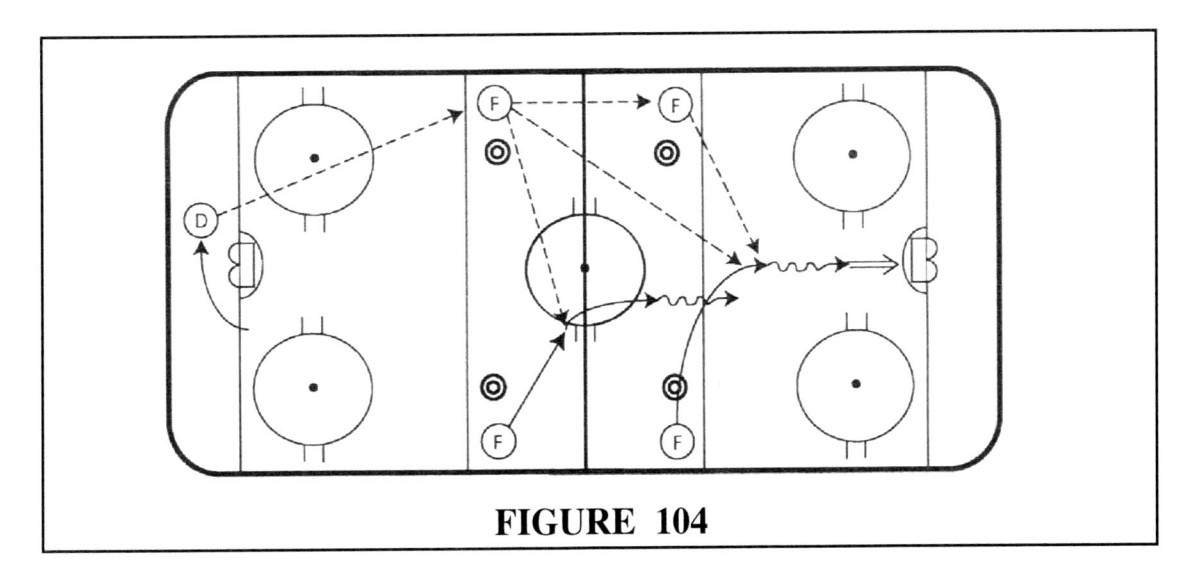

FIGURE 104

on the opposite side, who takes it in for a shot on goal. All of these options depend on the opponents positioning *(SEE FIGURE 104)*.

Regrouping Strategy

If the opponents penalty killing unit does manage to clear the puck or ball back down the rink, it might be wise to have a neutral zone regrouping plan. So the sooner your power play unit can get the puck or ball back into the attacking zone, the better. The most common play, an easiest to execute is the dump in, then try to get the puck or ball to your best player or shooter. However this does not always work too well. If the opponents are not pursuing the puck or ball deep in your zone after it has been cleared, your goalkeeper can come out and shoot the puck or ball quickly back up to one of your defensemen in the neutral zone *(SEE FIGURE 105)*. There are several plays then that can quickly be set up to regroup. First is the "posted forward or forward swinging", the "long regroup with swinging forward", then the "D to D and Ring" strategy.

Posted Forward or Forward Swinging

After the puck or ball has been chipped back up to the neutral zone, the 2 defensemen regroup there for the attack. First one defenseman passes to the defenseman on the opposite side. They may have to pass back and forth several times to allow the forwards time to move back to support positions for the next pass. The defenseman in the neutral zone starts out by receiving the pass, then they have two options. The first option is to pass to the posted outside forward winger. The second option is to pass to the swinging looping forward in the middle. This is where the defenseman making the pass has to learn how to read

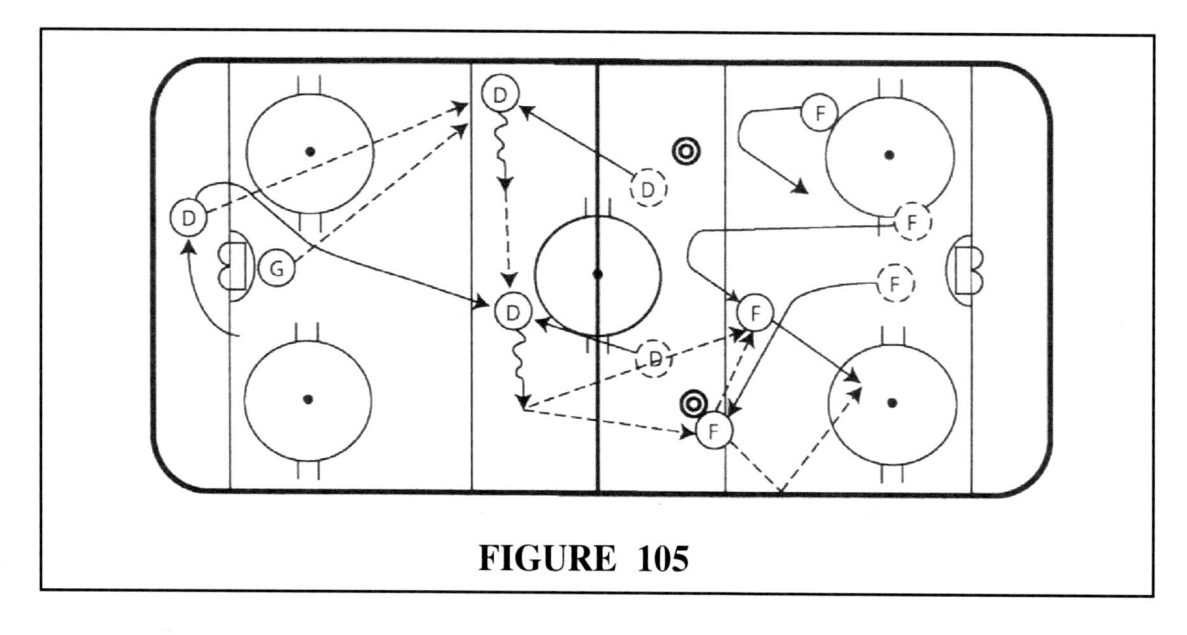

FIGURE 105

the opponents position. Most of the time the pass will probably have to go to the posted forward winger because it's crowded in the middle, and the swinging forward won't have much room to do anything with the puck or ball. When the posted forward gets the puck or ball, they have 2 options. They can carry the puck or ball over the blue line, then turn around and pass to the swinging forward in the middle. Or they can chip the puck or ball off the boards behind the defenders, to be received by the swinging forward looping back from the middle. All of these options will depend on the opponents positioning *(SEE FIGURE 105)*.

Long Regroup with Swinging Forward

When the puck or ball goes back into your own zone from a clear out, a long regroup with a swinging forward is a good play. On this tactic, your defensemen drop back along with one looping back forward in support. The patterns now become similar to the power play breakout from the defensive zone. First one defenseman goes back for the puck or ball. Then they pass the puck or ball to the other defenseman, who takes it and moves to the neutral zone on the strong side. At the same time the deep looping forward turns, and moves back toward the attacking zone blue line. Also at the same time, the middle forward has moved back towards the red line, turned, and loops back to the middle of the attacking zone. Meanwhile, the remaining forward moves back towards the attacking zone blue line, posts up, and acts like a stretch player. The defenseman with the puck or ball now has 3 optional passes, to either of the 3 forwards. Again all of these options will depend on the opponents positioning *(SEE FIGURE 106)*.

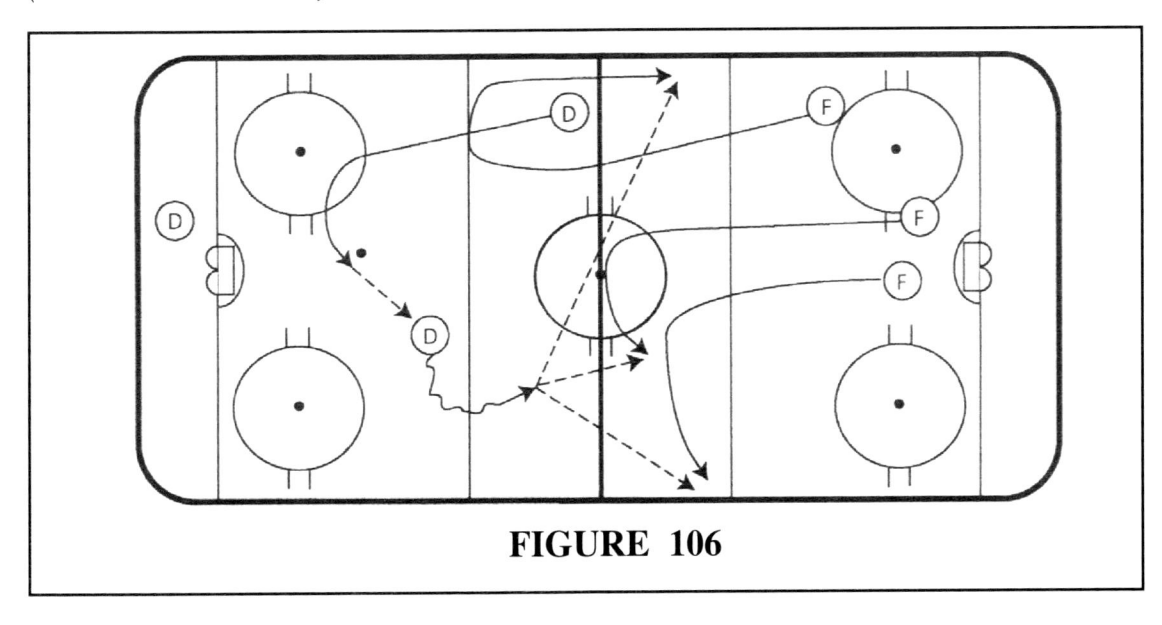

FIGURE 106

D to D and Ring

On this play version, the defensemen pass the puck or ball back and forth to give the forwards a chance to regroup back in the neutral zone. From the neutral zone the forwards move back towards the net for a possible pass, or to retrieve a dump in. In order for this play to work, the forwards have to recognize the defenseman starting to dump the puck or ball in from the red line. Then they have to sprint towards the net area, to recapture the puck or ball in the attacking zone. All of these options will depend on the opponents positioning *(SEE FIGURE 107)*.

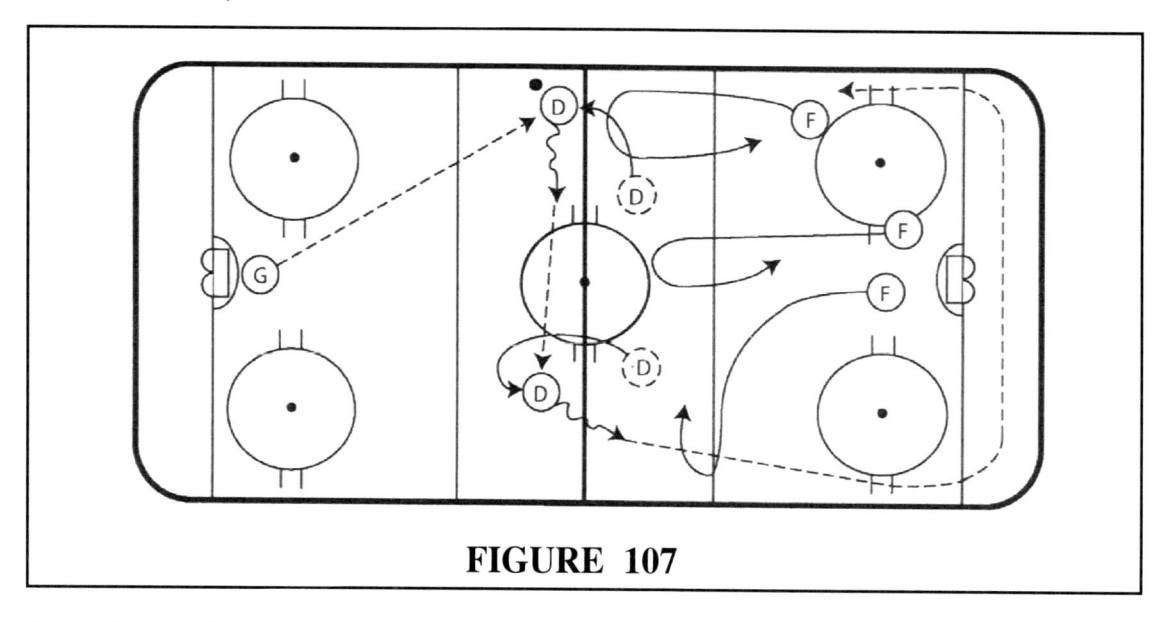

FIGURE 107

Penalty Killing Strategy

Penalty killing is related to the power play. This is because when the offensive team is on a power play, the defense needs a penalty killing unit to keep the offense from scoring until their penalty time is up, and they go back to full strength. I know young players need to experience everything, but if you do not have a specialized unit to kill penalties, your team is probably going to get killed on the scoreboard. Penalty killing units should have similar skills to a power play unit. However, they focus on stopping the opponents from scoring. Penalty killing units have to quickly read and react to what the power play unit is doing. Since they are undermanned, they have to be very effective and smart in using their defensive skills. The biggest key to killing penalties is, having a goalkeeper with excellent skills and ability.

The other key area for the penalty killing unit is Face-offs. If the penalty killing unit has a good Face-off player, there is a good chance they can recover

FIGURE 108

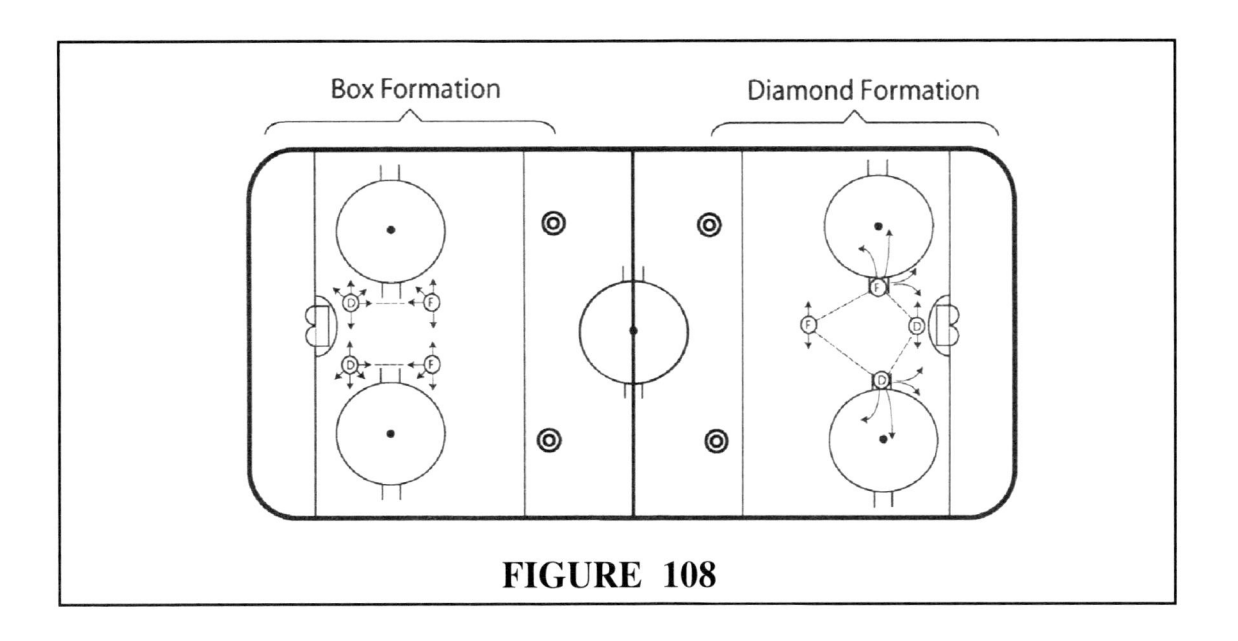

the puck or ball and effectively kill some time off the clock. Another key factor for penalty killing units is being able to control the area in front of their net, and block shots. Penalty killing unit players need to be quick, but patient. When you have one or two less players, you have to wait for opportunities, then jump on them so to speak.

When a 5 on 5 youth hockey team has one less player (5 on 4), there are 3 common basic formations they can use to kill penalties. They are the "box formation", the "diamond formation" *(SEE FIGURE 108)*, and the triangle +1 formation" *(SEE FIGURE 109)*. Each formation has it's disadvantages though. One of the main disadvantages of the box formation is, the opponents offense can collapse the box. One of the main disadvantages of the diamond formation is, one front player has to cover the offense's 2 point players right down the middle of the zone. This usually results in one of these players taking a long clear shot on goal. However if your front player is your best quickest, and smartest players, they can occasionally steal the puck or ball for a shorthanded breakaway goal. The triangle + 1 may be the best of the 3 formations.

When you have a 5 on 3 in youth ice hockey, or a 4 on 3 in youth roller

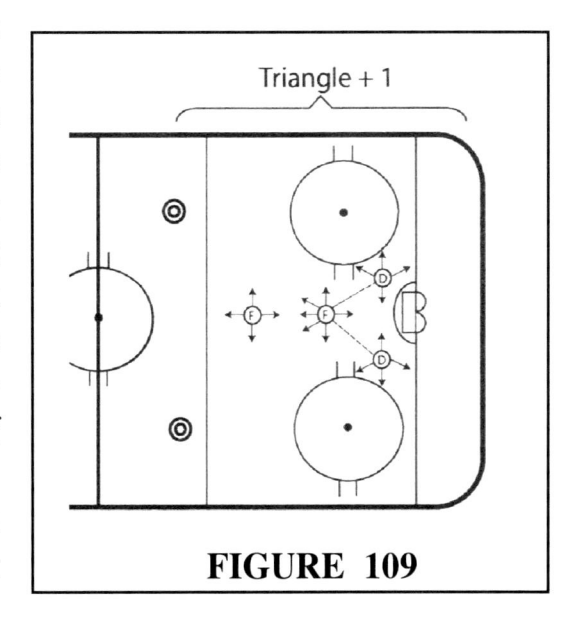

FIGURE 109

135

FIGURE 110

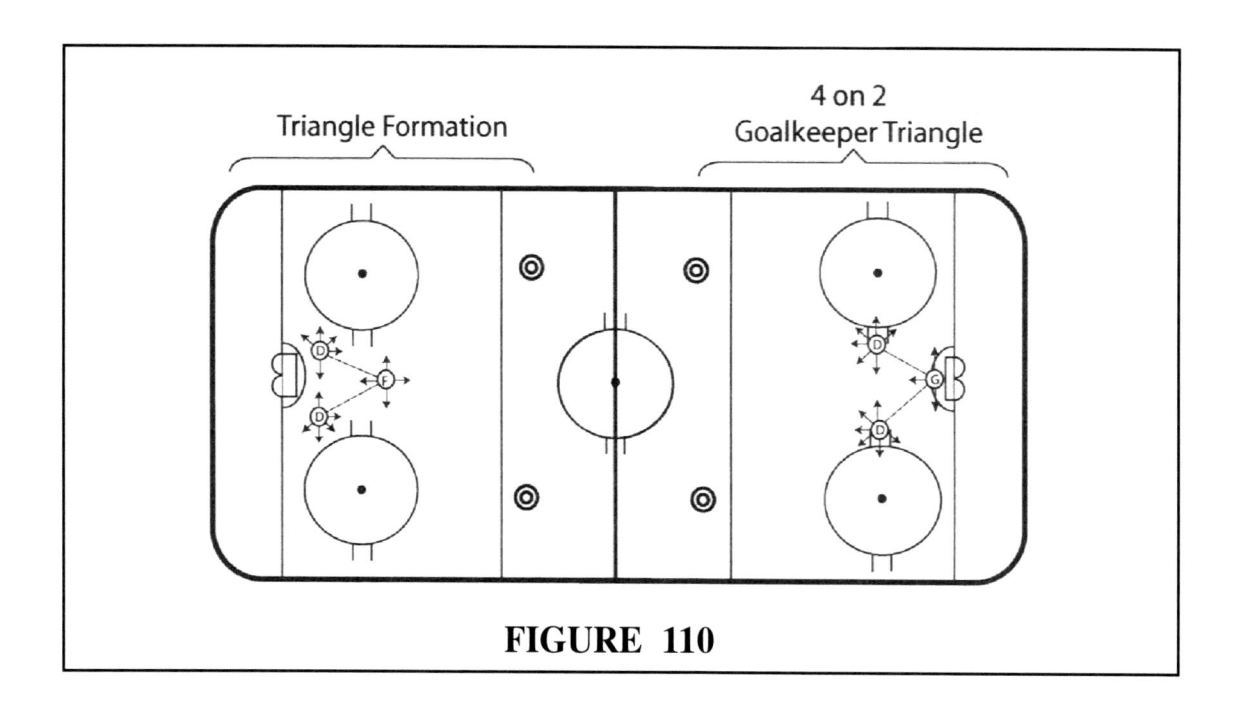

hockey, one the best common basic formations to use is the "triangle formation" *(SEE FIGURE 110)*. For the best chance to stop the offense, the base of the triangle has to be located down close to the net. The reason is because that area represents the highest percentage scoring area for the offense. When you have a 4 on 2 in youth roller hockey, the triangle becomes a 2 player with the goalkeeper triangle formation *(SEE FIGURE 110)*. When in this situation an excellent goalkeeper along with your 2 best fastest defensive players is required.

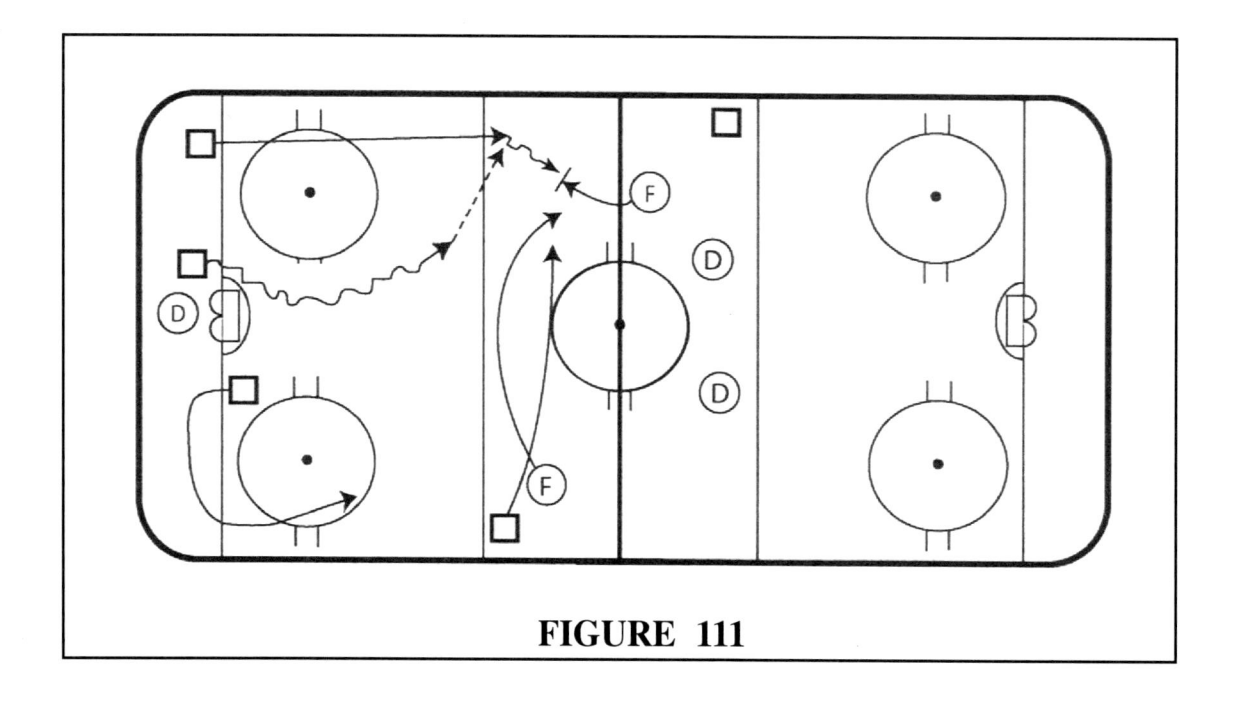

FIGURE 111

136

Penalty Killing Traps

Traps are very good to stop a power play and recapture the puck or ball. And one of the best traps to use is one called the "Hamilton Trap". This may be way to complex for the real little kids, but it might work for 12 year olds and teenage teams. This trap is based on a 5 on 4 power play team. How it works in the first version is, a penalty killing forward comes from down near the first blue line and angles up forcing the puck or ball carrier towards the second forechecking forward. The puck or ball carrier can see the forward coming up, so they pass off to their team mate coming up along the boards. The forward then steps up and "denies" the new puck or ball carrier the red line. The other forward goes toward the new puck or ball carrier, and both forwards trap the puck or ball carrier near the red line *(SEE FIGURE 111)*. However, if the second puck or ball carrier can see the trap coming, they cut right toward the oncoming forward and that breaks the trap.

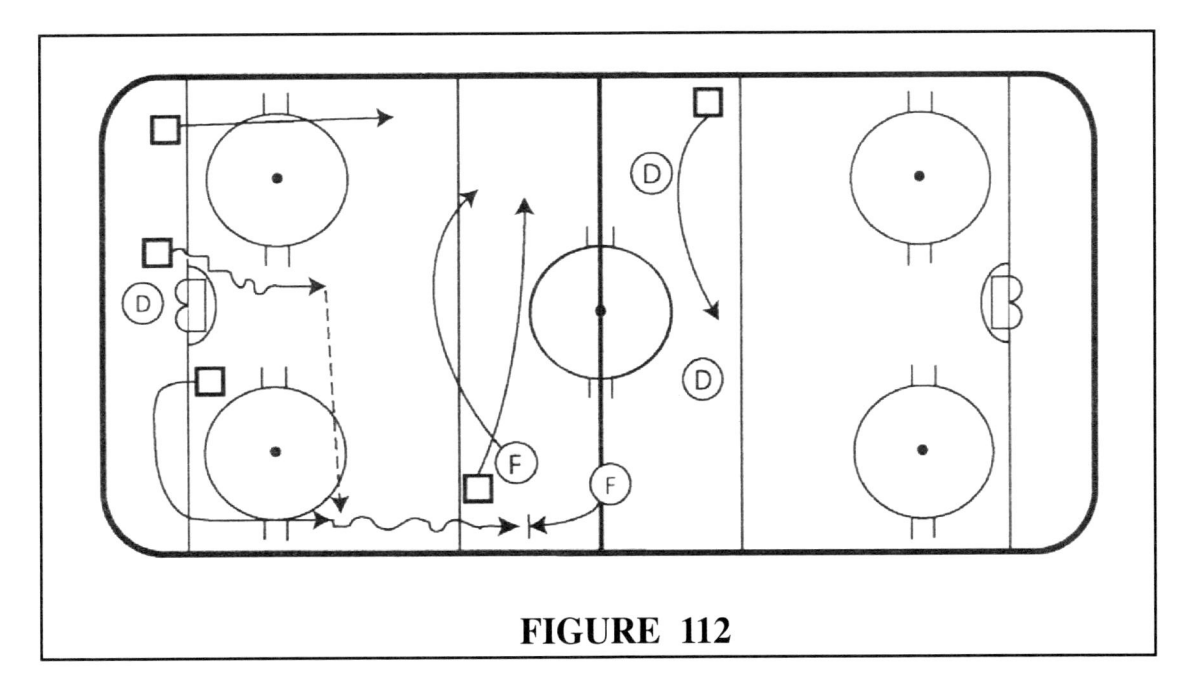

FIGURE 112

"Hamilton" was smart though, they had a counter version, for the counter, so to speak. The next time when they were on penalty killing, they lined up both forwards together down on the other side. So when the power play puck or ball carrier thinks they see what looks like the same trap again, they pass off down to their other player coming around the boards on the opposite side of the rink. Then just when that forward gets up towards the red line with the puck or ball, here is the penalty killing forechecking forward over on that side to trap them again *(SEE FIGURE 112)*.

137

Hockey Terminology

All parents and kids should learn the terminology associated with hockey. Then they will know what the coaches are talking about.

Altercation: Physical incident between at least two players resulting in a penalty.

Assist: The last one or two passes which immediately proceed a goal.

Angle, Playing the: Playing the angle is a method a goalkeeper can use to minimize the uncovered parts of the net. They do this by turning so they are directly in line with a shooter coming from the side.

Attacking Zone: This is the area between the opponents blue line and their goal line.

Back Check: This is when a player attempts to check or harass a player on the opposite team as they are reentering their defensive zone.

Backhand Shot: This is a shot or pass made by a player using their weaker shooting hand.

Ball: This is a special ball (usually hard rubber) used only in some roller hockey leagues.

Bench Penalty: This is the removal of a player from the game for two minutes, following a breach of the rules. Any player on the team, except the goalkeeper, may serve the penalty.

Biscuit: This is a slang term for the puck.

Blind Pass: This is a pass that is made without first looking up to see to whom the puck or ball is going to be passed.

Blocker: This is the pad the goalkeeper wears on the arm used to hold the stick.

Blueliner: This is another name for a defenseman. The players are so named because they line up on the blue line to start a game. They play near the blue line in the offensive zone, to protect the defensive blue line against opposing forwards trying to advance into the area behind them.

Blue Lines: This is a pair of one foot wide blue lines, which break the ice or floor into thirds. They are located 60 feet from each goal. These lines mark the attacking, neutral, and defending zones. There are no blue lines in roller hockey.

Board Checking: This is the body checking, cross-checking, elbowing, charging, or tripping, of an opponent in such a way that they are thrown violently into the boards around the edges of the rink. This is also known as "boarding". It can incur a penalty if done illegally. At the discretion of the referee, players shall be penalized, based upon the degree of violence of the impact with the boards.

Boards: These are the panels surrounding the rink that are 42 inches high. They are topped by glass or clear plastic panels that protect the spectators from flying pucks, balls, and players.

Body Check: This is the legal use of the body (most often the hip or shoulder) to knock an opponent off the puck or ball.

Box: This is a penalty killing set up in the defensive zone where the defensive team forms a box in front of their goalkeeper, to keep the opponents on the outskirts and away from a scoring chance.

Breakaway: This is a rush by the offensive team, in which the player carrying the puck or ball moves past all the other teams defensemen, and has a clear shot on the goalkeeper.

Breaking Pass: This is a pass to a team mate who is accelerating, and ready for a breakaway. This is also called a **Breakout**.

Butt Ending: This is an infraction resulting from the player using the shaft of the stick above the upper hand, in a jab or an attempt to jab an opposing player.

Butterfly Save: This is a save that the goalkeeper makes. It is so named because of the low position to the ice or floor, the way the pads splay along the ice or floor, and the position of the stick in front of the five hole. The glove is kept up and open in this position.

Captain: A player, other than the goalkeeper, selected to represent the team with the officials.

Center: This is the middle of the 3 attacking players, who are all forwards.

Center Face-Off circle: This is another name for the center circle. In this circle is where the opening face-off to start the game is conducted. Every subsequent face-off after a goal is scores is conducted in this circle.

Center Red Line: This is the line that divides the rink in half. The little circle in the middle of the red line is referred to as "center Ice".

Changing on the Fly: This is when teams switch players (lines) during play.

Charging: Charging is deemed to have been committed if, taking two steps or strides, a player runs, jumps into, charges into, body checks, or pushes an opponent from behind.

Check/ Checking: A player has been checked when an opponent shoves or pushes them with their body or their stick. The act is called "checking". The hit itself is called a "check". Intentional checking is not allowed in roller hockey.

Clearing the Puck or Ball (Clearing): This is when the puck or ball is knocked away from in front of the net, or after being dumped in is recovered and shot back down to the other end of the rink.

Corners: This is the four curved areas of the hockey rink. This is also a place where a lot of action takes place.

Covering: This is sticking close to an attacker, and thus preventing them from breaking away.

Crease: This is the blue semicircle directly in front of the goalkeeper. It is 6 feet in radius. If a player does not have possession of the puck or ball, they can not enter the crease. If a player scores a goal while another player is in the crease, the goal will be deemed illegal and not credited to the scoring team.

Criss Cross Attack: This is when two wingmen swap sides while skating down the ice or floor during an attack.

Crossbar: This is the horizontal bar along the top edge of the goal.

Cross Checking: This is holding a stick with both hands to check an opponent by using the shaft of the stick with no part of the stick on the ice or floor. This act incurs a penalty.

Cross Over: This is a skating move in which one foot is crossed over the other alternately. It is mostly used for circling, or turning on the ice or floor.

Cupping: This is illegally closing your hand around the puck or ball.

Dead Puck or Ball: This is a puck or ball that is shot over the boards and out of play by a player, or a puck or ball which is taken out of play when a player closes their hand around it.

Defensive Zone: This is the area where the opponents goal is located.

Defensemen: Defensively, these are two players that stay back, on the left and right side, that try to stop the incoming play from the other team before they have a chance to score. They block shots, clear the puck or ball from in front of their own net, and cover the other team's forwards. Offensively, they pass the puck or ball up the ice or floor to the forwards. Then they follow the play into the attacking zone, and try to keep it there.

Deke: This is when a player fakes their opponent out of position, by moving the puck or ball or part of the body to one side, then moving in the opposite direction. It is also sometimes just referred to as "faking".

Delayed Offside: When an attacking player crosses the attacking blue line ahead of the puck or ball, but the defending team collects the puck or ball, and is in a position to bring it out of their defending zone without any delay or contact with an attacking player, the offside call is delayed. However, if the puck or ball goes beyond the top of the end of the face-off circles, the offside is called immediately. There are no offside calls in roller hockey.

Dig: This is an attempt to win possession of the puck or ball in the corners of the rink.

Dive: This is when a player falls to the ice or floor in an attempt to draw a penalty against the opponent.

Draw: This is the act of successfully getting the puck or ball to a team mate at a face-off.

Dribbling: This is another term for handling, or moving, the puck or ball down the ice or floor.

Drop Pass: This is the act of a player leaving the puck or ball for player trailing behind them, to pick up.

Dump and Chase: This is a style of hockey where a team shoots the puck or ball into one of the far corners of the offensive zone, and then pursues it. This is opposed to carrying, or dribbling, the puck or ball into the zone.

Elbowing: This is an infraction resulting from a player using their elbow in any way to foul an opponent.

Empty Net goal: This is a goal that is scored after the opponent's goalkeeper has been pulled in favor of an extra skater. This is usually an end of the game, last minute, desperate attempt to score a goal.

Face-Off: This is dropping the puck or ball between two players, one from each team. It marks the start of play. Initial face-offs take place at center ice, and the puck or ball is always dropped by a referee.

Face-Off circles: These are two special areas, to the right and left of each goal mouth, where the puck or ball is dropped for face-offs.

Five Hole: This is an open area between the goalkeepers pads where a shooter would attempt to score a goal.

Flat Pass: This is a pass in which the puck or ball travels entirely along the ice or floor.

Flip Pass: This is a pass in which the puck or ball is lifted so that it goes over an opponent, or their stick.

Forecheck: This is when a player checks or harasses a player on the opposite team, in that teams defensive zone. Or it is also when a player is checking in their own offensive zone.

Forwards: This is a collective term for the center and the wingers, who have the primary offensive objective of scoring a goal.

Freeze the Puck or Ball: This is the act of holding the puck or ball against the boards, with either the stick or skates in order to stop play.

Game Disqualification: This is the result of a serious infraction in which a player is ejected from a game. The player must leave the area of the players bench and in no way direct, coach, or assist the team in any manner for the remainder of the game.

Game Suspension: This is the result of a serious infraction in which a player, coach, or manager is ineligible to participate in the next scheduled game.

Glove: The goalkeeper wears this on the nonstick hand.

Goal: The only way a point can be scored in hockey is achieved when the whole puck or ball crosses the goal line, and enters the net. It may not be deliberately kicked in with a skate, nor batted in with a glove, but it can be deflected off a players body. A goal scores one point.

Goal Cage: This is usually referred to as the "net". It is 6 feet wide and 4 feet high. As the word "net" describes, it catches the puck or ball.

Goal Judge: This is an office official who signals when a goal is scored, by turning on a goal, or red light.

Goal Line: This is the red line that runs between the goal posts, and extends in both directions all the way across the ice or floor to the boards. It is crucial in making icing calls.

Goal Mouth: This is the area right in front of the goal and crease line.

Goalkeeper: It is this players job to keep the puck or ball out of their team's net. They can use any part of their body, or any piece of their equipment to do so, and they are allowed to catch or smother the puck or ball.

Halves: This is a period of time that a roller hockey game has been divided into. USA Hockey In-line has two 15 to 20 minute halves. USA Roller hockey has two 15 minute halves.

Hat Trick: This is the scoring of 3 or more goals by a player in one game. This term came about when the owner of a hat store in Toronto, Ontario promised that he would give a hat to any player who scored 3 goals in one game. Fans used to throw their hats out onto the ice to celebrate a "hat trick", but this practice has become less common these days.

Heel of the Stick: This is the part of the stick between the straight part of the shaft, and the flat part of the bottom of the blade.

High Sticking: This is carrying the stick above the normal height of the shoulder. It is illegal.

Hip Checking: This is using the hip to knock an opponent off stride while they are skating.

Holding: This is an infraction resulting from a player impeding the progress of an opponent.

Hooking: This is impeding the progress of an opponent by using the blade of the stick to pull or tug against their body, or their stick.

Icing the puck: This is intentionally shooting the puck down the length of the ice, from behind the center line to over the opponent's goal line. It usually causes a stoppage in play unless the team icing the puck is on a power play. There are no "icing" calls in roller hockey.

Interference: This is interfering with an opponent who is not in possession of the puck or ball. Interference can be in the form of deliberately knocking the stick out of their hand, preventing them from recovering a dropped stick, or simply impeding their progress across the ice or floor.

Kicked Goal: A goal can not be intentionally kicked into the opponents net. It is disallowed, unless it is ruled that the puck or ball bounced off the skate, and was not intentionally directed into the gaol net.

Kicking: This is an infraction resulting from a player deliberately using the skate(s), with a kicking motion, to contact an opponent. And with no apparent intention to play the puck or ball.

Kneeing: This is an infraction resulting from a player using the knee in any way to foul the opponent.

Left Defensemen: This is the player that is playing on the left side of the defense.

Left Wing: This is the forward player that is playing on the left side.

Lie: The lie is the angle created between the handle of the goalkeepers stick and the paddle. The higher the lie is, the closer the stick resembles the letter "L".

Linesmen: They help officiate the game along with the referee. Each game has 1 or 2 linesmen, who are responsible for calling "icing", "offsides", and 2 line passes. They also drop the puck or ball for the face-offs that are not at center ice. They can also recommend penalties to the referee.

Major Penalty: This is usually called for fighting, or any other more extreme penalty. This penalty lasts 5 minutes, and can be imposed on any player.

Man Advantage: This is the team with one or more players on the ice or floor than the opposing team.

Minor Penalty: Most of the penalties fall under this category. They are called for 2 minutes, and can be imposed on any player.

Misconduct Penalty: This is a 10 minute penalty usually called against a player who becomes excessively abusive in language. They have to sit out 10 minutes, but their team can substitute another player for them.

Natural Hat Trick: This is 3 or more goals scored in consecutive shots by the same player. Doesn't happen very often.

Neutral Zone: This is the center third of the playing area in Ice Hockey. It extends from blue line to blue line. There is no "neutral zone" in Roller Hockey.

Offensive Zone: This is the part of the playing area where a teams goal is located.

Off Ice Officials: These are also known as minor officials. They are the officials that are not positioned on the ice or floor, but play an important role in assisting the referee. They include the official scorer, game time keeper, penalty timekeeper, and the judges.

Off Sides: When an attacking player precedes the puck over the blue line into the attacking zone, play is halted and restarted with a face-off in that teams defensive zone (or wherever the pass originated). An "off sides" can be called when a 2 line pass is made (a pass that crosses 2 lines). There are no off sides called in roller hockey.

Off Side Pass: The puck must not be passed over 2 lines (goal line excepted, unless the puck precedes the receiving player over the center red line. This is an offside pass and play restarts from the face-off spot nearest to the point where the pass was made. There is no off side pass in roller hockey.

One Timer or One Timed it: This is when a player redirects a pass, usually a shot on goal, without stopping the puck or ball to first shoot. It is called "one timing" the puck or ball.

Overtime: If the score is tied after 3 periods of play, there will be an extra 5 minute overtime period to decide a winner. The first team to score wins the game, but if no team can score in the 5 minute period, the game ends in a tie.

Paddle: This is the thick flat widened part of the goalkeepers stick just above the blade. It should remain on the ice or floor as much as possible. It is used for poking the puck or ball away, clearing the puck or ball, and covering the five hole.

Penalty: If a player or a team official breaks any rules a penalty is awarded. The form a penalty takes varies according to the severity of the violation.

Penalty Box: This is the area where the penalized players are sent, to serve their time. Sometimes just referred to as "the Box".

Penalty Killing: Defensive play of a special team which, because of penalty or penalties, has fewer players on the ice or floor than it's opponents have.

Penalty Shot: When a player is fouled from the rear when they had a clear path to the goal, a penalty is called. The penalty shot is a free shot given that player, where only the goalkeeper remains to defend the goal.

Periods: Ice hockey games usually consist of three 20 minute periods of time. Some roller hockey leagues have adopted this same rule. USA roller hockey has divided their game into halves.

Pipes: This is a slang name given to the goal posts.

Player Lines: Because hockey doesn't demand a stop in play for substitutions, players can go on and off the ice or floor while the play is in progress. A team then has "lines", each of which consists of groups of 3 forwards and 2 defensemen. Each team usually carries three lines of forwards (center, right wing and left wing) and 3 sets of defensemen. On large teams these lines change about every minute. In youth hockey they don't have that many players on a team, so the players have to be on several units and play longer.

Point: This is a position taken by an attacking player, during a power play, just on or inside of the opponents blue line (near the boards) to keep the puck or ball from escaping (cleared out) the opponents end zone.

Poke Check: This is when a player jabs with their stick at the puck or ball, or the stick of another player, in an attempt to get the puck or ball away from them. It's called "poke Checking". Goalkeepers use this technique many times.

Possession: This is the state of a player, other than the goalkeeper, who has most recently come in contact with the puck or ball.

Power Play: A power play occurs when one team has a one or two man advantage during the time period while members of the other team are serving penalties in the box.

Puck: This is a vulcanized rubber disc which is hit around the ice or floor. It is frozen for several hours before game time to minimize bouncing. It is used as a method of scoring a goal. In roller hockey it can be made from different materials, or it can even be a ball.

Pull the Goalkeeper: This is replacing the goalkeeper with another attacker. This is usually done when the game is nearing the end of the third period or half, and one team is losing (usually by 1 goal) in the final few minutes. It is done in the hopes that the extra attacker will give the losing team an edge they need to score the tying or winning goal.

Red Line: This is the line dividing the rink equally at the center.

Right Defenseman: This is the player who plays on the right side of the defense.

Right Wing: This is a forward player who is playing on the right side.

Rink: This is the inclosed surface area where the game is played. The dimensions of a hockey rink are about 200 feet long by 85 feet wide. They are sometimes a little smaller for in-line roller hockey. International competition, and world championship, games are played on rinks which measure about 200 feet in length and 100 feet in width.

Roughing: This is any undue physical treatment of an opponent. It may earn a minor or major penalty.

Rushing: This is a combined attack towards the net by some, or all, players of the team in possession of the puck or ball.

Save: This is a shot blocked by the goalkeeper which would have been a goal if not directly stopped. If the goalkeeper does not make a direct save, the shot is referred to as a scoring chance.

Screen Shot: This occurs when the goalkeepers view is blocked by players between the shooter and the goalkeeper.

Short Handed: When a team is on a power play, the other team is said to be short handed. This usually in reference to scoring a goal short handed.

Shuffle: This is a technique a goalkeeper uses for lateral movement. It is used when the puck or ball is relatively far from the net. The goalkeeper slides their legs, one at a time, in the desired direction. The disadvantage of this is that this can leave the five hole open.

Slap Shot: This is a shot on goal made by raising the stick backwards, then bringing it hard through the puck or ball, somewhat in the manner of an abbreviated golf swing, in order to impart maximum force to the shot.

Slashing: This is the action of striking, or attempting to strike, an opponent with your stick. Striking your opponent's stick with your own stick is not slashing.

Slot: This is the area immediately in front of the goal. It is the area from which most goals are scored, and where most of the action takes place.

Spearing: This is poking, or attempting to poke, an opponent with the top of the blade of your stick.

Split the Defense: This is when a player with the puck or ball attempts to squeeze between two or more of the opponents defensemen.

Stacking the Pads: This is a type of save where the goalkeeper attempts to place their body across the length of the net, pads on top of each other, to keep the puck or ball from entering a relatively unguarded net. This is also known as a two pad save.

Stanley Cup: this is the oldest trophy competed for by professionals in North America. This trophy has been awarded to the "National Hockey League" (NHL) champion since 1926. The trophy was purchased in 1893 by Frederick Arthur, Lord Stanley of Preston at a cost of $48.67. Lord Stanley then decreed that the trophy be awarded annually to the best hockey club in Canada.

Stick: Sticks may not exceed 56 inches in length. The blade is 1 foot 2-1/2 inches in length and 3 inches wide. The handle is one piece with a lamented blade attached to it. The blade of a goalkeeper stick is 1 foot 2-1/2 inches in length and 3-1/2 inches wide. The handle varies according to the goalkeepers height and reach.

Stick Checking: This is a technique involving a player's use of the stick or blade to poke or strike an opponent's stick blade, or a puck or ball in the opponent's possession.

Stick Save: This is also called a "set", or stance, position the goalkeeper takes during the majority of the time they are not actively making saves. A proper stance has the goalkeeper's weight on their toes, their knees bent, their catch glove at their knee, and their stick flat on the ice or floor.

Stickhandle: This is to control the puck or ball along the ice or floor.

T-Push: This is a technique used by the goalkeeper to move in a lateral direction. They perform a t-push by directing their outside skate (pointing) in the direction they wish to move, then pushing with both legs. This method is most effective when the puck or ball is close to the net, provided the five hole can be covered.

Team official: This is any person involved with the operation of a team. They may be the team director, manager, trainer, coach, or even the "kit" man.

Telescoping: This technique is an advanced form of "playing the angles" where the goalkeeper moves in and out into position so that the net is effectively covered, and the distance they have to travel is minimized.

Top Shelf: This is a term used to describe when an offensive player shoots high, in an attempt to beat the goalkeeper by putting the puck or ball in the top part of the net.

Trap: These are formations that are designed to keep the other team from scoring. It is usually accomplished by 2 players double teaming, or blocking, the puck or ball carrier.

Trapper: The trapper is a piece of equipment worn on the left hand (for right handed goalkeeper's) and on the right hand (for left handed goalkeeper's), and is similar in shape to a fielder's mitt in baseball. It is commonly referred to as the "catch glove", and is a strong point for many goalkeeper's. The catch glove can be used to stop play when the goalkeeper catches the puck or ball in it, then brings the glove in close to their body to prevent it from being knocked away. Trapper saves are often called glove saves.

Tripping: As the name implies, this is when a player trips their opponent. It can be with either a stick, knee, foot, hand, or elbow.

Two-Line Pass: This is when a player passes the puck or ball to a team mate, and it crosses two lines (red line - blue line) to reach them.

Walkout: This is when a player steps away from the boards with the puck or ball, then skates toward the area in front of the goal.

Wings: Right and left wings are players (forwards) that predominately move up and down the sides of the rink with the direction of play. Offensively, they skate alongside the center, passing back and forth and positioning themselves for a shot on goal. In the defensive zone, they guard the opponents point men and try to keep them from shooting.

Wraparound: This is when a player skates around the opponents goal, then using their stick attempts to wrap the puck or ball around the goat post and under the goalkeeper.

Wrist Shot: This is hitting the puck or ball with the blade of the stick by using a quick snap of the wrist rather than a full back swing.

Zamboni: This is a vehicle used to get the ice resurfaced, smoothed out, and ready for the start of the game and between periods. American Frank Zamboni invented this machine in southern California during the early 1940's. It is used all over the world now to resurface the ice in rinks.

The Legend or Key to the Diagrams

(Unless otherwise depicted)

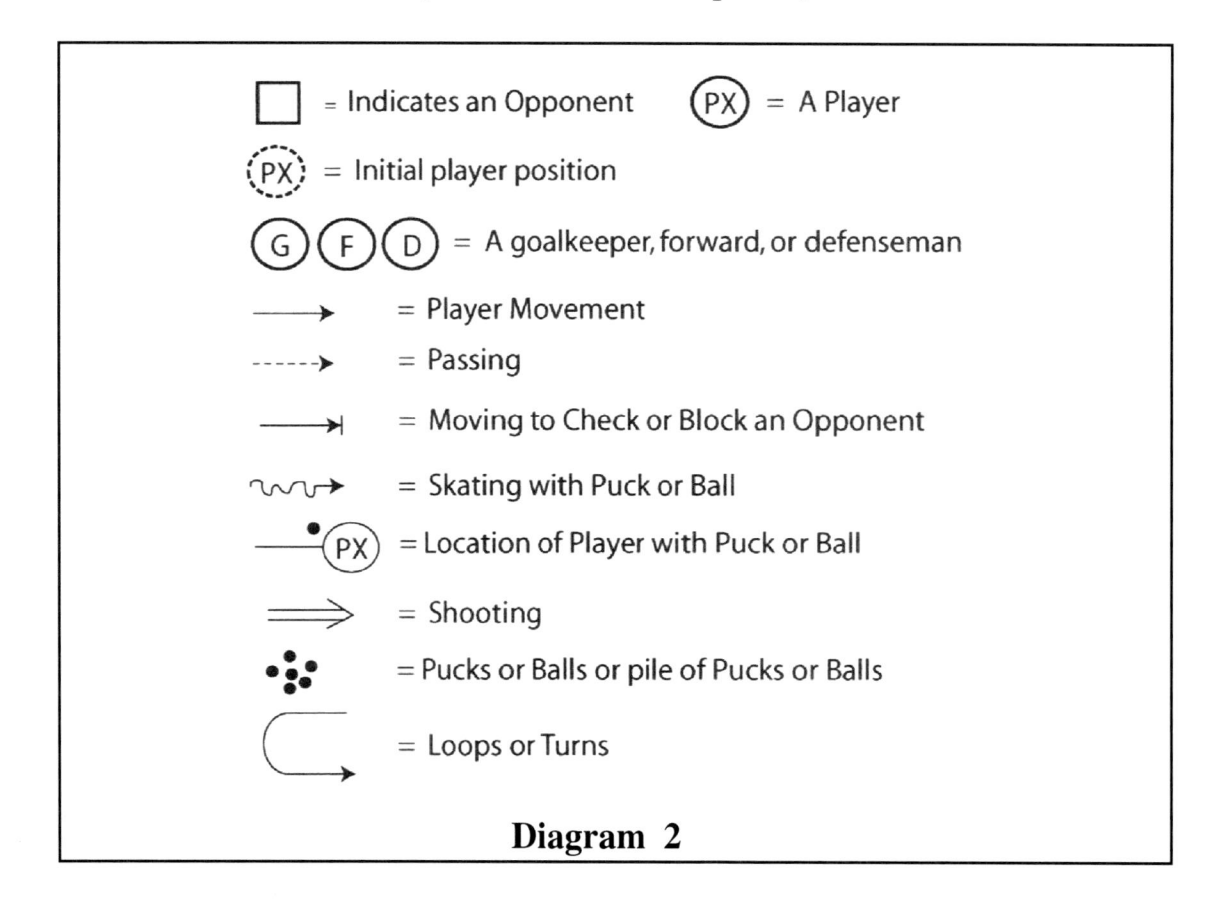

☐ = Indicates an Opponent   (PX) = A Player

(PX) = Initial player position

(G) (F) (D) = A goalkeeper, forward, or defenseman

⟶ = Player Movement

----▶ = Passing

⟶▌ = Moving to Check or Block an Opponent

∿▶ = Skating with Puck or Ball

⟶•(PX) = Location of Player with Puck or Ball

⟹ = Shooting

•:• = Pucks or Balls or pile of Pucks or Balls

⊃ = Loops or Turns

Diagram 2

New Parent Orientation

The Game of Hockey

This section is for those mom and dads that may not know much about the game of Hockey, or how it is played (sort of like a Hockey 101). The game is basically divided into three phases. They are offensive hockey, defensive hockey, and the transition phase. And within the transition phase, you also have power plays and penalty killing. The team that scores the most points (goals) wins the game.

There are two different types of games. First there is ice hockey, and then you have roller hockey. Roller hockey is similar in many ways to ice hockey, except it is played on a wood, cement, asphalt, or plastic surface known as a "Rink". Ice hockey players of course play on an ice surface. Roller hockey players wear in-line skates as opposed to ice skates, and play on a non-ice surface. Ice hockey teams have 5 players plus a goalkeeper. Ice hockey uses a puck to score goals. Roller hockey may use several different types of pucks, or a ball, to score with. Roller hockey teams usually have 4 players plus a goalkeeper, but some leagues have 5 plus a goalkeeper to a team. Ice hockey games have 3 periods of play. Roller hockey games usually have two halves of play. However, some leagues have 2, 3, or 4 periods of play. Rink sizes are a little different from ice hockey to roller hockey. Basically the roller hockey rink is a little bit smaller. Rink markings are different from ice to roller hockey *(SEE FIGURE 113, 114)*. For the time and duration of a game, for all levels, *SEE FIGURE 115.*

Offensive Game

The Scoring

When the team is in the offensive phase, the object is to score points. The offensive phase is when your team is in possession of the puck or ball, and they are moving towards their offensive goal. A goal counts as one point. In order for a shot to count as a goal, the whole puck or ball has to enter the net, then cross the goal line. The minute the other team intercepts the puck or ball, and gains control, they are on offense. This is called the "transition". In order to keep players fresh, a team has different groups of players called "lines". Hockey is played on the fly, so to speak. They do not have time outs in hockey while teams change players. This is all done on the fly. So it has to be very well coordinated by the team coaches. In youth hockey, the puck or ball can go back and forth between teams fairly quickly. As to which phase they are in while you are watching, the key word is "control". In other words, which player has control of the puck or ball.

How Goals are Scored

Goals are scored by shooting the puck or ball into the net. Players use a piece of equipment called a "stick", to whack, hit, or push, the puck or ball towards the net. The hit or whack has to be made by a players stick, and the contact has to be made below the waist. A goal can also be scored by ricocheting off of a players skate. They can not directly kick it in with the skate though. When a team is in the offensive phase, they may send out a specialized "line" consisting of fast players, and good shooters, that can score goals. Or if the team only has 2 or 3 good goal scorers, they may spread them out one to a "line". This way whichever "line" is out on the floor or ice, they will have at least one good shooter on the "line" with the potential to score. Teams will use different plays and formations, in order to give them a scoring advantage. Sometimes, near the end of the game one team will pull it's goalkeeper, and add a player in an attempt to score. Then if the other team is clever, they will get a shot off that will go into the empty net for a goal.

What the Offense does

Play starts with both teams lining up, opposing each other at the center circle for a face-off. The team gaining control of the puck or ball off the face-off, immediately goes on offense. They may "dump and chase" the puck or ball into the offensive zone, or they may go into a set attack formation in an attempt to score. They will keep doing this until they either score a goal, or they lose control of the puck or ball. When they lose control of the puck or ball they immediately go into "transition", and switch to defense. The other team then goes on offense, and counter attacks.

Offensive Team Members

The "ice hockey" offensive team can have 5 players, plus a goalkeeper, on the ice at one time. Those players are usually 1 center, 2 forwards (wingers), and 2 defensemen. The "roller hockey" offensive team will usually have 4 players, plus a goalkeeper, on the floor at one time. Some roller hockey teams will have 5 players on the floor at the same time. When they have 4 players, they usually are 1 center, 2 forwards (wingers), and 1 defenseman. When they have 5 players, their makeup is usually the same as on the ice hockey team. When a team goes on a "power play", they might have different combinations of players with special skills. As an example, all 5 of the players may be forwards or centers, fast with good shooting and puck or ball handling skills. Sometimes near the end of a close game, the team that is behind by a point may pull their goalkeeper and add an extra attacker (forward or center) in order to score quickly and tie the game. In this case the team would have 6 players out skating on the ice or floor.

What Offensive Players do

The main job of the "center" is to act like a quarterback and direct the attack. Sometimes what they do is a lot like centering the ball for a volleyball spiker to hit. In other words they pass the puck or ball out a little in front of a forward, so they can set up to make a good shot on goal. This might be like a "slap shot". The job of a "forward" is to move out in front, then try to get into position to make a shot on goal. The job of the "defensemen" is basically to stay to the rear, and stop the opposition from making any quick counterattack breakouts, or breakaways if they gain control of the puck or ball. You might say they are "safety valve" players. The offensive team's goalkeeper has basically the job of staying right near the front of the goal net, does some directing of the offensive play out ahead of them, stops any counterattack shots on goal, and clears out any dump in shots back in their defensive zone if they can easily get to them.

Defensive Game

What the Defense does

The object of the defense is to stop the other team from scoring. They usually have one or two designated defensemen towards the rear of the defensive formation. The defense has different formations they can go into to give them an advantage in stopping the offense from scoring. As an example, they can go into a zone type defense or a man-to-man type defense. When the team is on "penalty killing" defense, they can go into a "box" formation, a "diamond" formation, a "triangle" formation, or a "triangle+1" formation. Actually being on defense is probably easier than being on offense.

What Defensive Players do

It is the defenseman's job to keep the puck or ball away from the net. They stay at the rear of the formation, to stop the offense from making any kind of attacks that break through the front players in the formation. This would be like breakaways, breakouts, and 2 on 1's. They can use checking and blocking to stop opponents. They can steal the puck or ball and start counter attacks. They have to be very quick and smart, to stop the opposing team from scoring. When the team is on "penalty killing", and undermanned, they have to dump and clear the puck or ball to run time off the penalty clock. It is the goalkeeper's job to keep the puck or ball from going into the net.

Defensive Team Members

At full strength there are either 4 (Roller) or 5 (Ice) players plus a goalkeeper on the rink during defense. Normally when in the defensive phase, only two of these players are defensemen, depending on the defensive alignment they are in. Except in rare cases, a goal keeper is always there to defend the goal against shooters. On "penalty killing" teams, they may have all defensemen plus a goalkeeper. It depends on what the coach wants to use.

Transition Phase of the Game

The transition phase is when players have to change from offense to defense while on the fly. Again this is because they don't have time outs, to change teams or "lines" in hockey, as these phases change. Other sports have time to make these changes before play starts again. It also involves going on a "power play" when the opponents have a player, or players, on the penalty bench or box. And when the other team is on the "power play" the defensive team is in their "penalty killing" phase.

The Playing Rink

There are two basic sizes and layouts for hockey rinks. The overall rink size for youth ice hockey is 100 feet wide by 200 feet long maximum *(SEE FIGURE 113)*. The overall rink size for youth roller hockey, and in-line hockey is typically 85 feet wide by 185 feet long, but must be a minium of 65 feet wide by 145 feet long *(SEE FIGURE 114)*. Many roller hockey rinks are the same size as the ice hockey rinks. There are goals located at each end of the rink. The posts are 6 feet apart and the top bar is 4 feet off the surface. They are centered within the width of the rink. They are placed 12 to 15 feet in from the ends of the rink for ice hockey, and 10 to 15 feet in from the ends for roller hockey. Attached to the goal is a net that has to capable of stopping a puck or ball. Both ice hockey and roller hockey rinks are surrounded by a wooden or fiberglass wall or fence know as the "boards'. These boards commonly have a height of 40 to 48 inches. There may be a kick plate at the bottom of the "boards". And it is recommended that this kick plate be painted yellow or a light color. On top of the boards, in some rinks, is a safety glass shield to separate the players from the spectators. It is to also there to give some protection to the spectators, from flying pucks or balls. In the center of the rink is a 12 inch diameter blue spot. Across the center of the rink is a 12 inch wide red line, called the "center line", separating the rink in half. This line may be a solid line or a dashed line to distinguish it from the blue lines. For ice hockey two 12 inch wide blue lines extend across the rink, on both sided of the red line, to designate the neutral zone. There is no neutral zone for roller hockey. The face-off circles are 30 foot in diameter, with 2 inch wide blue lines. For their exact detail **SEE PAGE 89.** Four red face-off spots 2 feet in diameter are marked in the neutral zone for ice hockey. They are on both sides of the center line, for both ice hockey and roller hockey. For the goal crease detail **SEE PAGE 98**. High school teams basically play on the same size rink.

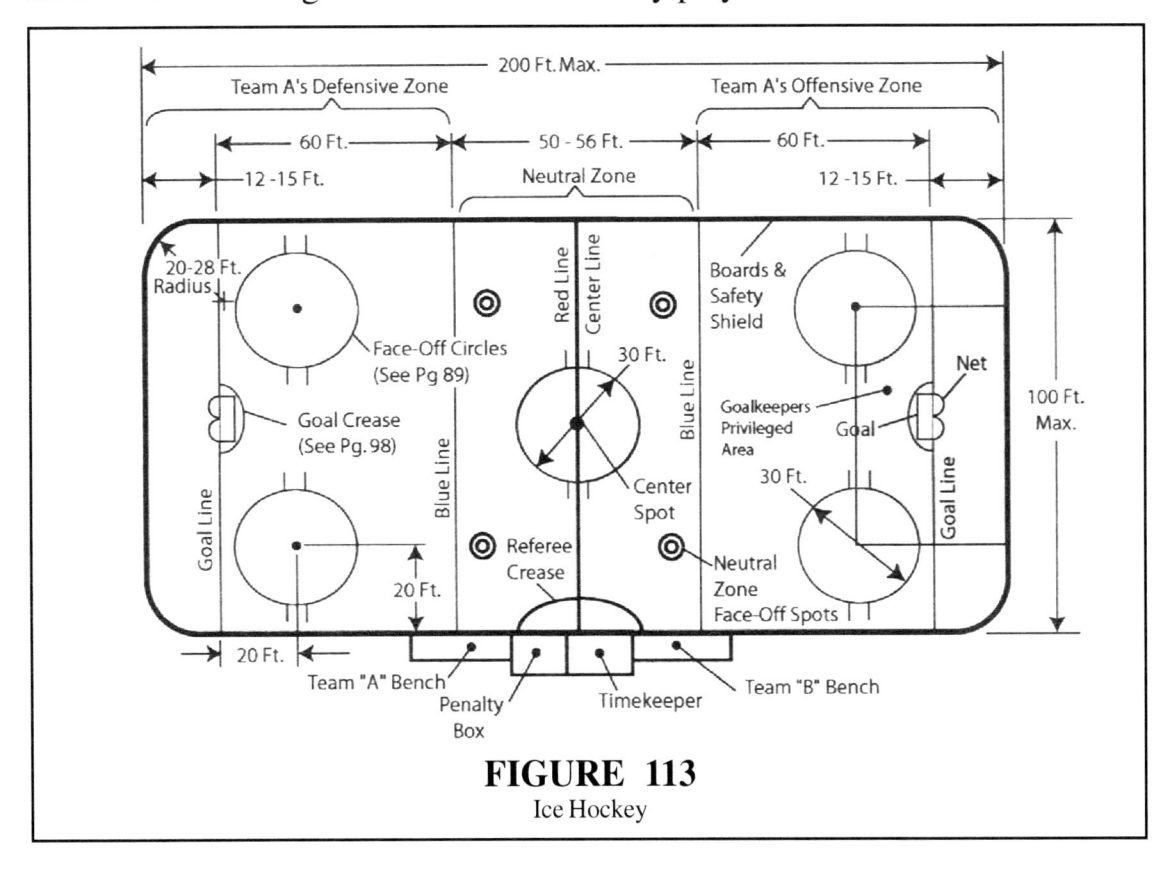

FIGURE 113
Ice Hockey

General Game Rules

There are just too many rules for us to list all of them here. So what we will do is list, and go over, the more common ones that come up. If you really want to look at all the rules, you can get a copy in libraries or on the InterNet. Or possibly even get a copy from your son or daughters coach.

151

FIGURE 114
Roller Hockey

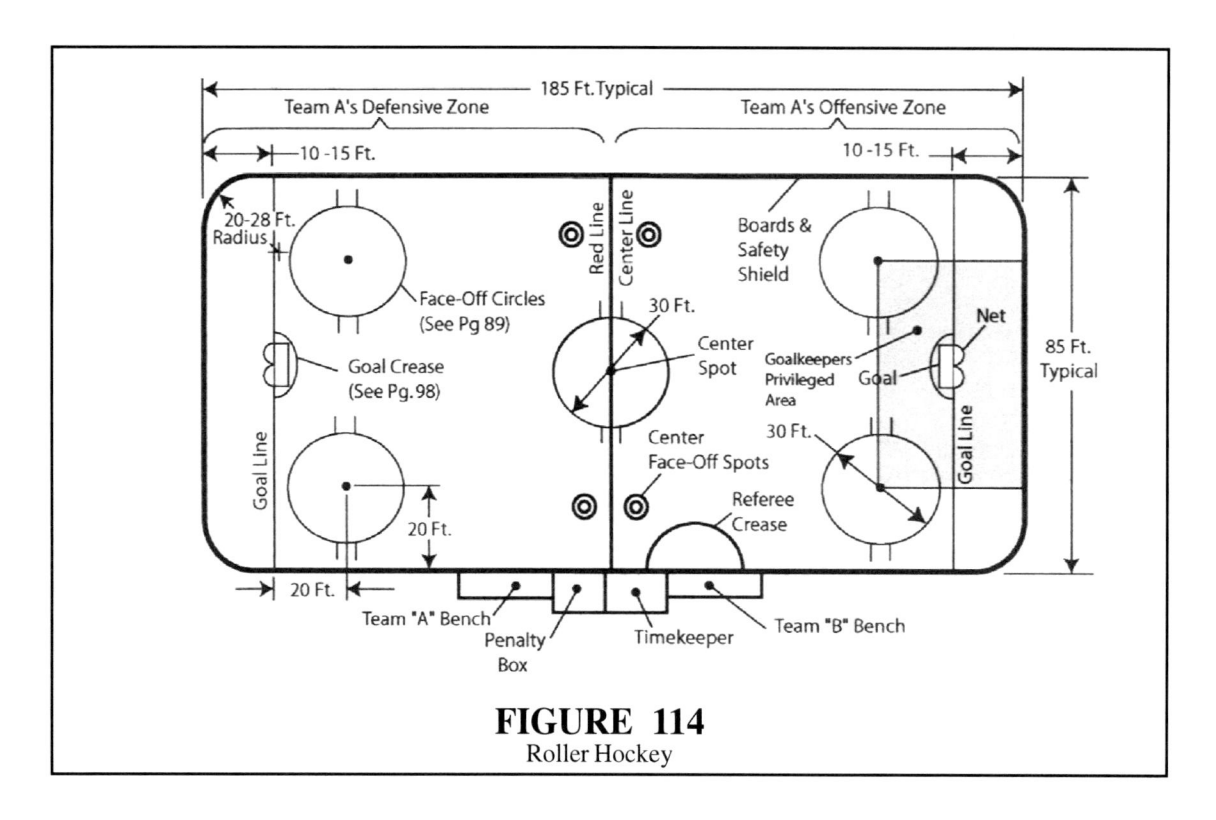

Rules Establishment

Ice hockey rules are established by "USA Hockey" located in Colorado Springs, Co. In Line hockey rules depend on which organization your area is associated with. There is USA Hockey In-line, in Colorado Springs, Co. Or there is USA Roller Hockey in Lincoln, Ne. which is part of USA Roller Sports (USARS). Most other offshoot leagues have their own special rules. Check with them if you have questions. However, for youth hockey it appears all these rules are usually similar to, or based upon the "National Federation of State High School Associations" (NFSHSA) rules book for hockey.

The Game

The game of "Ice Hockey" is played with three 20 minute periods of play, with a rest intermission between periods. Each team is allowed a single 1 minute time out per game. If one team is ahead by 1 or more points after the 3 periods, they win the game. If the game is tied after the 3 regulation periods, the game can be extended for one or more periods of play. Or the winner can be determined by a shoot-out. This is where a predetermined number of players from each team skates in on the goalkeeper, and attempts to score a goal. They keep doing this until there is a one goal advantage, and that team wins the game.

It is suggested by USA Hockey In-line that the game of "In-line Roller Hockey" be played with two 15 to 25 minute halves of play, with a rest intermission between halves. As in ice hockey, each team is allowed a single 1 minute time out per game. And the same rules apply for tie games, as in ice hockey.

It is recommended by USA Roller Hockey that the game of "Roller Hockey" be played with two 15 minute halves of play, with a rest intermission between periods. As in ice hockey, each team is allowed a single 1 minute time out per game. And the same rules apply for tie games, as in ice hockey. Training and instructional leagues may have different rules.

Scoring

A point is scored when a player shoots the puck or ball all the way into the net, and goes completely over the goal line.

Time of Games

For the time or duration of games **SEE FIGURE 115**. The main thing you need to do is, make sure you son or daughter is aware of the time left in the game, and the number of points their team has as they come down to the end of the game. Training and instructional leagues may have different rules.

Time Intervals vs Age Groups

Organization	Division	Age (Yrs.)	* Period/Half (Min.)	Intermission (Min.)
USA Hockey (Ice)	Mites	8 or Under	20	2
	Squirts	10 or Under	20	2
	PeeWees	12 or Under	20	2
	Bantams	14 or Under	20	2
USA Hockey InLine	Mites	8 or Under	15 to 25	2
	Squirts	10 or Under	15 to 25	2
	PeeWees	12 or Under	15 to 25	2
	Bantams	14 or Under	15 to 25	2
USA Roller Hockey	Mites	8 or Under	15	3
	Squirts	10 or Under	15	3
	PeeWees	12 or Under	15	3
	Bantams	14 or Under	15	3

Notes:
✱ = Time shown is regulation. This may vary due to available rink time (1 Hr.).
Ice Hockey has 3 time periods to the game. Roller Hockey has 2 halves to a game.

FIGURE 115

Team Members

USA Hockey rules say a team shall consist of players who are identified for the game on a roster. The number of members on a team might vary, depending on the league they play in . Basically there are a maximum of 18 players and 2 goalkeepers on a team. Only 6 of these players can be on the rink at the same time (5 players and 1 goalkeeper). Only players on the roster can play in games and matches. After the game starts, there can be no roster changes. Only team members and coaches can sit on the bench. Parents that are at the game as spectators can not sit on the bench. The team captain has to be identified with a 3 inch high letter "C" , in a conspicuous place on the front of their jersey. Training and instructional leagues may have different rules on team members.

Players

The players on a team should know the rules of the game and abide by them. They should use sportsmanlike conduct, and accept the referee's decisions. They should behave respectfully towards team mates, their coaches, the officials, the opponents, and the spectators. And I might add this coaches, be careful because they usually learn their behavior (good or bad) by watching and listening to you.

Substitutions

Hockey is an on going almost continuous game. They have substitutions, but they are called "line changes". However the "line change" substitutions have to be made smoothly and correctly, so they do not delay the game. And any player or players leaving the ice shall always be at the players bench, and out of the play before any change is made. The goalkeeper can be substituted for separately. However, they have to abide by the same rules as the rest of the players on their team while making the change. The goalkeeper can not be changed with a non goalkeeper player, taking their place at the net. They can be changed for a 6th attacking player, but that player has to be playing center, forward, or defenseman.

Injured Players

When a player, other than the goalkeeper, is injured and has to leave the rink during the game, they may retire from the game and be replaced by a substitute. However play must continue without players leaving the ice or floor. If a goalkeeper has an injury or becomes sick, they must be ready to resume play immediately or be replaced by a substitute goalkeeper. A player who is obviously bleeding shall be ruled off the ice or floor immediately if observed during a stoppage of play. If observed during play, play shall be stopped immediately, and the bleeding player then ruled off the ice or floor. Bleeding players can not return to the game until the bleeding has stopped, and the cut or wound is covered properly.

Play on the Puck or Ball

At the start of the game or period, and after a stoppage, play on the puck or ball starts with a face-off. Any player who shoots the puck or ball after a whistle has been blown shall be assessed a minor penalty for unsportsmanlike conduct if, in the opinion of the referee, the player had sufficient time after the whistle, to refrain from taking the shot. If a player knocks, throws, or shoots, the puck or ball out of the reach of an official who is retrieving it during a stoppage, they shall be assessed a misconduct penalty. If a player rolls the opponents puck or ball carrier along the boards where the player is trying to squeeze through too small of an opening, boarding is not called. However, if the player being boarded is not the puck or ball carrier, a penalty will be called.

On face-offs, the attacking team player shall be the first player to place their stick on the ice or floor. For face-offs along the center red line, the visiting team player shall place their stick on the ice or floor first. No other player shall be allowed to enter the face-off circle or come within 15 feet of the players facing-off the puck or ball. And all players other than the player facing-off must stand on their side of the rink, on all face-offs. If a player, other than the player facing-off, fails to maintain their proper position, the center of their team shall be ejected from the face-off. In the conduct of any face-off anywhere on the playing surface, no player facing-off shall make any physical contact with their opponent's body by means of their own body or by their stick, except in the course of playing the puck or ball after the face-off has been completed. For violation of this rule the referee shall impose a minor penalty on the player(s) whose action caused the physical contact.

A minor penalty shall be imposed on a player, other than the goalkeeper, who deliberately falls on or gathers the puck or ball into their body. A player who drops to their knees to block a shot should not be penalized if the puck or ball is shot under them, or becomes lodged in their clothing or equipment. However, any use of their hands to make the puck or ball unplayable should be penalized.

If a player, except a goalkeeper, closes their hand on the puck or ball, play shall be stopped and a face-off shall follow. However, if the puck or ball is dropped to the ice or floor immediately, play shall not be stopped. A player or goalkeeper shall be permitted to stop or "bat" the puck or ball in the air with their hand, or push it along the ice or floor with their hand, and play shall not be stopped unless they have directed the puck or ball to a team mate in any zone other than their defending zone. In that case play shall be stopped and the puck or ball faced-off at the spot where the offense occurred unless otherwise provided by the rules. Batting the puck or ball above the normal height of the shoulders with the stick is prohibited, and when it occurs there shall be a whistle and the ensuing face-off shall take place at one of the end face-off spots adjacent to the goal of the team causing the stoppage, unless:

(1) the puck or ball is batted to an opponent and the opponent gains possession and control of the puck or ball, in which case the play shall continue, or

(2) a player of the defending team shall bat the puck or ball accidentally into their own goal in which case the goal shall be allowed.

A minor penalty shall be imposed on a player who interferes with or impedes the progress of an opponent who is not in possession of the puck or ball, or who deliberately knocks the stick out of the opponents hands, or who prevents a player who has dropped their stick or any other piece of equipment from regaining possession of it, or who knocks or shoots any abandoned or broken stick or illegal puck or ball or other debris towards an opposing puck or ball carrier in a manner that could cause them to be distracted.

If the puck or ball precedes all players of the attacking team into their attacking zone, any player is eligible to take possession of the puck or ball , except when rule 620 "icing" applies (youth rule). When the puck or ball goes outside the playing area or strikes any obstacles above the playing surface other than the boards, glass or wire, or deflects off an official out of the playing area, it shall be faced-off from where it was shot or deflected by a player unless otherwise provided for in the rules.

The puck or ball must at all times be kept in motion. Play shall not be stopped because the puck or ball is frozen along the boards by two or more opposing players, unless a player falls on or is knocked down onto the puck or ball. If one player freezes the puck or ball along the boards, or if a player deliberately falls on the puck or ball, a minor penalty for delaying the game shall be assessed.

Play Around the Net

A minor penalty shall be imposed on any player who makes stick contact with an opposing goalkeeper while they are in the goal crease, who has covered or caught the puck or ball, regardless of whether or not the referee has stopped play. A minor penalty shall be imposed on a goalkeeper who deliberately drops the puck or ball on the goal netting to cause a stoppage of play. When the puck or ball becomes lodged in the netting on the outside of either goal so as to make it unplayable, or if it is frozen between opposing players intentionally or otherwise, the referee shall stop play and face-off the puck or ball at either of the adjacent face-off spots unless in the opinion of the referee the stoppage was caused by a player of the attacking team, in which case the resulting face-off shall be conducted in the neutral zone.

When the puck or ball is in the attacking zone and not in the goal crease, a player on the attacking team may not stand on the goal crease line or in the goal crease, hold their stick in the goal crease, or skate through the goal crease. If the puck or ball should enter the goal while such a condition prevails, a goal shall not be allowed. For violation of this rule, while the attacking team has possession of the puck or ball, play shall be stopped and a face-off held at the nearest neutral zone face-off spot. This rule shall not apply when the goalkeeper is out of their goal crease. If a player of the attacking team has been physically interfered with by the action of the defending player so as to cause them to be in the goal crease, and the puck or ball should enter the goal while the player so interfered with is still within the goal crease, the goal shall be allowed. A goal scored by a player using a high stick (above the shoulder) shall not be allowed, except accidentally by a player on the defending team.

A minor penalty shall be imposed on a goalkeeper who deliberately falls on or gathers the puck or ball into their body, when their body is entirely outside the boundaries of the goal crease and the puck or ball is behind the goal line. This also applies when the puck or ball is outside the boundaries of the goalkeepers "privileged area", or who holds or places the puck or ball against any part of the goal or against the boards, when having an opportunity to play the puck or ball with their stick prior to being pressured by an attacking player. No defending player, except the goalkeeper, shall be permitted to fall on the puck or ball, hold the puck or ball, or gather the puck or ball into their body or hands, when the puck or ball is within the goal crease. For a violation of this rule, play shall be immediately stopped and a penalty shot/ optional minor shall be awarded to the nonoffending team.

A goal shall be scored when the puck or ball has been put into the goal in any way by the defending team accidentally. The player of the attacking team who last played the puck or ball shall be credited with the goal, but no assist shall be awarded. If an attacking player kicks the puck or ball and it goes directly into the goal, or is deflected off the kick into the goal by any player, including the goalkeeper, a goal shall not be allowed. If the puck or ball shall have been deflected into the goal from the shot of an attacking player by striking any part of a player from the same team, a goal shall be allowed. The player who deflected the puck or ball shall be credited with the goal. Goals shall not be allowed if the puck or ball has been kicked, thrown, or otherwise deliberately directed into the goal by any means other than a stick. If a goal is scored as a result of a puck or ball being deflected directly into the goal off an official, the goal shall not be allowed.

The goalkeeper may not leave their stick or any part thereof in front of their goal. If they do and if the puck or ball hits the stick, thereby preventing an obvious and eminent goal while the goalkeeper is on the ice or floor, but in the act of leaving the ice or floor, or going off the ice or floor, the referee shall stop play and award a goal to the nonoffending team. A goal shall not be allowed if the puck or ball was propelled by the hand of an attacking player, and entered the goal either directly or after deflecting off any player including the goalkeeper. If a player from the defending team deliberately displaces the goal and, in the opinion of the referee, the puck or ball would have entered the goal had it not been displaced, thereby preventing an obvious goal, a goal shall be awarded in lieu of a penalty shot. There will be a minor/major penalty imposed on any player who "body checks" or "charges" a goalkeeper who is in the goalkeepers "privileged area".

Fisticuffs (Fighting)

A major penalty shall be imposed on any player who engages in fighting. An additional minor penalty shall be imposed on any player who starts or instigates a fight. A minor penalty shall be imposed on a player who, having been struck, shall retaliate with a blow, or an attempted blow. However, at the discretion of the referee, a double minor or a major penalty may be imposed if such player continues the altercation. As parents, remember the referee is provided a very wide latitude in the penalties they may impose under this rule.

A major penalty shall be imposed on any player involved in fights off the playing surface, or with another player who is off the playing surface before, during, or after the game. A game misconduct penalty shall be imposed on any player, or goalkeeper, who is the first to intervene in an altercation then in progress. This penalty is in addition to any other penalty incurred in the same incident. When an altercation does occur on the ice or floor, at the signal of the referee, all players (nonparticipant), excluding goalkeepers, must proceed immediately and directly to their respective players bench. Goalkeepers must remain in the immediate vicinity of their goal crease.

A minor penalty shall be imposed on any player, including a goalkeeper, who removes their glove or gloves and/or drops their stick during an altercation, and who is not a participant in the original altercation. A game misconduct penalty may be added to the minor penalty if, in the judgement of the referee, the player is the instigator of a subsequent altercation. This penalty shall be in addition to any other penalty incurred in the same incident.

Rules for Injuries

A match penalty shall be imposed on any player who deliberately injures or attempts to injure an opponent, and the circumstances shall be reported to the proper authorities for further action. A substitute for the penalized player shall be permitted at the end of the fifth minute.

A match penalty shall be imposed on any player or team official who deliberately injures or attempts to injure a team official or game official in any manner, and the circumstances shall be reported to the proper authorities for further action.

A major, plus a game misconduct, penalty shall be imposed on any player who "head-butts" in such a manner as to in any way foul an opponent.

Any player wearing tape or any other material on their hands, who cuts or injures an opponent during an altercation, shall receive a match penalty under this rule.

In the case where it is obvious that a player has sustained a serious injury, the referee and/or linesman may stop play immediately. A player other than the goalkeeper, whose injury appears serious enough to warrant the stoppage of play, may not participate further in the game until the completion of the ensuing face-off.

A player or a goalkeeper who is obviously bleeding shall be ruled off the ice or floor immediately if observed during a stoppage of play. If observed during play, play shall be stopped immediately, and the bleeding player or goalkeeper then ruled off the ice or floor. Said player or goalkeeper shall not be allowed to return to play until the bleeding has been stopped, and the cut or abrasion covered. It is required that any affected equipment/ uniform be properly decontaminated or exchanged.

Players Uniforms

USA Hockey requires each player and goalkeeper listed in the lineup of each team shall wear a visible, individually identifying, number at least 10 inches high on the back of their sweater. The number may be 8 inches in the Midget and

Bantam classifications, and 6 inches in height in the Squirt, Peewee, and Mite classifications. All players of each team shall be dressed uniformly. All players must wear approved skates (ice or roller), and an HECC approved helmet and face mask. The USA Hockey organization also recommends a full face mask, shin pads, elbow pads, hip pads or padded pants, shoulder pads, tendon pads, and a protective cup (males only). Most youth players are required to wear an internal mouth guard and gloves. Additional equipment is required for goalkeepers, such as a blocker, a catch glove, a special stick, and special leg pads *(SEE FIGURE 69)*.

In addition to the same uniform and equipment required by ice hockey, USA Hockey In-line requires a chinstrap, and hockey gloves. They recommend a pelvic protector, chest protection, and throat protector. Goalkeepers must wear chest protection.

In addition to the same uniform and equipment required by ice hockey, USA Roller Hockey requires all players to wear gloves. They also require goalkeepers to wear HECC approved masks, and eyeglass wearers must have plastic lenses, not glass. Suspenders, socks, and neck guards are optional in most leagues. Because some requirements might vary in other leagues, check with the coach or league to make sure your son or daughters equipment meets league standards. For more information on the uniform and equipment *SEE THE SECTION ON EQUIPMENT.*

Hockey Age Groups

Hockey breaks down into different age groups as you go around the country. Most established hockey teams go by the age group standards set by USA Hockey, USA Hockey In-line, or USA Roller Hockey *(SEE THE CHART IN FIGURE 115)*.

Officials

Why have Officials (Referee's)
In this book the term "official" and "referee" is used many times. They are the same person. Some coaches just like to call the officials, referee's. I think it's obvious why we have referee's, without them the game could get real ugly, arguments, kids getting hurt, fan rioting, and who knows what else could happen. Hockey games have referee's, to judge whether the rules have been followed. The game of hockey is more complicated than you might think, and that is why we need referee's to keep track of the rules.

All levels of hockey teams should have at least one official at the game. Usually there will be two officials in the upper divisions. However, in some lower level youth games you may only see one official. USA Hockey rules call for a referee and two linesmen. Where there are two, one will be the head referee, and the other one is the linesman. However, in some special cases they may both be referee's. All referees and linesman must have some kind of training in youth hockey. They usually receive this training in a certified referee clinic given by USA Hockey or USA Hockey In-line, or in USA Roller Hockey's certification program.

If the hockey games your son or daughter takes part in have two officials, you are lucky because two sets of eyes are going to see more than one. The reason there may be only one referee is probably because in some leagues it is hard to get anyone to volunteer. And I think it's mostly because fans, and parents, don't want to be the one hollered at if they are the referee making the call. And then if some of the fans, friends, or other parents watching don't like the call, they don't want them to be mad at them. And I think that is why too few officials has a lot to do with people getting mad at games. When there are too few officials, just one official is more than likely not going to be able to see every rule infraction that occurs on the rink. It's a lot easier to watch for infractions of the rules when you have 2 or 3 officials present, on the ice or floor all during the game, and that is their only job.

So please try to be tolerant of the situation as parents while you are watching your son or daughter's game. I have been at other youth sports games where one of the two officials (referee's) got sick and had to leave. Now you have only one referee, and the teams were left with the decision of whether to play the game with one official or not at all. Because the game was at the lowest level of teams in the league, and late in the season with no championship on the line, both teams agreed to go with one official. And he had a very tough job, believe me. A good game for a referee is a quiet game. This means he was unnoticed, and did his job.

When an infraction of the rules occurs, either the referee or the linesman (assistant referee) will make the call. Or in some cases both. If the linesman and the head referee do not agree on the call, the head referee's decision is final. The referee will make calls by blowing his whistle, and making a hand signal, indicating the infraction or foul *(SEE FIGURE 116 & 117)*. In some cases the referee may have to blow the whistle a second time, to make their indication. For this book we will use the "official's signals", and other information, from the "USA Hockey" rules book. They are a little more expanded than some of the signal illustrations I have seen in other books for youth hockey.

1. Boarding Striking the closed fist of the hand once into the open palm of the other hand.	**2. Body Checking** The palm of the nonwhistle hand is brought across the body and placed on the opposite shoulder.	**3. Butt-Ending** Moving the forearm, fist closed, under the forearm of the other hand which is held palm down.
4. Charging Rotating clenched fists around one another in front of the chest.	**5. Checking from Behind** Arm placed behind the back, elbow bent, forearm parallel to the ice surface	**6. Cross Checking** Moving the forearm, fist closed, under the forearm of the other hand which is held palm down.
7. Delayed Calling of Penalty The nonwhistle hand is extended straight above the head.	**8. Delayed (Slow) Whistle** The nonwhistle hand is extended straight above the head. If play returns to neutral zone without stoppage, and the offending team clears, arm is brought down.	**9. Delaying the Game** The nonwhistle hand, palm open, is placed across the chest and then fully extended directly in front of the body.
10. Elbowing Tapping the elbow with the opposite hand.	**11. Fighting (Roughing)** One punching motion to the side, with the arm extending from the shoulder.	**12. Goal Scored** A single point, with the nonwhistle hand, directly at the goal in which the puck or ball legally entered, while simultaneously blowing the whistle
13. Hand Pass The nonwhistle hand (open hand) and arm placed straight down alongside the body, swung forward and up once in an underhand motion.	**14. Head Contact** Nonwhistle hand placed palm inward on the back of the helmet.	**15. High Sticking** Holding both fists, clenched, one immediately above the other, at the side of the head.
16. Holding Clasping the wrist of the whistle hand well in front of the chest.	**17. Holding the Face Mask** Closed fist held in front of face, palm in, and pulled down in one straight motion.	**18. Hooking** A tugging motion with both arms, as if pulling something toward the stomach.
19. Icing Front referee gives slow whistle signal first. The minute the condition occurs, the back linesman gives signal by foldig arms across chest.	**20. Interference** Crossed arms stationary in front of chest, with fists closed.	**21. Kneeing** A single tap on the right knee, with the right hand, keeping both skates on the ice.

FIGURE 116

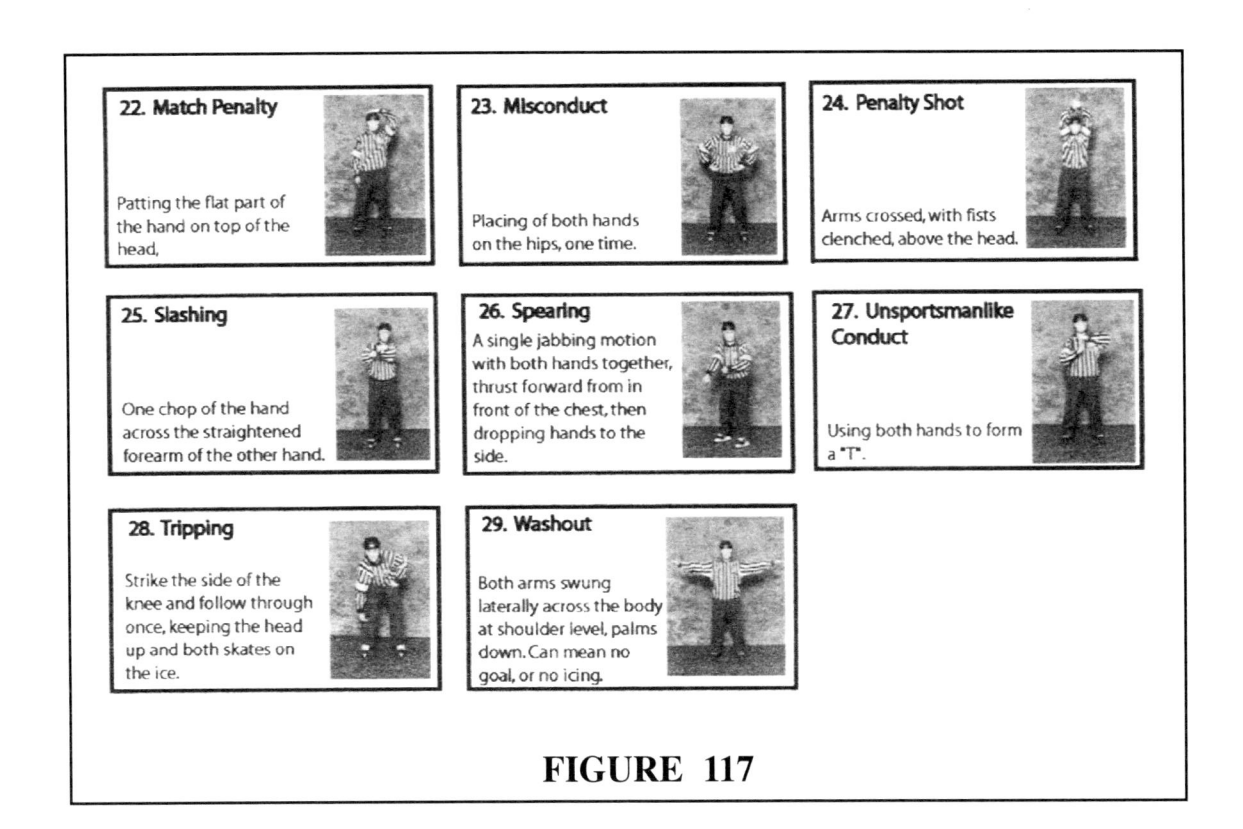

22. Match Penalty	23. Misconduct	24. Penalty Shot
Patting the flat part of the hand on top of the head.	Placing of both hands on the hips, one time.	Arms crossed, with fists clenched, above the head.
25. Slashing	**26. Spearing**	**27. Unsportsmanlike Conduct**
One chop of the hand across the straightened forearm of the other hand.	A single jabbing motion with both hands together, thrust forward from in front of the chest, then dropping hands to the side.	Using both hands to form a "T".
28. Tripping	**29. Washout**	
Strike the side of the knee and follow through once, keeping the head up and both skates on the ice.	Both arms swung laterally across the body at shoulder level, palms down. Can mean no goal, or no icing.	

FIGURE 117

Who are the Officials

Referee's and linesmen (officials) are easily recognized on the rink by their uniform, which is usually black pants, a black and white striped sweater, and a black hockey helmet. And they are usually adults, or young adults, which makes them stand out bigger than the kids. We will not attempt to show all of the referee's and linesmen's duties. We will show a short list of some of their duties, so you can see what kinds of things they have to do during games. The other officials duties are just as their name implies.

The game on the ice or floor should be administered to by a referee and linesmen. Other officials at a game might include a game timekeeper, official scorer, penalty timekeeper, and 2 goal judges. The head referee and the linesman have the authority to make decisions about rule infractions. Jurisdiction by the officials begin with their arrival on the ice or floor prior to warm-ups, and extends through the verification of the final score, and until all players have proceeded to their dressing rooms. There should be no exchange of duties by the referee and the linesman unless during the game they are hurt, sick, or unable to continue.

Referee's Responsibilities

The referee has general supervision of the game, and full control of all officials. It is their duty to see that the required equipment is in use. Before the game starts, it is their duty to see that all the other officials are in place, also that the timing and signaling equipment all work correctly. On occasion they may consult with the linesman, or other officials before making their decision. They report to the official scorer the name or number of the goal scorer, and any players entitled to assists. They check all team rosters, and all players in uniform before signing a report of the game.

Linesman's Responsibilities

It is the duty of the linesman to determine any rules infractions, concerning "off sides" or "icing". They will conduct all face-offs, except at the start of the game and at the beginning of each period (referee conducts). At the next stoppage of play, they report their version, that just occured, of any rules infractions that they believe constitutes a penalty.

Penalties

Penalties, infractions, and fouls are called by the referee, with the help of the linesman, or a second referee. We are not going to indicate every possible penalty or infraction in this section. There are just too many. We will try to go over the ones you might normally see in a game, or are the most controversial. The penalties, and explanations we will go over are based on the USA Hockey rules book. The reason we are indicating it this way is because their rules are pretty "normal", and some leagues over the USA have their own slightly different versions of these same rules. And there is no way we can find and identify all of them.

Most of the penalties, and fouls, are called by the head referee. The linesman mostly makes determinations and indications. Penalties are basically grouped into 6 categories. They are "minor", "major", "misconduct", "match penalties", "penalty shots", and "goalkeepers penalties". Some infractions may have several different assessments, depending on the intent of the player committing them.

Minor Penalties

Generally:

Ice = 2 Min.

For: Holding, hooking, interference, tripping, delay of game, high sticking, charging, slashing, elbowing, roughing, cross checking, grasping the face mask, checking from behind, playing with illegal equipment, and abusing the official.

Roller = 2 or 3 Min.
For: Same as ice hockey except "grasping the face mask", and "checking from behind" are not called.

Major Penalties (Some come with a misconduct or game misconduct)
Generally:
Ice = 5 Min.
For: Cross checking, boarding, elbowing, kneeing, slashing, checking after a whistle, checking from behind, fighting, spearing, butt-ending, and attempting to injure.
Roller = 5 Min.
For: Same as ice hockey except, "grasping the face mask", and "boarding" are called.

Misconduct (There are several types)
　General Misconduct
　Ice and Roller = Removal of player for 10 Min.
　For: Most of the "minor" and "major" penalties above come with a "misconduct" or a "game misconduct", also for "not surrendering a stick for measurement", abusing the official, and a mouthguard violation.
　Game Misconduct
　Ice and Roller = Suspension of player for the rest of game.
　For: Leaving the bench during an altercation, striking, attempting to injure, touching, and holding a game official.

　Gross Misconduct
　Ice and Roller = Suspension of player for the rest of game, and with the possibility of further suspension of that player from the league.
　For: = Same as "game misconduct", except with more than a 1 game suspension, and possibly suspension from the league.

Match Penalties
　Ice and Roller = Suspension of player for the rest of game, and with further suspension of that player from the league.
　For: = Attempting to injure an opponent, deliberately injuring an opponent, swinging stick at opponent, and taped hand cutting an opponent in an altercation.

Penalty Shots
>**Ice and Roller** = A goal instead of a penalty shot can be awarded if in the eyes of the official the puck or ball would have gone into the net.
>
>For: Deliberate illegal substitution, goalkeeper deliberately displaces goal (nonbreakaway), deliberate removal of goalkeepers helmet/ face mask, player falling on puck or ball in the crease, picking up the puck or ball in the crease, throwing stick at puck or ball in defensive end, and illegal entry into a game on a breakaway.

Goalkeepers Penalties
>**Ice and Roller** = Besides the regular "minor" penalties, a goalkeeper can receive additional major and misconduct penalties.
>
>For: Wearing or playing with illegal equipment, leaving crease during altercations, participating in play across centerline, going to bench for a stick during stoppage, piling up obstacles in front of goal cage, holding puck or ball more than 3 seconds after warning from official, and shooting puck or ball directly out of play.

Equipment

Each level of Hockey, from professional to youth teams, has slightly different rules on what equipment can and can not be used. Mostly, this is to protect the players from injury. In this book we will talk about youth equipment. Most youth Hockey organizations and leagues have very similar rules, compared to the higher level Hockey teams. Since there is hard contact with the ice or floor of the rink, and between the players, rules have to be set up to protect the participants. Also flying pucks or balls can cause some major injuries. Another piece of equipment that is dangerous is the ice skate. It is very sharp, and has been known to inflict some very bad cuts. The protection is directed to all parts of the body, but the critical area is the head. In almost every league the head gear must be approved by the league governing body. The "Hockey Equipment Certification Council" (signified by HECC in this book) is an independent organization responsible for the development, evaluation, and testing of performance standards for protective ice hockey equipment. There are strict standards for helmets, face masks, and skates, as of the writing of this book. Some ice and roller hockey players will attempt to modify their equipment, to give them an edge. Do not let your son or daughter do this. It may be illegal. Make sure all their equipment is approved by the league.

Health Concerns

Another very important thing to mention is, that rotten smell that is associated with sports equipment is caused by sweat, mucus, dander, dirt, blood, and drinks that have soaked into the equipment. The mix of all these different things is an ideal breeding ground for the growth of bacteria, mold, and fungus. And they all pose a health threat to your son or daughter. So when you see a rash or blisters developing on your son or daughter, guess what, there is a good chance they have an infection from all that stuff on their uniform or equipment. So you mom or dad are going to have to be the one to make sure their equipment stays clean, don't leave it up to your son or daughter.

So how do you do this. If you do it yourself, you need a cleaning solution that will kill Staphylococcus Epidermidis, Staphylococcus Aureus, Streptococcus Viridans, Streptococcus Faecalis, Coliform, Enterics, Fungus, Mold, and Yeast. There is an easier way though, find out where they have an ***"Esporta"*** wash system center. Take everything there except maybe their Jersey, and get it cleaned. And don't buy into your teenager telling you, "It's bad luck to wash or clean your equipment, when your on a winning streak". I know it's probably going to be another expense, as if you didn't have enough already, but it's you son or daughter's health we are talking about here. It looks like a 3 month interval is pretty common for cleaning. So you are looking at maybe about $45 for a whole set of equipment every 3 months.

Worn Equipment
Uniform

Most youth hockey organization rule books require a jersey (sweater), hockey pants, stockings, gloves, approved skates, an approved stick for regular players ***(SEE FIGURE 118 & 120)*** and for goalkeeper's ***(SEE FIGURE 122)***, approved helmet and face mask, shin pads, elbow pads, hip pads or the padded hockey pants, tendon pads, shoulder pads, a protective cup (males only), and an internal mouth guard ***(SEE FIGURE 118 & 119)***. There are two kinds of mouth guards. First the one that just fits around your teeth, and second a type that you heat up in hot water, then bite into it so that it fits the shape of your teeth. Approved skates should have an HECC label, or marking of some kind, for easy checking by the referee. And referee's do inspect the skates before a game starts. All the pads should be made of foam or rubber, and they are usually covered with a soft elastic material. All equipment and pads should fit snugly, and be comfortable for long periods. Goalkeepers are required to have special pads such as special

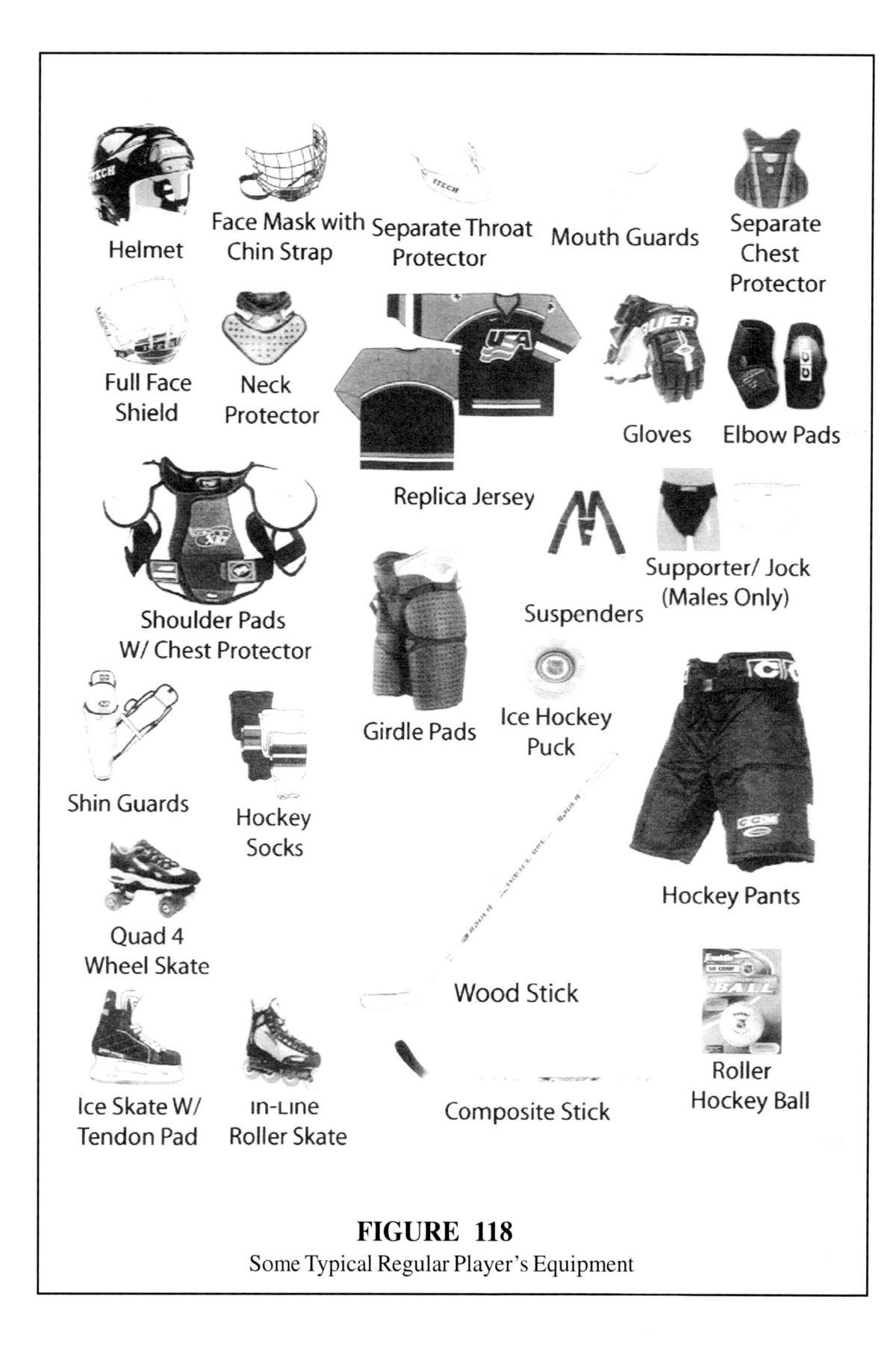

FIGURE 118
Some Typical Regular Player's Equipment

FIGURE 119
Some Typical Goalkeeper's Equipment

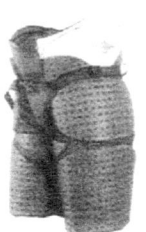

FIGURE 120
Player's Stick

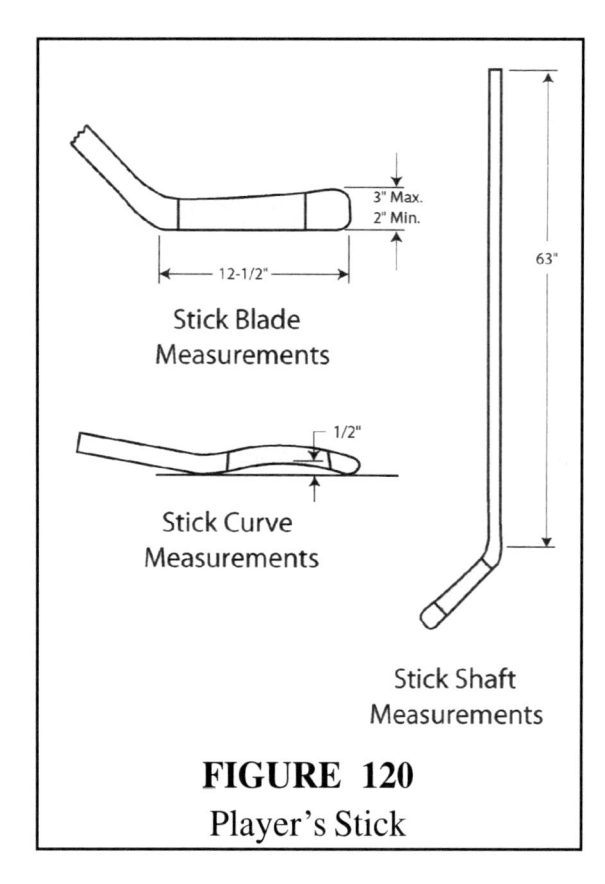

leg pads (12" wide), a blocker (8" wide x 16" high), and a special catching glove with cuff *(SEE FIGURE 121)*. Suspenders, and socks are not always required, but many players wear them.

Roller Hockey was developed and started in New York state, using the old traditional quad or four-wheel skate *(SEE FIGURE 118)*, but today the in-line skate is mostly used. Roller hockey requires some additional equipment such as a chin cup with their face masks *(SEE FIGURE 118 & 119)*, pelvic protector, chest protector, and a throat protector. Also in Roller hockey the goalkeeper is required to have a chest protector *(SEE FIGURE 119)*, and all eyeglass wearers must be using plastic lenses, not glass. For Ice Hockey and Roller Hockey the jersey, pants, helmet, and stockings, of each player on the team should be the same color. All jerseys must have a number permanently attached to it. The size is up to the league. For enjoyment of the game, freedom of movement, and their own protection, make sure all of their equipment fits properly. And it's probably a good idea to wash their Jersey and pants, at least after every other practice or game if possible, just for good measure so to speak.

Miscellaneous

Players may **_not_** wear a cast, splints, braces, made of an unyielding material, even if padded, unless directed in writing by a licensed medical physican. And even then they have to be covered on all exterior surfaces with a 1/2 inch thick, high density closed cell polyurethane, or similar material with the same properties. All gloves have to be complete, that is no cutting off fingers, or the part of the palm. And even though I don't see it in the rules book, any prosthetic limbs would probably

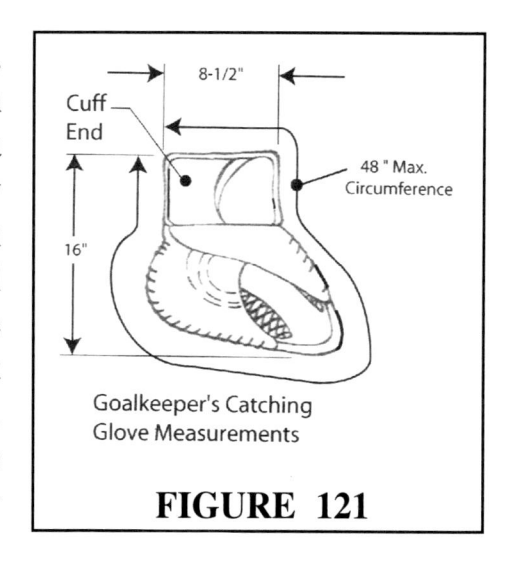

FIGURE 121

have to be covered, made of a pliable material, and approved by the league in writing. They can *not* wear earrings, or jewelry unless it is completely covered by equipment or taped to the body. They can wear religious or medical medallions, but the chain should be removed, and they must be taped to the body under the uniform. When they get a little older and are really moving fast and hard, it's probably a good idea to tape their ankles, or have them wear pliable ankle braces, especially if they have bad ankles or they have a history of ankle problems.

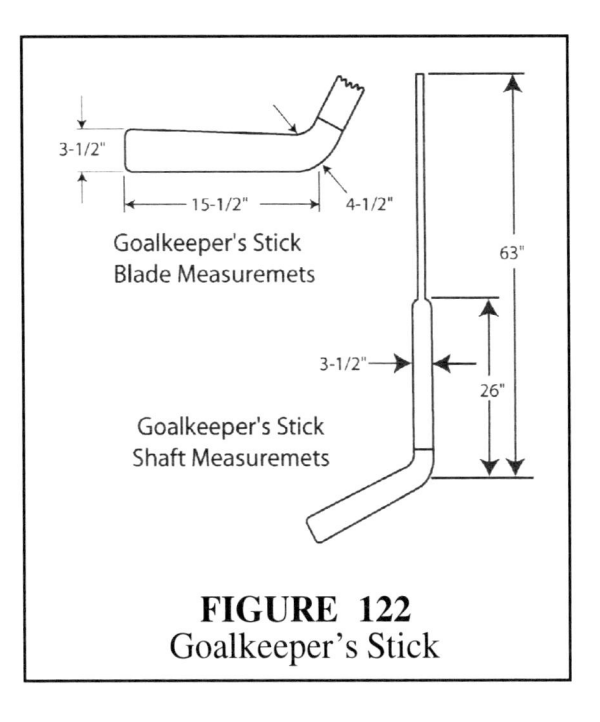

FIGURE 122
Goalkeeper's Stick

Other Equipment

One of the most important, and necessary, pieces of equipment required during the game is a puck or a ball. Pucks and balls don't vary in size, but some do vary in weight. The same size puck is used for ice hockey and in-line hockey *(SEE FIGURE 123)*, except the weight can be a little lighter for in-line hockey. For the 10 and under youth ice hockey league, and the 10 and under girls ice hockey league, the puck is the same standard size but weighs less, and is a different color *(SEE FIGURE 123)*. For most games the puck is used for ice and in-line hockey. However, if the rink the "In-Line" game is being played on has boards that are less than 40 inches in height, a ball has to be used. All balls are the same size but might vary just a little bit in weight, depending on who makes them. They have to be a style called "no bounce", and they can be liquid filled *(SEE FIGURE 123)*.

Other available equipment used mostly in Hockey training are street or driveway goal nets for shooting targets and goalkeeper practice, protect a garage door shooting tarps, the "Accu-Pass" passing trainer, "Power Skater" trainer, Speed and agility ladder, stick handler trainer, "Sharp Shooter" net attach target, "Kolka" speed trainer, a Mylec goal target set, a "Mr. Assist" puck skill trainer, "SkillPad" for shooters, moving Goalie dummy, a balance board for agility and balance training, a "Swiss" ball for strength training, and a "Staubar goalkeeper trainer *(SEE FIGURE 124)*. For other training aids, cone sets are helpful to

PUCK/BALL SIZE vs AGE GROUPS (8 & Under Thru 14 Yrs.)			BALL SIZE - Dia. ✱ Inches (Wt.)	PUCK Dia. x Thick. (INCHES)	# Puck Color	PUCK WEIGHT (OUNCES)
Ice Hockey	Mites	—	3 x 1	Blue	4 - 4 1/2
	Squirts	—	3 x 1	Blue	4 - 4 1/2
	PeeWees	—	3 x 1	Black	5 1/2 - 6
	Bantams	—	3 x 1	Black	5 1/2 - 6
In-Line Hockey	Mites	2 1/2 - 2 3/4 (3 Oz.)	3 x 1	#	3 1/2 - 6 1/2
	Squirts	2 1/2 - 2 3/4 (3 Oz.)	3 x 1	#	3 1/2 - 6 1/2
	PeeWees	2 1/2 - 2 3/4 (3 Oz.)	3 x 1	#	3 1/2 - 6 1/2
	Bantams	2 1/2 - 2 3/4 (3 Oz.)	3 x 1	#	3 1/2 - 6 1/2
Roller Hockey	Mites	2 1/2 - 2 3/4 (3 Oz.)	3 x 1	#	3 1/2 - 6 1/2
	Squirts	2 1/2 - 2 3/4 (3 Oz.)	3 x 1	#	3 1/2 - 6 1/2
	PeeWees	2 1/2 - 2 3/4 (3 Oz.)	3 x 1	#	3 1/2 - 6 1/2
	Bantams	2 1/2 - 2 3/4 (3 Oz.)	3 x 1	#	3 1/2 - 6 1/2

Notes:
✱ = All balls are no bounce, and may be liquid filled.
All age groups and divisions are per USA Hockey, USA In-Line Hockey, or USA Roller Hockey.
 # = Color is optional, but it must contrast with the color of the playing surface of the rink. This applies to balls also.

FIGURE 123

have around. They are used to mark training lanes, or areas, on the rink and out in the back yard or street.

Some of this equipment is available in sporting goods stores, and athletic equipment stores. Many of the training aids are available on the "InterNet". And believe it or not, many of them are not to expensive. Another thought is to use birthdays and christmas to buy them as presents, instead of clothing or video games.

FIGURE 124
Some Typical Training Equipment

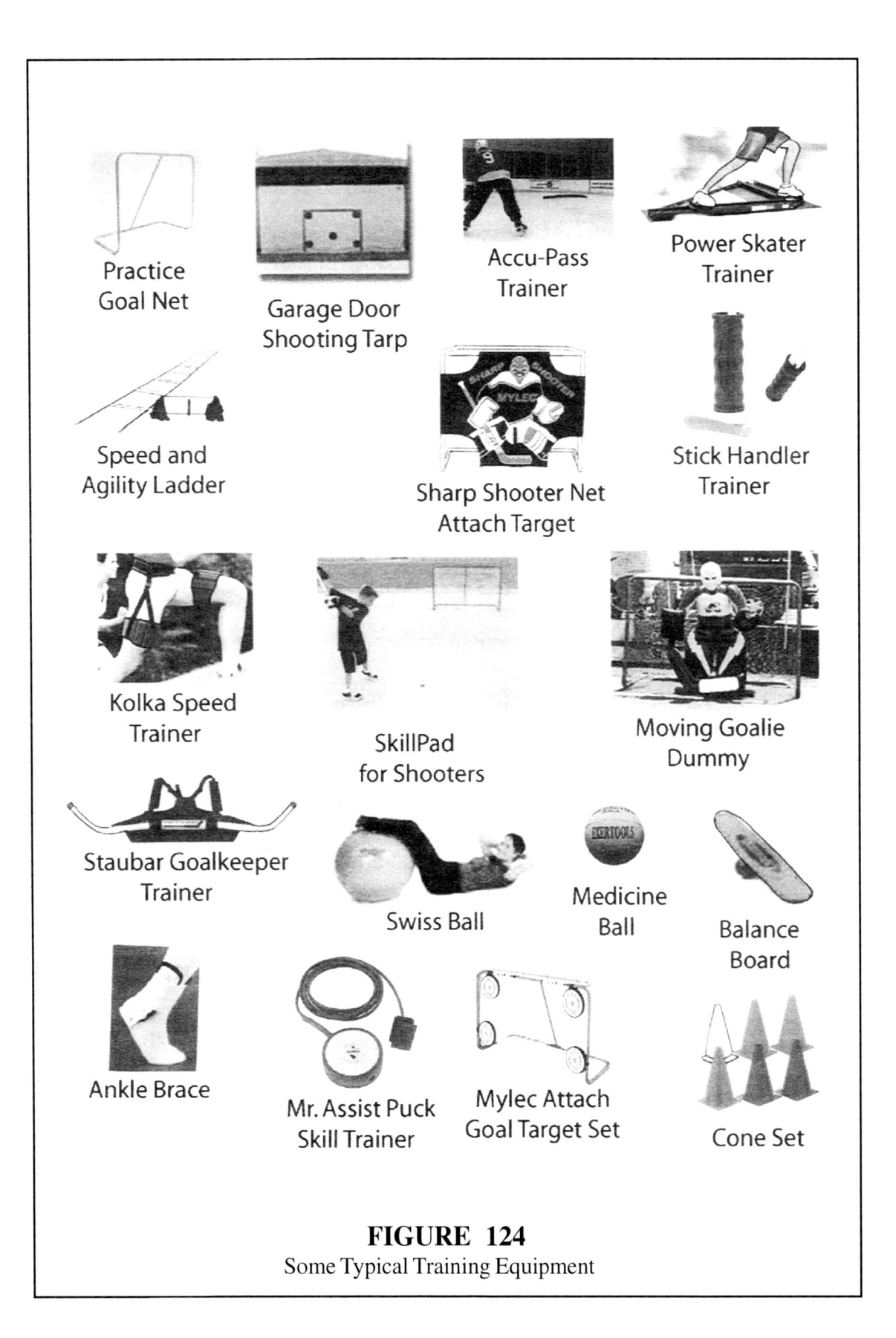

Try these other excellent books for teaching your Son or Daughter sports Fundamentals

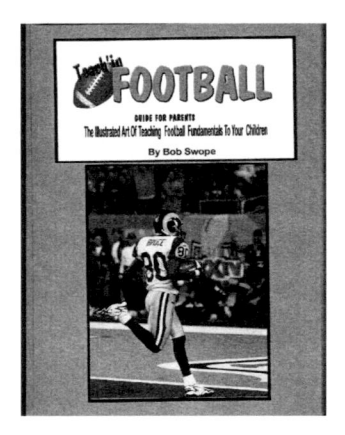

Teach'in Football - Teach your son all the basic fundamentals he needs, to play the game of football. Mom and dad, you will have fun teaching him, and he will have more fun playing the game because he will feel like he knows what he is doing. This book is complete with everything both of you need to know. It covers all the positions, new parent orientation to football, equipment required, field size, and general game rules.
ISBN 0-9705827-4-9, second edition, soft cover paperback, 8 x 10-1/2, 138 pages.

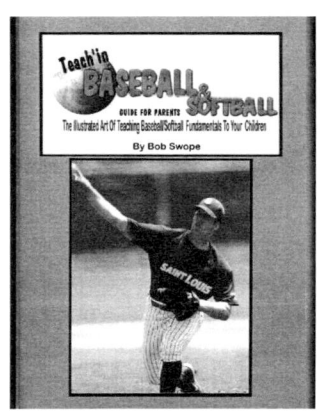

Teach'in Baseball & Softball - Teach your son or daughter all the basic fundamentals they need, to play the game of baseball or softball, and all in one book. Mom and dad, you will have fun teaching them, and they will have more fun playing the game because they will feel like they know what they are doing. This book is complete with everything both of you need to know. It covers all the positions, new parent orientation to the game, equipment required, field size, and general game rules.
ISBN 0-9705827-2-2, soft cover paperback, 8 x 10-1/2, 161 pages.

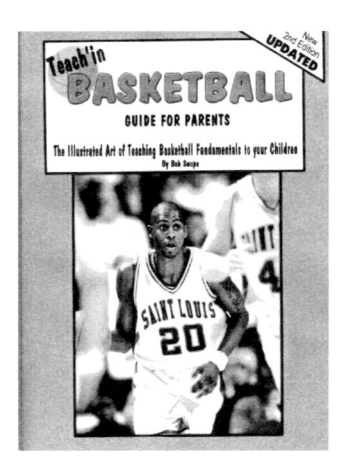

Teach'in Basketball - Teach your son or daughter all the basic fundamentals they need to play the game of basketball. Mom and dad, you will have fun teaching them, and they will have more fun playing the game because they will feel like they know what they are doing. This book is complete with everything both of you need to know. It covers all the positions, new parent orientation to the game, equipment required, court size, and general game rules.
ISBN 0-9705827-1-4, second edition, soft cover paperback, 8 x 10-1/2, 151 pages.

Teach'in Soccer - Teach your son or daughter all the basic fundamentals they need, to play the game of soccer. Mom and dad, you will have fun teaching them, and they will have more fun playing the game because they will feel like they know what they are doing. This book is complete with everything both of you need to know. It covers all the positions, new parent orientation to soccer, equipment required, field size, and general game rules.
ISBN 0-9705827-3-0, soft cover paperback,
8 x 10-1/2, 138 pages.

Teach'in Track & Field - Teach your son or daughter all the basic fundamentals they need, to excell in track and field events, and all in one book. Mom and dad, you will have fun teaching them, and they will have more fun learning the events because they will feel like they know what they are doing. This book is complete with everything both of you need to know. It covers all the events, new parent orientation to the track and field, equipment required, track size, and most basic rules.
ISBN 0-9705827-5-7, soft cover paperback,
8 x 10-1/2, 180 pages.

Teach'in Volleyball - Teach your son or daughter all the basic fundamentals they need, to play the game of volleyball, and all in one book. Mom and dad, you will have fun teaching them, and they will have more fun playing the game because they will feel like they know what they are doing. This book is complete with everything both of you need to know. It covers all the positions, new parent orientation to volleyball, equipment required, court size, and general game rules.
ISBN 0-9705827-7-3, soft cover paperback,
8 x 10-1/2, 144 pages

These books and other Jacobob Press Ltd. books are available from your local bookstore, just ask for them, or by calling the supplier at (314) 843-4829

Index

1-2-2 Dbl. Swing Power Play...............130
1-2-2 Spread Power Play....................131
3-1-1 Power Play.............................127
3-2 Power Play................................127
3 on 2/ 2 on 1 Save Strategy................111

A
ASEP...17
About the Author................................7
Abductors Stretch..............................22
Abs, strengthening.............................30
Age Groups, Hockey...............153, 160,172
Agility Drills...................................25
American Sport Education Program........17
Angle, Playing the (Goalkeeper).........108
Angling Out Strategy........................123
Ankle Strengthening...........................32
Ankle Stretch...................................24
Ankles, Taping................................171
Athletic Equipment Stores.................172
Attack Triangle........................117, 118
Attackers.......................................124
Attacking, Zone..............................138
Attitude Development........................10
Authors Acknowlegement.....................3

B
Backchecking Strategy.......................123
Backhand Sweep Wrist Shot................68
Ball, Hockey.............................171, 172
Ball, Medicine............................34,173
Ball, Swiss.............................34,171,173
Behavior..10
Behind the Net Strategy...................110
Bleeding..159
Blocker Glove.............105,160,169,170
Blocker Glove Save..........................105
Blocking...84
Books, Other Excellent..............174, 175
Breakaway Strategy, Goalkeeper.........109
Breakaways....................................77
Butterfly Save, Goalkeeper................101
Butterfly Slide Save, Goalkeeper.........103

C
C-Cut Footwork..........................47,94
Calf Stretch....................................23
Captain...................................139,154
Cardiorespiratory Fitness...................13
Carrying Puck or Ball........................77
Casts..170
Catch Glove Save............................105
Catching (Stick)...............................84
Catching Glove.............105,160,169,170
Catching the Puck or Ball..................84
Centers, General..............................15
Checking..71
Chest Protector.....................160,168-170
Chin Strap............................160,168,170
Cleaning.......................................167
Communicating..........................52, 115
Compacting.................................72,73
Cone Sets...............................171,173
Controlled Falling Drills....................28
Cool Downs....................................39
Coordination & Agility, Gen...............25
Counterattacking, Neutral Zone..........124
Covering Up Strategy......................108
Crossover Foot Drill.........................25
Crossover Stepping Drill....................45
Cup, Protective (Male)..............160,167

D
Deke..54
Defenders, General......................16,149
Defensive Game...........................149
    Defensive Team Members........150
    Transition Phase..................150
    What Defense Does..................149
    What Defensive Players Do.......149
Defensive Formations....................135
    Box Penalty Killing..................135
    Diamond Penalty Killing...........135
    Hamilton Trap Penalty Kill....137
    Triangle Penalty Killing..........136
    Triangle +1 Penalty Killing.....135
    4 on 2 Goalkeeper Triangle......136
Defensive Strategies.......................120
    Covering in front of Net......121

    Cover the Point..................122
    Pressuring Puck or Ball..............121
    Reading & Reacting............121
Defensemen, General..........................16
Deflection Save Strategy....................109
Diving, Saving the Puck or Ball.........104
Drills & Exercises................................19
    How do they help.................19
Drills Blocking, Catching, Stopping....84
    Techniques..........................84
Drills for Carrying Puck or Ball.........77
    Open Surface.........................77
Drills for Checking............................71
    Body...................................71
    Stick............................73,74
    Tight Checking Game...............76
Drills For Controlled Falling...............28
    Monkey Walk.......................28
    Roll Over come up to Feet.........29
Drills for Coordination & Agility........25
    Crossover Foot.......................25
    Dodging..............................27
    Running Backwards 26
Drills for Communicating..................52
    Non-Verbal..........................54
    Passing...............................54
    Verbal................................53
Drills for Facing Off...........................87
    Techniques..........................87
Drills for Faking................................78
    Body...................................79
    Eyes....................................79
    Head..................................78
Drills for Goaltending......................90
    99 Percent Game.................97
    Fool Goalkeeper Game...............94
    Glove Saves..........................105
    Hot Shot Game....................112
    Magic 7 Rules......................113
    Movements..........................92
    Positioning..........................96
    Save Strategies....................107
    Save Techniques...................99
    Stance................................91

Drills for Passing & Receiving......59
    Backhand Receiving.................63
    Backhand Sweep Pass...............60
    Flip Pass.............................61
    Forehand Receiving.................63
    Forehand Sweep Pass...............60
    Monkey in the Middle..........64, 66
Drills for Pressuring..........................84
    Techniques..........................84
Drills for Protecting Puck or Ball......82
    Techniques..........................82
Drills for Puck & Ball Handling..........55
    King of Circle Game.................58
    Moving Handling.....................58
    Stationary Handling.................56
Drills for Reading & Reacting............85
    Reacting to Play Around You.....86
    Reading Opposition.................86
Drills for Rebounding.........................80
    Techniques..........................80
Drills for Running & Leg Strength......36
    Balance Conditioning.................39
    Speed Burst Running..............37
    Stair Climbing......................36
    Wind Sprint Ladders.................36
Drills for Shooting............................67
    Backhand Sweep Wrist...............68
    Coaches Choice Game.............70
    Flip Shot.............................69
    Forehand Sweep Wrist.............67
    Snapshot.............................69
Drills for Skating & Movement...........40
    Backwards..........................47
    Forward..............................40
    Stopping.............................42
    T-Push Start.......................51
    To the Side........................51
    Turning..............................45
Drills for Strength & Power.............30
    Ankle Strengthening.................32
    Biceps Curl.............................35
    Dumbbell Pullover 33
    Knee Bend Pulls 31
    Finger Strengthening.................35
    Half Squats (Hamstrings)...........31

Sit Up Crunches 30
Wrist Curls................................33
Upper Body.............................34
Drinks...14
Dumbbells Pullover Drill.................33
E
Earrings..171
Elbow Pads......................160,167,169
Endurance, General.....................13, 38
Ephedra (Warning)...........................12
Equipment, Accessory...................171
Equipment, Cleaning......................167
Equipment, General......................166
Equipment, Goalkeepers......167,169,170
Equipment, Training...............171-173
Equipment, Typical Players............168
"Esporta" Wash System...................167
Exercises Warm Up/Stretching.................19
F
Face Mask..........................160,167-169
Face-Off Circles.........................88,89
Face-Off Strategy, Neutral Zone..........123
Face-Off strategy, Goalkeeper..............110
Facing Off......................................87
Faking..78
Fighting...158
Finger Strengthening.......................35
Fitness, Cardio/Muscular.....................13
Flip Pass..61
Flip Shot..69
Forechecking Strategy....................123
Forehand Sweep Wrist Shot..................67
Formations, Defensive.............135-137
Formations, Offensive..........118,126-134
Forwards, General...........................15
Fundamentals..................................14
G
Game of Hockey..........................147
Game Rules, General.............151-160
Attacking...............................157
Attacking Opponent........156,159
Batting Puck or Ball..............156
Equipment.....................160
Face-Offs............................155
Fighting............................158
Goalkeepers Privledges....157,158
Handling Puck or Ball.............155
High Sticking.....................157
Icing...............................156
Injuries............................154,159
Misconduct.........................127
Play Around the Net................156
Play on the Puck or Ball........155
Players.............................154
Players Uniforms.....................159
Rules Establishment................152
Scoring.........................153,157
Substitutions.....................154
Team Members........................154
The Puck or Ball.............171,172
The Captain........................154
The Game.........................152
Time of Games.....................153
Time Outs..........................153
Games..40
10 Yard War.......................119
99 Percent.........................97
Coaches Choice Shooting..........70
Dodge Ball........................27
Fool the Goalkeeper.................94
Hot Shot............................112
King of the Circle................58
Monkey in the middle.............64, 66
Passing Communication..........54
Tight Checking...................76
Games, Approach & Training...........17, 40
Gator Aid.......................................14
Glasses.................................160,170
Glove, Blocker..............................105
Glove, Catching....................105,169,170
Glove Saves..................................105
Gloves............................160, 167-170
Goal..................................55,173
Goal Crease Detail...........................98
Goalkeeper Penalties.......................166
Goalkeepers, General......................16
Goaltending....................................90
Grip, Hand (on Stick)......................56
Groin Stretch..................................21

178

Guarding a Player..........................75
H
HECC (Testing).....................160,166
Half Squats Drill.........................31
Hamstring Stretch........................24
Head Coach...............................11
Health Concerns.........................167
Health Habits............................12
Helmets.......................160,167-169
High Forwards & Wings, General..........15
Hip Flexor Stretch.......................21
Hip Stretch..............................20
Hockey Strategies, Basic................114
    Attack Formations..............118
    Communicating..................115
    Defensive......................120
    Goalkeeper.................107-112
    Offensive......................116
    One on One....................119
    Team...........................115
Hockey Terminology.....................138
Hustle...................................12
I
Improving................................10
Increase Scoring Productivity............116
Influence, Parental......................10
Injuries..........................9,71,154
Injury Rules........................154,159
InterNet Shopping......................172
Introduction..............................8
J
Jersey's (sweaters)..............159,167-170
Jewelry.................................171
Jogging..................................19
K
Key to Diagrams (Legends)..............146
Knee Bend Pulls..........................31
Knee to Chest Stretch....................23
L
Leg Pads, Goalkeeper...........160,169,170
Legend for Diagrams....................146
Lifting the Stick.........................74
Linesman............................161,164
Linesman, Responsibilities........161,164

List, Make a.............................17
Low Forwards & Centers, General.........15
M
Magic 7 Rules, Goalkeeper's..............113
Major Penalties.........................165
Match Penalties.........................165
Medallions, medical or religious.........171
Medicine Ball........................34,173
Minor Penalties.........................164
Misconduct..............................158
Misconduct Penalties....................165
Misconduct Rules........................158
Monkey Walk Drill.......................28
Mouth Guard........................160,167
Muscle Memory.......................28,40
Muscular Fitness.........................13
N
NFSHSA (High School)..................152
Net..................................55,173
Neutral Zone............................151
Neutral Zone Play.......................123
New Parent Orientation..................147
Nonverbal Communications..............115
O
Offensive Formations...........118,126-134
    1-2-2 Double Swing Pwr.Play....130
    1-2-2 Spread Power Play..........131
    3-1-1 Power Play..................127
    3-2 Power Play....................127
    5 on 5 Movement..................118
    Attack Triangle...................118
    D to D Ring......................134
    Forward Swinging..................132
    Long Regroup....................133
    Secondary Triangle................118
Offensive Game........................147
    How goals are Scored............148
    The Scoring.......................147
    Offensive Team Members.........148
    What Offensive Players Do.......149
    What Offense does................148
Offensive Strategies......................116
    Increase Scoring..................116

       Make Goalkeeper Move..........117
       Read & React......................116
Officials...160
       Who are the Officials..........161,163
       Why have Officials.................160
Organize Your Teaching.......................17
Orientation, New Parents...................147
"Over" (Verbal)..............................53
Overhead Stretch............................20
Overtime Games.......................152,153

P
Pad Saves, Goalkeeper.....................101
Pads, Protective.....................160,167-169
Pants................................160,167-169
Pass, Backhand Sweep........................60
Pass, Flip..................................61
Pass, Forehand Sweep........................60
Passing....................................59
Penalties 164
Penalty Killing Strategy......................134
Penalty Shot..............................166
Playing Rink..........................150-152
Playing the Angle, Goalkeeper............108
Poke Checks................................74
Poke Check Saves, Goalkeeper..........104
Positioning, Goalkeeper.....................96
Power Play Strategies....................124
       Addressing Problems................125
       Battle for Pucks/Balls............126
       Breakout Strategy.................126
       Create 2 on 1 Rush................125
       Develop skills........................126
       Manage Time Limit................126
       Regrouping............................132
       Spread Out Defense................125
       Win Neutral Zone Face-Offs.....126
Power Poke Check Save...................104
Pressuring..................................84
Protecting Puck or Ball....................82
Protective Cup (Males)...............160,167
Prosthetic Limbs............................170
Puck...................................171,172
Puck or Ball Handling.......................55

Q
Quickness, General..........................38
R
Rapid Puck/Ball Movement..............124
Reading & Reacting...................85,116
Ready Position, Goalkeeper................91
Ready Position, Player.....................41
Rebounding................................80
Receiving..................................59
Receiving, Backhand.......................63
Receiving, Forehand.......................63
Referee's................................160,163
Referee's Responsibilities............161,163
Regrouping, Neutral Zone................124
Respect....................................11
Reverse....................................53
Ring (Dumping)...........................53
Rink, Ice Hockey...........................151
Rink, In-Line Hockey......................152
Rink Presence..............................28
Roll Over Drill.............................29
Running Backwards Drill....................26
Running, General..........................36
Rules, General Game...............151-160
Rules Establishment.......................152
S
Safety, General............................166
Saves, Goalkeeper.........................99
Scoring.............................147,148,153
Screen the Shot Strategy...................107
Screening............................107,116
Seated Leg Stretch.........................24
Seated Pelvic Stretch......................20
Seated Straddle Groin Stretch..............21
Secondary Attack Triangles........117-119
Shooting...................................67
Shoulder Pads.....................160,167-169
Shuffle Step, Goalkeeper..................92
Signals, Officials....................161-163
Sit Ups Drill...............................30
Skates...............................160,167-170
Skate Saves, Goalkeeper.................100
Skating, General...........................40
Slap Shot..................................67

Snapshot..69
Socks...167-170
Speed Burst Running........................37
Speed, General..................................37
Speed Strategy.................................124
Spots, Face-Off..................................90
Stair Climbing...................................36
Stacked Pads Save..........................102
Steroids (Warning).............................13
Sticks...167-171
Stick Saves, Goalkeeper....................99
Stockings (socks)........................167-170
Stopping Puck or Ball........................84
Strategies..114
Strength, General..............................30
Strength Drills....................................30
Stretching..19
Substitutions....................................154
Supporters, Jock (Males)..........168,169
Suspenders..............................160,168-170
Sweater (Jersey)...............159,167-170
Swiss Ball............................34,171,173

T
Tactics (see strategies)....................114
T-Push, Players..................................51
T-Push, Goalkeeper's........................93
Teaching, Organize Your...................17
Team Members................................154
Telescoping, Goalkeeper...................94
Terminology, Hockey.......................138
Throat Protector...................160, 168-170
Time Interval (For game)..................153
Time Out Rules................................153
Training Equipment....................171-173
Training, Games.................................17
Transition...................................122,150
Transition Strategies.....................122
    Countering.............................122
    Neutral Zone Play.................123
    Regrouping............................123
Trapping..123
Triceps Stretch...................................22
Tricking..78
"Turn Up" (Verbal).............................53

U
USA Hockey...............................152,161
USA Hockey Age Groups.........153,160
USA Hockey In-Line..................152,161
USA Roller Hockey...................152,161
Uniform.............................159,167-170

V
Verbal Communicating....................115

W
Warm Up/Stretch Exercises...............19
    Abductors Stretch..................22
    Ankle Stretch..........................24
    Calf Stretch.............................23
    Hip Flexor...............................21
    Hip Stretch..............................20
    Jogging...................................19
    Knee to Chest Stretch...........23
    Overhead Stretch...................20
    Seated Leg Stretch................24
    Seated Pelvic Stretch.............20
    Seated Straddle Groin...........21
    Triceps Stretch.......................22
Warnings..6
"Wheel" (Verbal)................................53
Where they Play................................18
Wind Sprint Ladders.........................36
Wings, General..................................15
Wrist Curls...33

Y
Yard Line Markers.............................36
Youth Hockey Teams......................113

Z
Zamboni..146